ABBOTT'S
ENCYCLOPEDIA OF
ROPE TRICKS
For Magicians

ABBOTT'S ENCYCLOPEDIA OF ROPE TRICKS

For Magicians

COMPILED BY STEWART JAMES

Illustrations by

Sid Lorraine and Howard Melson

DOVER PUBLICATIONS, INC.
New York

Published in Canada by General Publishing Company, Ltd., 30 Lesmill Road, Don Mills, Toronto,
Ontario.
Published in the United Kingdom by Constable
and Company, Ltd., 10 Orange Street, London WC 2.

This Dover edition, first published in 1975, is a
republication of the third (1945) printing of the
work originally published by Abbott's Magic
Novelty Co., Colon, Michigan, under the title
Abbott's Encyclopedia of Rope Tricks. The Illustrations Section of that edition, duplicating illustrations in the text, is omitted from the present
edition.

International Standard Book Number: 0-486-23206-9
Library of Congress Catalog Card Number: 75-12132

Manufactured in the United States of America
Dover Publications, Inc.
180 Varick Street
New York, N.Y. 10014

Publisher's Foreword

We are indeed happy to present to the Magic Fraternity the Encyclopedia of Rope Tricks as an authoritative and comprehensive work on the Art of Rope Magic — the most complete reference on this subject extant.

To those who have eagerly awaited its publication, we believe we are giving them a work that was worth waiting for.

In producing this volume, we have strived to make it a real compendium of rope tricks — not merely a collection of rope effects, but rather a reference work as complete and informative as possible. This we feel confident has been achieved.

Many months have been spent in research and the compilation necessary to give workers in the realm of magic the best of rope effects that through repetition have become standard — classics if you will — also others not so well known, and some that appear in print for the first time. All of these effects represent the cream of the crop in this branch of the magic art.

Grouping of the various tricks and their variations has been made in such a manner and carefully indexed as to make every item easily accessible.

It is our sincere hope that this work will provide magicians — professional and amateur — with pleasure in the reading and profit in performance through the addition to their repertoires of some of the rope tricks contained in this volume.

With this thought we leave you to the perusal and study of the effects of the master workers in rope magic.

Percy Abbott

Colon, Michigan.

We Dedicate

THE ENCYCLOPEDIA OF ROPE TRICKS

to

Dr. Harlan Tarbell

who unquestionably is responsible for the

present-day popularity of Rope Magic

The Tarbell Rope Trick is a classic in this field of magic endeavor — one that will endure for many years to come — and its originator merits a profound salaam for this effect, aside from continued acclaim for his many contributions to magic in general.

INDEX

INDEX

CHAPTER THREE. PENETRATIONS (One Rope)

INDEX

CHAPTER FOUR. CUT AND RESTORED CORD

INDEX

INDEX

CHAPTER SEVEN. CUT AND RESTORED ROPE
(Prepared Rope)

INDEX

CHAPTER EIGHT. MISCELLANEOUS ROPE TRICKS

INDEX

CHAPTER 1
KNOTS

Chapter 1. KNOTS

G. W. HUNTER'S PUZZLE KNOT

You are probably familiar with the quite ancient puzzle where you would be given a rope to hold, one end in each hand, and would be challenged to tie a knot therein without releasing either end. This was accomplished by folding the arms BEFORE picking up the rope. The simple act of unfolding the arms pro-

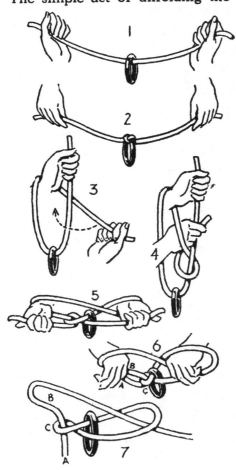

duces a knot in the rope. This "catch" might well serve as an introduction to the following really baffling trick.

The performer holds a rope as in Fig. 1. The use of a ring, as illustrated, is an effective addition. He states that he will tie the ring on the rope without releasing either end. Impossible as that seems, that is apparently what happens and the result is depicted in Fig. 2.

The first move is clearly shown in Fig. 3. The right hand goes into the loop as indicated by the arrow. Its further progress is shown in Fig. 4 and the result of these moves is to have an arrangement as in Fig. 5. If the hands were brought together and the loops dropped off the wrists, you would return to the position shown in Fig. 1.

To produce the knot it is necessary to secretly make an additional move. As the hands are brought together, to drop off the loops that encircle them, the backs are uppermost as in Fig. 6. The right hand releases end A and regains it again at point B after it has passed through loop C. Fig. 7 is of further assistance in understanding this move.

The dropping of the loops, the releasing and regaining of end A, and the separating of the hands to the position in Fig. 2, all blend together in one continuous movement. When properly made, it is absolutely indetectible.

An interesting presentation is to give a spectator a similar length of rope and have him try to do as you do. You get a knot but he does not although he will believe that he did exactly as you did. This is one trick that may be safely repeated.

A further surprise for the spectator is when you slowly and deliberately weave the rope into the position illustrated in Fig. 5. It is evident to the most critical that there has been no trickery. Instead of proceeding as previously, direct the spectator to grasp the two ends of the rope and pull it from your wrists. Imagine his surprise when he sees the knot forming before his very eyes.

This climax is produced with little or no effort on your part. Once the rope is in position Fig. 5, the act of removal by some other person is all that is needed to create the knot. The secret move must not be made.

Some performers have the ends of the rope tied around their thumbs, to preclude any thought of manipulation, up to the point where the rope is removed by a spectator.

THE ONE HAND KNOT

A two foot length of rope is sufficient to demonstrate this feat of dexterity. Extend the right hand vertically in front of the body, thumb upwards and resting lightly against the first finger. Lay the middle of the rope over the second joint of the thumb. That portion of the rope that lies across the palm is clipped between the third and little finger. Turn the hand palm downwards. Grasp the end of the rope that crosses the back of the hand between the thumb and forefinger, quickly snap the hand, first down and then up, and the rope will drop out straight with a single knot neatly formed at about the middle.

The rapid down and up movement serves to cover the action. It is best concluded by tossing the rope in the air on the upward swing and catching it, to display the knot, as it falls.

THE FLIP KNOT

Both ends of the rope are held in the right hand. The rope is snapped in the air at the same time as one end is released. A single knot is disclosed near the end of the rope.

The knot is secretly tied in advance about three inches from one end. The rope may vary considerably in length but four or five feet is about the most effective. The thumb, first and second fingers of the left hand effectually conceal the knot as the rope is held up to display. In taking the rope by the right hand, it is clipped between the first and second fingers with the knot again safely concealed behind them and toward the palm.

The other end of the rope is brought up and held between the first finger and thumb. As you snap the rope, you release this end. Appear surprised that nothing happened and again place it between first finger and thumb. Repeat the second time but at the third attempt you retain this end and allow the knotted end, from between the first and second finger, to fly in the air. Of course, this time it bears a knot.

THE LIGHTNING KNOT

One end of the rope is clipped between the thumb and first finger of the right hand. Allow about four or five inches to extend over the back of the hand. The other end of the rope is clipped between the thumb and first finger of the left hand but in a directly opposite manner. The main body of the rope passes across the back of the hand and four or five inches extend across the palm.

Bring the hands together, fingers pointed toward each other, and the right hand nearest the body. Left first and second fingers clip the end of the rope hanging over the back of right hand, and the right first and second fingers clip the end of rope that is hanging across the palm of left hand. On parting the hands, the knot appears at the center of the rope.

TWO AT A TIME

The hands are held about fifteen inches apart, palms up, arms half bent, and the rope lying across the wrists with an equal amount hanging down at both sides.

Turn the hands toward each other, at the same time turning them over, so that by the time they have made one complete revolution the backs will be uppermost and the ends of the rope will be hanging over that portion stretching horizontally between.

Grasp one end in each hand, let the loops drop off and two knots will appear evenly spaced from the center.

THE KNOT OF ENCHANTMENT

This is a feat that the average scientist will say is contrary to the laws of nature and utterly impossible. The principle on which it is performed is very little understood. The conjurer has a piece of rope at least three feet long which he allows to be examined. The ends of the rope are then tied to his wrists and, if the spectators are particularly suspicious, the knots may be sealed with wax, so that, if they are tampered with, the audience will find it out. (Figure 8.)

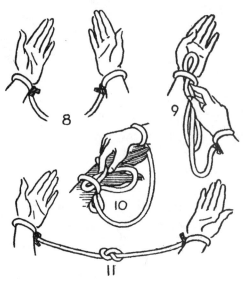

Now the performer announces that he will cause a genuine knot to appear on the rope, without disturbing the knots or removing the rope from his wrists. He turns his back to the spectators for a moment, and when again he faces them the knot—a plain, ordinary slipknot—has been tied in the rope. The knots on the wrists are undisturbed. (Figure 11.)

The secret depends upon a clever bit of manipulation of the rope. As soon as his back is turned the magician seizes the center of the rope in his right hand. He twists the rope twice around, forming a loop in the center of the rope. Holding his left hand before him, palm upward, he now thrusts the loop he has made under the rope around his left wrist. (Figure 9.) As it emerges on his palm, he passes his left hand completely through the loop. Reaching to the back of his left hand, he pushes the loop under the rope on the back of the wrist, just as he had done before on the other side. (Figure 10.) As the loop comes through, it has formed itself into a large knot which can be drawn tight, when it will be found to fit exactly in the center of the rope. (Figure 11.)

This may sound difficult, but in reality it is very simple, and will be found so after a little experimenting.

ANY NUMBER OF KNOTS

A rope is coiled and dropped on the floor. The magician grasps one end and quickly raises it. The rope now bears several knots.

The result is obtained entirely from the method used in coiling the rope. The magician takes the rope in his right hand at a position of about one foot from the end. (Figure 12.) The left hand now takes up

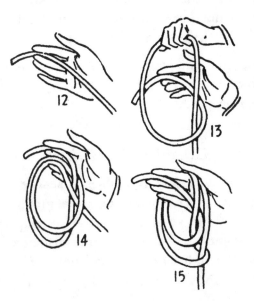

a loop of the rope in the manner shown in Figure 13. It is passed over the hand as shown in Figure 14. He does this with every loop made, and it will now be found that, at the conclusion of the coiling, when the end of the rope is reached, if the original end, first held in the hand, be passed through all the loops, the result will be to tie as many knots in the rope as there were loops made. (Figure 15.)

All that remains is to drop the coiled rope on the floor and later grasp the original end and jerk it in the air.

A variation is to make three loops in the rope and have a volunteer hold one end in each hand with the most part hanging behind his back. Force a three spot from a deck of cards on a second volunteer. Have first volunteer face the audience and you step behind him. The value of the selected card is now revealed and you tie that many knots in the rope without volunteer releasing either end. Worked in this manner, you apparently do not know the number of knots to be tied until AFTER the ends are firmly held.

Sometimes the rope is lowered in a basket or urn, the original end never going out of sight, and is raised again bearing the knots.

GUARDING THE LINE

This more closely resembles a seance test than a magician's trick. Each end of a lengthy rope is securely tied to the wrist of some volunteer, and sealed. The two volunteers stand at some distance from each other and the lights are extinguished. There are several knots on the rope when the lights are again snapped

24

on and the volunteers will insist that the ends of the rope have remained firmly fastened to their wrists throughout.

When the lights are extinguished, the medium picks up the coiled center portion of the rope and holds it in his right hand. Going to one of his volunteers, he slips it over his head, and allows it to drop to the floor,—all unknown to the volunteer, as the magician is particularly careful to see that the rope did not touch him in its passage to the floor. This volunteer is requested to alter his position a few feet, and he is guided to some place where he will be free of the coil. It will now be seen that the whole body of one of the volunteers has passed through the loops of rope, and there are, accordingly, a number of knots formed in the rope —as many knots as there were coils in the rope.

ADOLPH FERBER'S SPECTRE TIE

In addition to a four foot length of rope, a metal tube, three-quarters of an inch in diameter and three inches long, is used.

Magi hands out the apparatus for examination. He slips tube on center of rope, has two spectators each hold one end of rope, covers the tube and rope and explains that with the aid of the long past dead, he will tie a knot around tube. He reaches under the cover, makes the motion of tying a knot, and when covering is whisked away, a real knot is tied around tube. Knot cannot be removed without letting go of one end of the rope.

Shake out rope and double so that center rests over forefinger and thumb tip of right hand. Now while you are talking, cross rope right under fingers with aid of left hand so that rope on side marked (A) crosses

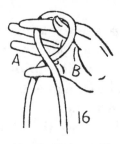

over rope on side marked (B). Place little finger of right hand under intersection as in illustration. Now with all three fingers remaining in position, take part of rope darkened in illustration between forefinger and thumb which are between loop, and pull rope through loop, all the time holding rope under little finger gently in left hand. Pull until you have about three or four inches of loop left over knot which results. Tighten knot gently. Now audience sees back of right hand holding rope with loop sticking out of top about three inches, fingers concealing knot. All these actions take place in a few seconds. Now slip tube over center of loop and pull rope through top of tube, that is, that part of rope that pulls freely through knot. Hold out rope with tube in center over knot which audience, of course, knows nothing about. Be sure tube conceals knot.

Have two spectators each hold one end of rope, throw covering (newspaper, handkerchief or scarf) over center and tube, reach under cover and slide tube off knot to the left, loosen knot and untie. Be sure to have both hands under cover and slide tube off knot to the left, loosen knot and push tube through knot until you feel knot tied around tube. Tighten knot around tube. Practice this a few times out in the open and soon it will be a simple matter to tie knot around tube under cover in just a few seconds. Let one of the spectators remove cover from rope and be sure and satisfy audience by letting several spectators examine knot. This has the effect of a small miracle if it is done properly.

THE VANISHING SQUARE KNOT

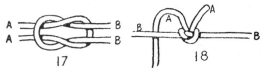

Figure 17 shows the proper way to tie the square knot. The top A and B mark the ends of the rope. If you grasp the rope at A-A in one hand and B-B in the other and tug with all your strength, you will form what seems to be a very hard knot.

This square knot may be quickly and simply altered to a slip knot. All you have to do is take hold of the rope at B-B, one portion in each hand, and a quick pull will form the knot depicted in Figure 18. Study it and you will see how the knot may be slid right over the end B and off the rope.

RALPH HULL'S FAMOUS VANISHING KNOT

This is one of the prettiest little sleights you have ever witnessed. It is so clean cut and so convincing that hundreds of magicians from all over the world have marveled at it. The knot is tied in such a fair manner it seems impossible for any trickery to be there, but it's there, just the same.

The moves for this beautiful effect will be shown in detail by a series of illustrations.

The eight drawings show what almost amounts to a slow moving picture of making and vanishing this knot. The whole when mastered is one complete movement. With a swing of the rope and a movement of the hands the knot is tied, placed in the hand, and fades away.

Hold the rope in the palms of the two open hands exactly as shown in Figure 19. The short end hangs

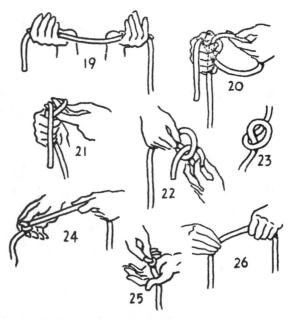

over the right hand about 10 inches in length. The right hand is closed up and turned to a perpendicular position as shown in Figure 20. The left thumb comes down on top of the rope to hold it and the left hand simply is turned over when the positions shown in Figure 20 will be attained. The hand that has been partially X-rayed is the right hand. Now the rope is in such a position that the long end of it may be taken hold of by the right thumb and the right forefinger, and the long end of the rope just hangs toward the floor a portion of it being hidden from sight by passing behind the four fingers of the right hand. This is shown exactly in Figure 20.

Now the left forefinger just reaches forward, going under the short end of the rope as shown in Figure 21, and it is pulled right on through what is to all appearances, a real loop formation of a knot. Figure 22 describes better than words the movement of pulling the rope right through and shows the right hand as the upper one holding what seems to be a perfect knot. Figure 23 shows the fake knot exactly as it would appear if the right thumb were removed from it, but of course this is not done at this stage of the game. Now the left hand takes hold of the rope about ten inches away from the fake knot exactly as shown in Figure 24 and gradually pulls on the rope, the right thumb and forefinger allowing it to slide under the upper fold, and at the same time kind of rolling the fake knot a little and to all appearances, this just tightens the rope up to a real and genuine knot. The right hand throws the short end of the rope across the palm of the left hand, and deposits the knot right in the center of the left palm, the right thumb merely pushing down on the lower section of the fake knot to cause it to appear real. This exact move is shown in Figure 25. The left fingers close on the knot, and the right hand is withdrawn and takes hold of the short end of the rope and left hand turned over (as in Figure 26). All that remains to be done is to gently pull with the right hand and the knot seems to melt away, as it were.

As said before, when this is properly performed it is a most bewildering illusion. It's perfect in every detail and a person may watch it over and over and not be able to detect but what it is a real knot that is tied. WHEN YOU GET THE KNACK OF IT, THE WHOLE OF THE MOVEMENTS JUST DESCRIBED ALL BLEND INTO ONE MOVEMENT, and apparently the knot (?) is tied with just a swing of the rope and the end pulled through. Practice this until you are fully acquainted with it.

CHEFALO'S VANISHING KNOT

The knot, with which Chefalo's name has been associated for many years is a most interesting one.

A double knot is tied and one end of the rope is threaded back and forth first through one and then the other of the loops thus formed. The ends of the rope are pulled and the knots dissolve.

The illustrations leave little to explain. Just be sure to follow the various steps exactly as pictured in

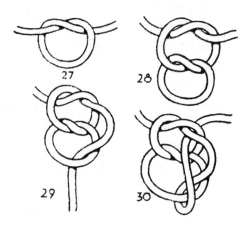

Figures 27, 28, 29 and 30. What will appear as a perfectly genuine knot will prove to be as intangible as the air.

THE CAPTIVE KNOT

A single knot is tied in the center of a rope and the ends are tied together with seven or eight more. All knots, in this case, may be tied by a volunteer and he may try to remove the captive single knot before handing it to you. Underneath the cover of a large cloth, you quickly remove the knot.

The apparent removal of the knot is accomplished by absurdly simple means. You slip your fingers into the loop of the knot, enlarge it and keep slipping the knot along the rope until it joins the rest where it appears to be one of the knots used in tying the ends together.

THE MAGIC SHOE LACES

The following is Ralph Hull's presentation of a clever little knot mystery of the late G. W. Hunter.

First you tie the knot (illustrated in Figures 31 to 36.) Take hold of the two ends of the rope and pull and it naturally pulls right out. The next time you tie it exactly the same and pull the two ends through the loops as illustrated in Figure 37. This makes it appear impossible to pull the knot out by pulling on the ends of the rope, yet strange to say, in some unaccountable manner this very thing happens.

You can tie the knot up to the point shown in Figure 36 in a second's time, after you master the

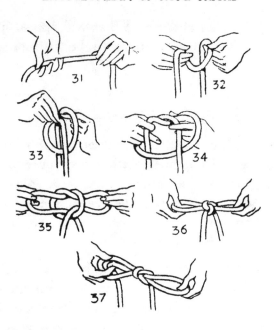

moves. Hold the rope as shown in Figure 31, right hand palm down and the left hand palm up, bringing them a little nearer each other and Figure 32 will be attained. Right index finger reaches over and catches end of rope hanging from left hand and the left forefinger catches the end of the rope hanging from right hand. This movement is shown in Figures 33 and 34. The hands are merely pulled apart pulling these two ends of rope along, and Figure 35 shows the result. Merely by tightening up on the loops (by pulling with each hand) Figure 36 is attained. This is a double loop that will pull right out if the ends of the rope are pulled. That is what you really do the first time. But the second time, you pull the ends through the loops as shown in Figure 37, and this makes a different looking proposition out of it. The little patter story that goes with this effect helps build it up. It runs as follows:

"Have you ever seen the MAGIC SHOE LACES? This is the way we learned to tie our shoe laces when we were mere youngsters. Of course it is handy for the kiddies to have their laces tied in nice bows like this (at this point you have tied the double bow as illustrated in Figure 36) for at night when they are tired and want to get their shoes off in a hurry and pile in bed, all they need to do is take hold of the ends and pull, and away goes the double knot, and off come the shoes! But do you know that sometimes when the kiddies are playing about all day, one end may happen to get up through the loop like this? (Here you have tied the double loop knot again as shown in Figure 36, and left forefinger goes right down through the loop and gets hold of the end and pulls it right up through, exactly as shown in Figure 37. The other forefinger (right) goes down through its loop and pulls end up through in exactly the same manner. To be sure you always go right on this, take Figure 36 as the guide— you will notice that the two thumbs both point down through the loops. Well, this is your cue—your forefinger goes right down through the loops as indicated by direction the thumbs point, and brings the ends up through.) Then to even complicate the matter, the other end is liable to get through the loop and now, not noticing this the kiddies in their usual hurry just take hold of the ends of the laces and jerk—and what is the result? You all know for no doubt every one of you have had this same experience. (At this point you pull on the two ends until you have apparently drawn the loops right into a hard knot). There would be no use in pulling harder, for the harder one would pull, the harder the knot would get. I used to hunt for a fork, or an old fashioned shoe buttoner to get the laces untied.

However that was before I knew magic, for by the aid of it, even though the ends had been pulled through the loops thus forming a hard knot, the magic words secretly pronounced is all it would take. (Here you hold the rope in left hand and right hand runs right down over the knot and it seems to melt right away just as before). Wonderful what magic will do isn't it?"

You will find this to be very effective.

JOHN BRAUN COMBINATION KNOT

In effect, tie a bow knot in a piece of rope, put the ends of the rope through the loops as explained in the "Shoe Laces" effect, and then pull the knot tight. Immediately tie the Chefalo Knot on top, following

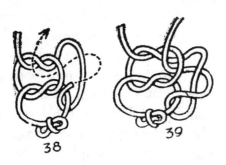

38   39

through as in Figure 38 and 39. Pull the knots tight, and you have what seems to be a hopeless tangle. While spectators hold the ends of the rope, you magically dissolve the knots, and the rope is untangled again! Follow the illustrations carefully. The various positions are as the hands appear to you. Pull the knots tight— that is, as tight as you dare without pulling them out. While the spectators hold the ends of the rope you apparently rub them away with your closed hand over them.

WHOLESALE KNOT REMOVAL

Two ropes are used this time. They are held side by side and a knot tied in the center of both of them simultaneously. Further knots are tied until the ropes can hardly bear more. Spectators may assist in tying the knots.

A volunteer holds the four ends bunched up in his hand while the knots are concealed beneath a cloth. Reaching under this cloth, you are able to remove every last one of the knots.

The two ropes are each doubled back on itself at the center. They are joined together with a loop of thread. They appear to be two complete ropes held side by side. The first knot should be tied by you. It hides the doubled centers and permits spectators to add more knots without detecting anything wrong. Under cover of the cloth it is an easy matter to break the thread and remove the knots.

GONE AGAIN

This is a follow-up to "Any Number of Knots" which is explained in an earlier portion of this chapter.

After the knots, which have magically appeared, have been displayed, the rope is bunched up and then let fall with one end only being retained. The knots are gone as mysteriously as they came.

In gathering up the rope, you open out the loop of each knot, under the pretext of showing it genuine, so that the rope again assumes the same position as when you coiled it up and passed the original end through as illustrated in Figure 15. All you have to do now is pass that original end back through the loops of the knot and retain it as you let the rest of the rope drop. The knots dissolve in exactly the reverse of the manner in which they were tied.

VISIBLY

After tying a knot that dissolves to nothingness, you offer to explain how it is done. Under cover of your hand ,you state that you actually remove the knot and place it in your pocket. That is exactly what appears to happen. A knot is tied in the rope, you cover it with your hand, the knot is revealed to be gone from the rope and you show it in your hand.

All you need is knot tied in a rope similar to that you are using and cut away with the ends trimmed quite closely to the knot itself. This is concealed in the hand and revealed only after the knot in the rope, it may be either "The Chefalo Vanishing Knot" or "The Magic Shoe Laces" has dissolved.

C. T. JORDAN'S MYSTIFYING KNOT TRICK

This is a simple but bewildering feat. A length of rope and a plain wooden curtain ring or unprepared bracelet is all the equipment required. The ring is threaded on the rope and three knots are tied over it.

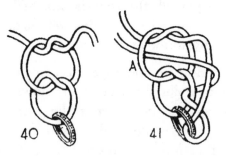

While the ends of the rope are held both the ring is removed and the knots are untied.

The first two knots are genuine (Figure 40) but the third works the trick. The ring is best laid on a table while the knot is tied. First, lay the right hand end down alongside the knots already tied and pull it up through the curtain ring; then under itself, down through the noose of the first knot, across and under that part of itself that lies beside the knots, over and down through the noose formed by the second knot. It will come out alongside the other end. (Figure 41).

The person who is going to help you grasps the ends and lets the center of the rope hang down behind his back. He must face the audience, so that what you do behind his back will not be observed.

On examining the knot you will find that there is one prominent loop. (A, Figure 41). The first thing to do is slip this loop right down and over all the knots and the ring. Now, by merely shaking the rope, it straightens out and the ring hangs suspended by one easily removed loop. This loop is similar to that employed in attaching price tags. Merely enlarge it and slip over the ring. The ring will drop off and leave the rope without a knot.

CHAPTER 2
PENETRATIONS
(Two Ropes)

Chapter 2. PENETRATIONS

(Using Two Ropes)

ROPES THROUGH THE NECK

Two lengths of rope, each about six feet long, are placed around your neck. The doubled ropes are crossed at your throat and a single overhand knot tied. Several spectators may each tie additional knots. Grasping the knots at your throat, you give a tug and the ropes apparently pass right through your neck. The ropes are freely displayed and still bear the loops which were but a moment before around your neck. The knots are undisturbed.

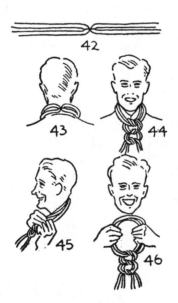

The ropes are prepared as in Fig. 42. They are doubled back upon themselves and the middle of each connected with a loop of thread. In placing the ropes about your neck, leave the secret joint concealed at the back as in Fig. 43. In Fig. 44 is depicted the appearance to the audience after the knots are tied.

When you are ready for the release, grasp the ropes above the knots as depicted in Fig. 45. A slight pull breaks the thread and the loops are spread apart with your fingers as the ropes apparently penetrate your neck.

As long as the secret joint is kept concealed, the ropes have every appearance of being single and lying parallel to each other.

VENABLE'S IMPROVED ROPES THROUGH NECK

In this version, the ropes are not prepared in advance but a hitch, as pictured in Fig. 47, is secretly made. Mr. Henry Venable stated that the method of

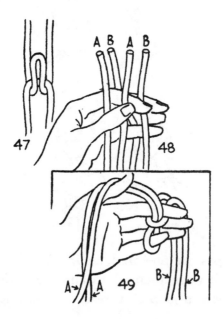

actually making this hitch had always been left vague in the descriptions of the trick which he had read. He asserts that the following method is indetectable.

The ropes are first exhibited separately, one held in each hand near the end, and shown to be separate and sound. The two ropes are now taken in the left hand, separated by the forefinger, and each held near the end. The right hand now brings up the other ends of the ropes, keeping them separated with the right forefinger, and places them in the left hand, each rope having both of its ends on the same side of the left forefinger. We shall denote the ropes between the thumb and forefinger as A and that between the first and second fingers as B. Now the little finger of the left hand is inserted through the loop of B and draws back one side of loop A; the condition now is that illustrated in Fig. 48.

The right hand now takes the ends of the ropes and draws them up vertically until the looped ends are in the left hand, which you find will have them as shown in Fig. 49, the end of loop A being around the little finger and through loop B.

The right hand can now drop the ends of loop B forward and A towards himself, take the ropes by the middle from the left hand, hitch already made, put them around his neck (under his collar to conceal the loop), tie them up, and there you are. A spectator can pull them as hard as he pleases, as the hitch will not come loose unless you work the rope back and forth from side to side.

The effect of the move described seems to the spectator to be merely the doubling of the ropes and taking them by the middle.

THE ROPES AND RINGS MYSTERY

Five or six curtain rings are strung upon two ropes and are tied with a single knot as in Fig. 53. Two ends

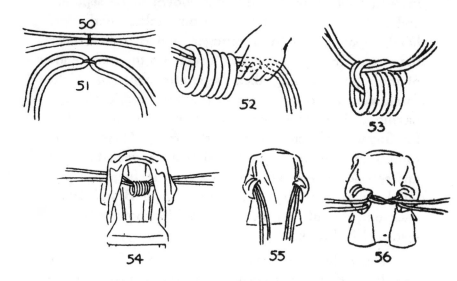

of the rope are threaded through the sleeve of a borrowed coat and held by one volunteer. The other two ends are threaded through the second sleeve and held by a second volunteer. Fig. 54 shows what the arrangement looks like to you and Fig. 55 is the view to the audience. (The rings should be tied on the ropes in Fig. 54.)

Another single knot is tied in one of the ropes so that the final appearance is as Fig. 56. While the volunteers hold tightly to their respective ends of the ropes, you remove the rings, the coat and the knots.

The ropes are at least twelve feet long. They are prepared in a similar manner to that described in Ropes Through The Neck. A piece of thread is wound once or twice about the middle of the ropes, as in Fig. 50, and then they are doubled back upon each other, as in Fig. 51.

In presenting the trick, you have one volunteer stand at each side of you. The rings may be examined and then are threaded on the rope while you keep the secret joint concealed in your hand, as in Fig. 52, at all times.

The rings are then tied with a single knot, using both ropes, as in Fig. 53.

After threading the ropes through the sleeves and having rested the coat on the back of a chair, have each volunteer hand you one end that he is holding and tie one more knot on the outside of the coat as in Fig. 56.

If you break the thread, under cover of the coat, as the volunteers pull on the ropes, the rings and coat will come free while the ropes will be stretched out straight between them.

A variation in presentation is to remove the rings but to retain the loops. Then, as an additional surprise, you release the loops and the coat is removed from the ropes as well.

STANLEY COLLINS NEW ROPES AND RINGS RELEASE

This method is performed with two long pieces of rope and three rings of large size. When the audience has thoroughly inspected these articles to their satisfaction, the conjurer passes both ropes through one of the rings. It is interesting to note that the ropes are passed through the ring separately, two different spectators each threading one rope if desired.

The ring having been secured with a knot, the second ring is threaded on the ropes over one pair of ends, and the last ring over the other ends.

The ropes are finally carried down the sleeves of a coat, then another knot having been tied, the ends are handed to two gentlemen, with the request that they pull against each other. Instantly the ropes are pulled straight and free from knots, the rings and coat being left in the hands of the conjurer.

The secret of this puzzling problem lies in the fact that really four rings are used instead of three, the presence of one being unknown to the audience. This fourth ring is exactly the same as the other three both in appearance and size, but has a slit similar to the "key" ring in the Chinese Linking Rings. This "key" ring is out of sight at the start. It can either be vested or on the table under some silks.

You invite two gentlemen up to examine the ropes and the three unprepared rings. While they are examining these articles, borrow a coat. As you return with the

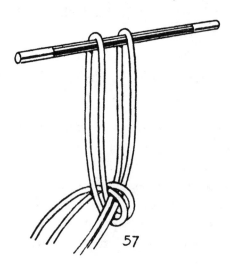

57

coat, ask for the three rings again and make the exchange of one unprepared ring for the "key." This "key" ring is threaded first, you concealing the cut in the ring with your thumb. The ropes are tied exactly as in Fig. 57, the "key" ring taking the place of the wand.

The two remaining rings are now threaded, one on each side of the tied ring, and the ends of the ropes are brought down the sleeves of the coat. One rope from one sleeve and one from the other are then tied with a single knot, as in Fig. 56.

You reach inside the coat, slide the ropes through the "cut," thus releasing all three rings, at the same time taking care to hold the rope together. Give the command to pull and the two assistants from the audience pull against each other, thus pulling the ropes out the sleeves of the coat and leaving the coat and the three rings in your possession.

Quickly place the "key" ring under your vest and remove the unprepared one therefrom under cover of the coat. The coat is now brought down into the audience to its owner and the three rings can be freely examined.

This trick is very easy to perform owing to the fact that you work behind the coat. To the audience it appears as if you are merely supporting the coat and the rings until you give the command to pull.

Mr. Collins asserts that it is very easy to split a wooden ring along the grain. Simply drop the ring edgewise on a very hard substance. A ring split in this manner may be handled most freely, and close to a spectator's eyes without any fear of the crack being observed.

RELUE'S ROPES AND CUPS

Two ropes are tied around the wand and held at their ends by volunteers. Two tin cups and then two china cups are threaded on the ropes. You withdraw the wand and wave it over the cups. The tin cups crash to the floor but the china cups remain hanging on the ropes.

There is no previous preparation of the ropes. Place them over the wand. Hold both ends of each rope in one hand. Cross the ropes (really both ends of one rope) in one hand over the ropes in the other hand and draw tight in a single knot (in such a manner that if you now remove the wand, you will have one rope complete in each hand). Have the volunteers on either side hold the ropes. Thread a tin cup on the ropes at either side. Now take one rope (either one) from each volunteer and tie the tin cups on. In this tie, just cross the ropes over (one from each side) and draw up a single knot as you have done in the previous tricks in this chapter.

After you hand these ropes back, each volunteer is really holding one end of each rope. Next place the china cups on the ropes—one from either end of ropes. As you withdraw the wand and wave it over the tie in the center, the volunteers pull the ropes tight—the tin cups fall—the china cups remain.

Refer to Fig. 57 for the manner in which the ropes are tied on the wand.

ORIENTAL OR SIMPLICITY ROPE RELEASE

Ottokar Fischer of Vienna is credited with first using the simplified method, just explained in the previous trick, of performing the release without previous preparation of the ropes.

In his routine, a fan took the place of the wand and brightly colored silks were used instead of cups. This makes a fine oriental presentation on any program.

WALKING THROUGH ROPES

Still another variation of this effective principle. Two long ropes are displayed and passed up under a gentleman's coat and behind him. He is further secured by tying one of the ropes in a single knot in front of him. Two volunteers stand, one to his right and the other to his left, and hold the ends of the ropes. The gentleman steps backward and the ropes, having apparently penetrated his body, are stretched straight and free in front of him. He has apparently walked through the two ropes.

Little needs to be explained. The ropes are prepared as in Fig. 51. Fake joint is kept concealed in the hand until it is safely hidden beneath the first volunteer's coat. Be sure that your audience is impressed with the fact that the ropes actually pass behind him at the start.

THE 3-IN-1 ROPES

Mr. A. C. Thompson suggests the following method of preparing the ropes for such tricks as Walking Through Ropes, Ropes and Rings, or Ropes Through Neck.

You will require a small piece of cloth for each rope. It need only be long enough to fit around the rope like a band and wide enough to accommodate two dress snap fasteners. The male halves of two fasteners are sewn to the center of one cloth band and the two female halves to the second cloth band.

Two male halves are sewn at one end of each cloth strip and two female halves at the other end of each strip and on the other side of the strip from the first pair.

You now have two cloth strips, one to snap around each rope to form a band at the rope's center. These two ropes many now be snapped together as shown in Fig. 58.

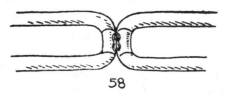

58

The ropes may first be shown held far apart and then snapped together as you place them both in one h nd. During the course of the trick, you need only to unsnap them instead of breaking the thread as in the original version. In conclusion, you have only to unsnap the cloth bands themselves to leave the ropes quite unprepared.

MIMI-CORDS — Adolph Ferber

Apparatus used consists of two ropes, each six feet long, and a block of wood approximately three and a half inches square, half an inch thick and with a half inch hole through the center.

The effect to the audience is that both ropes are threaded through hole in block, one is removed and the remaining rope is jerked right through the block.

Hand out the ropes and the block for examination. When the ropes are returned, take one by the extreme end in the left hand and the other in the same manner in the right. Now place both ropes in the right hand, hold near the ends and, while you talk, twist ropes' ends with left hand as in Fig. 59. The fact that the ropes

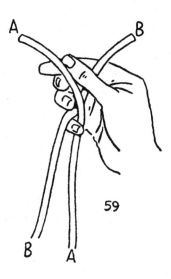

59

are crossed is hidden in the hand, thumb between ropes on top of cross and little finger between ropes on bottom. (After you are accustomed to the move, it may prove easier to do it with the right hand alone).

Pick up other end of A in left hand and join with first end. Do likewise with other end of B, keeping right hand fingers in position as much as possible. After a little practice, you will find it easy enough to bring up both ends of both ropes at once with your left hand and join them properly with ends in right hand. Always use this latter method when presenting the trick for an audience.

Hold ends of both ropes in left hand and pull with left hand until the right hand fingers reach the center of ropes. Result—ropes are linked to each other in center. Cover link naturally with right hand.

Thread two ends of rope through the center of the block, until centers reach back of block. Keep back of block, where link is, away from audience. The block is held in right hand, four fingers in front, thumb in back, fingers and palm covering front of block.

Pull at one end of back rope, pulling it completely away from block. Simultaneously slip second finger of right hand over one of two ropes (really one rope, of course) hanging from front of block and hold it around lower edge of block and under second finger. This is so it will appear that you have a length of rope hanging from the front of block and one from the back.

If necessary, the left hand may aid in this move while you are getting hold of back rope to withdraw it.

Then hold two ends of rope in left hand and pull it, seemingly through the block, while four right hand fingers are still over center of front of block.

CHAPTER 3

PENETRATIONS
(One Rope)

Chapter 3. PENETRATIONS
(Using One Rope)

LOOP THE LOOP

This is actually a puzzle but well worth knowing. Use a soft rope about nine feet long and tie the ends together. Remove your coat, put the loop of rope over your right arm and put your right hand in your vest pocket. Have anyone try to get it off without untying or cutting the rope and without you removing your hand from vest pocket.

The solution is to pull the loop through the armhole of your vest, over your head, out through the other armhole and over the other arm. You can now reach up under vest and pull the rope down. It will fall to the floor, leaving you only to step out of it and be free.

THE LEG TIE

Four feet of rope is a nice length to use for this trick. It is apparently wrapped twice around the leg, just above the knee. You grasp both ends in one hand, give a quick jerk, and the rope seems to pass right through your leg leaving the rope suspended in a loop from the hand that held it.

First stretch the rope above the leg as in Fig. 60. Place the center of the rope against your leg and wrap it around as in Fig. 61.

Demonstrate how secure it is and then remove and hold the rope again as in Fig. 60.

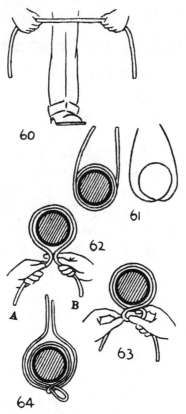

Once more the rope is placed around the leg in apparently the same manner. What you really do is quite different.

Let us suppose that it is being placed around the left leg. Place both hands and ends A and B at the rear of the leg. Right thumb is placed against B and right forefinger in front of A. See Fig. 62.

Engage A with right forefinger and pull it under B. Push B to left with right thumb. Grasp B with left thumb and forefinger. Refer now to Fig. 63.

With left thumb and forefinger, push A around under B and pull it through a little way to right with right thumb and forefinger. You will release A from left hand and B from right in order to do this.

Bring ends A and B up in front of leg and grasp both ends in the right hand. Give the rope a quick jerk and it remains suspended in a loop. Fig. 64 shows the actual position before the release is made.

NEVIL MASKELYNE'S LEG TIE

The performer sits down and bends one leg. Around the top of the calf he winds a piece of rope twice; he then carries the rope up to the thigh and passes it twice around the thigh and ties the two ends together. The binding appears to be absolutely genuine; yet, when the performer takes hold of the rope and straightens his leg he is able to pull the loop of rope away.

If the reader will experiment a few times, using the illustrations as a guide, he should have no difficulty in mastering the tie. The learner should remember that the rope goes twice around the calf and twice around the thigh and that the second two moves cancel the first two because the rope goes around in the opposite direction. Another point to remember is the crossing of the two ends of the rope; they cross below the knee and above it, but again the second move cancels the first. The loops around the thigh are made in such a way that the rope does not cross, as depicted in Fig. 69.

Every detail of the presentation is pictured and if the reader will follow the instructions, beginning with the rope in front of the leg, he should have no difficulty in performing the trick. Fig. 65 is a side view and Fig. 68 the appearance from the front of the com-

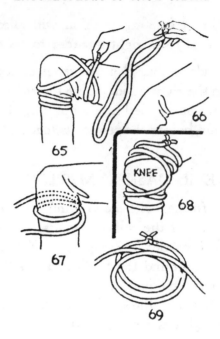

pleted tie. Fig. 67 shows how the rope goes around the calf and Fig. 69 shows the procedure to follow in winding the rope around the thigh. Fig. 66 is how the rope appears immediately after the release.

TENKAI ROPE TRICK THROUGH NECK

A rope is passed twice around the neck. A sharp tug on the ends and it apparently penetrates the neck.

The illustration shows the moves step by step. Note in Fig. 70 that end B, hanging on your left side, is a trifle longer than A.

Fig. 71 shows how you reach across the short piece with the right arm and grasp the long piece. You now reach across the long piece and grasp the short piece with the left arm as in Fig. 72.

When the loop, held in the right hand, is about half way around the neck, then the left hand starts with the short piece and follows right around the same way. The right hand stops when half way around and goes no further, but the left hand goes clear around.

Fig. 73 shows clearly that these moves have bound the loop securely in the rope. The appearance from the front is as Fig. 74. Because B was longer at the start, the ends now hang evenly.

By a quite different set of moves, you are really in a similar position to the manner in which the rope passes around your leg in Fig. 64. A sharp pull and the rope is straight and free in front of you.

NEW ROPE THROUGH NECK

Unfortunately, I am unfamiliar with the name of the originator of this clever method.

The rope is first tied in a circle and placed over the head and around the neck, represented by the dark

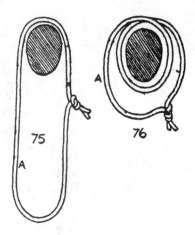

oval, in the manner shown in Fig. 75. Eight feet is about right for the length of the rope and note that the knot is well up toward the neck on the left side.

Grasp the rope at point A in the right hand and carry it around the neck once so that Fig. 76 illustrates the new position.

Next cross the rope in front of you as in Fig. 77.

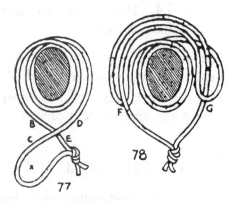

The rope at left of neck goes in front of the rope at right. Grasp points B and C in the right hand, D and E in the left hand, with the palms of the hand toward your body.

Raise the rope and drop loop X over your head so that rope, where it crosses, will be at the back of the neck. Fig. 78 discloses the formation the rope will assume. There will be a loop, F and G, at each side of the neck. The hands automatically arrive at these positions, F and G, and conceal the loops.

The release is affected by allowing the loops to slip out of your hand at the same time as you grasp the single rope, just below them, and pull quickly down and away from the neck.

THE HANDKERCHIEF RELEASE

Your hands are bound tightly together with a handkerchief looped around your wrists and tied in several knots. The end of a piece of soft rope, about twelve feet long, is dropped through the circle made by your arms and pulled tight by someone who holds both ends so you cannot escape. Fig. 79 will clarify these instructions.

Requesting a little slack, you move your hands up and down quite rapidly. At your command, volunteer pulls on the rope and is reasonably surprised to see it drop to the floor. Both ends of the rope are still in his possession and you are as securely bound, with the handkerchief, as you were at the beginning.

Fig. 79 shows your hands tied with the handkerchief, the rope slipped through your arms and pulled tight by someone who holds the ends.

The first secret move is apparent in Fig. 80. When the rope is first pulled tight, catch it between your hands at the base of the wrists. When it is slackened, grasp the loop with the tips of the right-hand fingers, as in

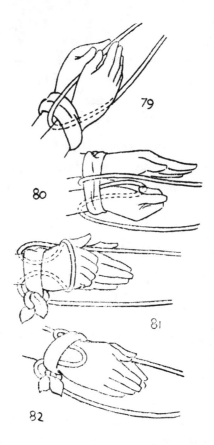

Fig. 80, and slip it over the back of your right hand, as in Fig. 81.

As soon as the loop is over your right hand, open your palm so that both palms are together, and then stop the up-and-down motion of your hands. Tell your assistant to pull tight again; the rope now being as shown in Fig. 82. Be sure not to let the back of your right hand be seen as you now pull hard on the rope.

When ready to break away, turn quickly to the left, at the same time slipping your right thumb under the upper part of the rope.

JAY-BEE'S UNDISTURBED KNOT

A six foot length of soft rope and a piece of silk are the essentials for this really baffling trick. The rope is handed to the person assisting you on your right, the silk to the other assistant on your left, requesting both to thoroughly examine the articles handed them. The

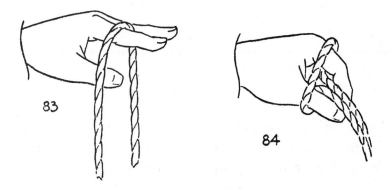

rope is taken back first, as in Fig. 83, with your left side to audience because you are facing your assistant.

Now, turn around to get the silk from the assistant at other side of stage. Drop the left hand to your side, first finger and thumb close on to each other BEHIND the doubled rope as it hangs down. Fig. 84.

Let the rope rest against your left side coat pocket, draw the hand upward and you will find the rope as in Fig. 85. Your aim should be to do these moves as one and part of your general movement from one side of stage to the other.

While your left hand has been executing these moves, your right takes the silk from the assistant on your left. Bring the left hand up in front of you and push the silk through, from the side nearest audience.

of the loop your first finger and thumb occupy. The back of the hand hides this loop and when you have tucked the end of the silk through, let the loop remain in the palm of the hand and slide it to the center of the silk. Tie a knot in the silk. This leaves the rope as

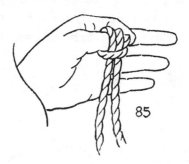

in Fig. 85 only, instead of the thumb and finger being in the loop, the silk occupies this space, and the loop is still hidden in the palm of the left hand.

There is no need to look at the rope or the silk during this operation. You have been telling the audience what you are doing, and that is how long it should take.

The rope is now handed to your assistants, one end to each. Hand an end to the assistant on your right, first of all. You are holding the rope with one hand on each side of the silk and, just before giving him an end, give the rope a smart pull. The other end of the rope is handed to your assistant on the left.

If you inspect the rope and silk at this stage, you will find the rope quite straight but the silk has TWO KNOTS, the one you tied, plus a slip-knot. Bunch these two slightly together and ask your assistants to hold the rope taut. To prove that the silk is securely tied, run it along from end to end of the rope while

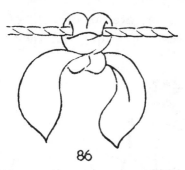

86

holding the slip-knot. See Fig. 86. This slip-knot must be at the back. If it is not, you can quite easily turn it around while showing silk to be tied.

Tell your audience that you are going to pull the piece of silk through the cords without disturbing the knot. Repeat your instructions to assistants to hold the rope straight and firm, get the silk to the center, still holding the slip-knot (which by now is fairly loose). Give a smart pull upwards on the silk and you will find it leaves the rope quite easily. Continue this movement upwards and let the silk fly into the air. Catch it as it falls and display The Undisturbed Knot.

Originator suggests using two ropes and a piece of silk oblong in shape 9" x 18" which, when held by the corner, has the appearance of a full size silk.

THE VEST TURNING TRICK

One end of a three foot length of rope is tied around your right wrist and the other end around your left wrist. The knots may be sealed with sealing wax if you wish. Retiring behind a screen, or into the next room, you return in a minute or so with your vest turned inside out and buttoned up the back. The knots at your wrists have not been tampered with.

As soon as you are out of sight of your audience, unbutton the vest, reach up and draw it over your head.

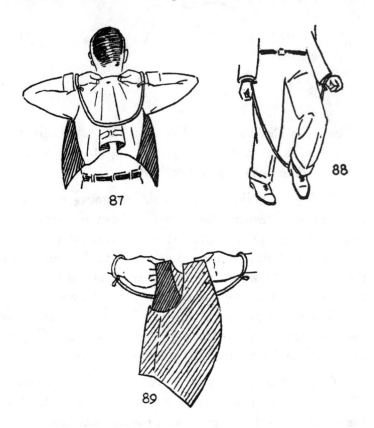

Fig. 87. Now turn the vest inside out by drawing it through one armhole. Fig. 89. Put the vest back on with the back to the front. Step over the rope in order to bring your hands behind you so that you may button the vest up the back. Bring your hands again to the front before returning to your audience. Fig. 88.

The trick may even be performed with the coat on by pulling the vest through the sleeve of the coat before turning it and drawing it back to position again.

THE RING ON THE ROPE

A large ring or bracelet is examined. As in the last trick, your wrists are bound with a three foot length of rope and the knots may be sealed. Regaining possession of the ring, you turn your back to the audience for a brief moment. When you again face them, the ring is threaded on the rope, while the knots on your wrists remain intact.

In reality two rings are used. Before presenting the trick, slip one of the rings over your left wrist and up the sleeve out of sight.

Immediately you turn your back, with your wrists tied and the examined ring in your possession, you slip this ring up under your vest out of sight. Draw the duplicate ring down the left sleeve on to the rope and turn around.

Naturally the ring on the rope and the knots may be examined indefinitely without revealing any trickery.

Sometimes the sleeves are rolled up and the duplicate ring is concealed under the roll of the sleeve.

THE RING KNOTTED ON THE ROPE

An additional touch to the last trick. The ring is not only threaded on the rope but securely tied with a single knot as well.

After the ring is on the rope, as previously explained, slide it close to the knot on the wrist. Grasp the center of the rope and proceed exactly as explained in The Knot of Enchantment, paying particular attention to Fig. 9 and Fig. 10.

Entirely disregard the ring until the knot is made and then you will find that it is around the ring itself.

PUZZLING RING ON THE ROPE

Oscar S. Teale has added an additional subterfuge. Two rings are used, as before, but they are of iron and there is a slight difference. One is slightly distorted to permit it to pass over the left hand on a line with the third joints of the fingers. This is only possible when the hand conforms itself to the shape of the ring and by pressure. The ring will not go over the right hand. A little known fact is that the left hand is invariably smaller than the right. This is the ring that is concealed up the sleeve. Although the ring first displayed is perfectly round, it will not pass over either hand. The variation is so slight as to pass unnoticed.

Now, at the introduction and again at the conclusion of the trick, the ring may be proven too small to pass over your hand. Be sure and use the distorted ring on the right hand when proving (?) this statement.

THE NEW RING ON ROPE

Here is an improved version which should prove mystifying even to the man that knows the original method. Only one ring is used and it can be thoroughly examined both before and after the presentation. May be performed with the sleeves rolled above the elbows.

The big secret is that the ring used is a flexible wire bracelet. After the rope on your wrists and the ring have been examined, you turn your back on the audience and slip the bangle over your wrist. Slide it

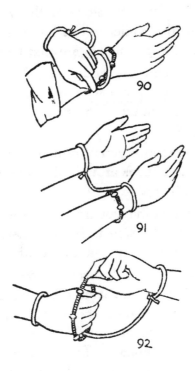

under the rope around the wrist, as in Fig. 90, until the ring is in the position shown in Fig. 91. Remove it from the wrist but over the encircling rope this time. Fig. 92.

The ring is now on the cord, although the knots on the wrists have not been touched.

For impromptu presentation, use a heavy elastic band.

SLATER'S RING ON THE ROPE

This lengthens the item and makes it appear more mysterious.

A ring is given for examination. Your hands are tied as in the previous versions of this mystery. Any volunteer from the audience has his hands tied with a similar length of rope but his are tied behind him.

Volunteer faces the audience. You step behind him, with the ring. Almost immediately the volunteer is asked to turn around. The ring is on the slack between his wrists.

You both resume your original positions. When next the volunteer turns around, the ring is threaded on the slack in both ropes.

For the final time you resume your former positions. This time the ring is on the performer's rope only and everything may again be examined.

Three rings are really used. One ring has a fine slit or break in it so that it may be slipped on and off the ropes at will. One of the remaining two unprepared rings is slipped on the arm and up the sleeve as in the original version. The remaining ring is for the examination at the first. The slit ring is vested.

First Effect. Examined ring is vested. Slit ring removed from vest and slipped on volunteer's rope.

Second Effect. Slit ring is slipped on your own rope as well.

Third Effect. Slit ring is vested again. Unprepared ring brought out of your sleeve and on to your rope.

Rupert Slater is to be congratulated on this interesting and mystifying routine.

BORROWED RING ON ROPE

This may follow any of the previous tricks in this series of rope and ring tricks. You borrow a ring, turn your back, and a moment later show it tied on the center of the rope.

Pass the center of the rope through the ring. Push this loop under the rope encircling the left wrist. Fig. 9. Put your hand through the loop and the loop back under the rope around the wrist. Fig. 10. Drop the loop off your hand and you will find it forms a knot around the ring.

This knot is not quite the same as in The Ring Knotted On The Rope explained earlier.

THE "CHEEKY" ROPE AND RING TRICK

You display a large ring threaded on a three or four foot length of soft rope. Two spectators each hold one end of the rope while its center and the ring is covered with a large handkerchief. Practically the moment your hand is covered, you withdraw it with the ring free of

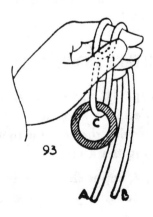

the rope. The ring and rope may both be thoroughly examined.

Secret: The ring is never actually threaded on the rope at all. An extra bit of rope, six or seven inches long, is used and it is the short piece that appears to be the middle of the rope due to the manner in which it is held. See Fig. 93. The ends of the short loop C and the center of the rope itself are concealed between the thumb and fingers of the left hand.

One spectator stands at your left and grasps end A while the other spectator stands at your right and holds end B. This has the appearance of stretching the rope out straight with the exception of the center which is apparently looped down between your fingers and bears the ring.

Another spectator covers your hand with an opaque handkerchief. Immediately crumple the short loop C in your hand and conceal it under the rest of the fingers as you display the ring held at the tips of the forefinger and thumb.

It is easier, but not quite as effective, to place both hands under the handkerchief. The short loop C is still most readily concealed in the same hand that holds the ring.

EDWARD SMITH'S ROPE AND RING TRICK

A rope, perhaps 18 inches long, looped around a ring and its ends tied in a knot, as shown in Fig. 94, is handed to a person with the request that he remove the ring without untying the knot.

This seemingly impossible task is quickly accomplished by you on turning your back to the group for a moment. Or the trick may be performed beneath a large handkerchief spread over the rope and your two hands.

94   95

Fig. 95 reveals the secret. Before the knot is tied the rope is cut near one end and a small brass bolt is inserted in the end of the long piece of rope while a small nut is imbedded in the end of the short piece. The screw end of the longer length is then screwed to the nut end of the short piece and the rope is tied in such a manner that the knot conceals the joint. The sealing wax on the ends of the rope and around the knot serve the double purpose of keeping the knot in place and in adding to the mystery.

To perform the trick you have merely to unscrew the right-hand part of the loop close to the knot, remove the ring and screw the rope back in place.

The rope may be easily prepared by anyone. Procure a suitable ring, either iron or wood, from one to two inches across. It has already been suggested that the rope be 18 inches or more in length. Window-sash cord will be found to be very satisfactory. Remove the brass screw and its nut from a used dry cell. File the nut to the smallest possible diameter. With a file, square the unthreaded part of the post. Cut a two or three inch piece off one end of the rope and wind the two severed ends with a string to a distance of half an inch. With a round awl or nail make a hole in each severed end. Work some glue into each hole. In the hole in the long length of rope insert the squared end of the brass post and in the hole of the short piece of cord insert a nut. A bit of glue may be spread across the two severed ends

When the glue has thoroughly dried, unwind the strings on the two ends of the two pieces of rope, screw the rope together and make a knot in the looped rope as in Fig. 94. Make sure that the joined part of the rope is completely hidden inside the knot. Make the knot permanent by smearing both it and the ends of the rope with melted sealing wax.

Before screwing up the rope give the long side of the loop a few backward twists to prevent it from curling; also put the ring on the rope as in Fig. 94.

THE DROPPING RING

The requirements for this bit of mystery are a two foot length of soft rope, a borrowed finger ring, and a handkerchief. With these simple articles you apparently accomplish the impossibility of passing one solid object through another.

First the rope is tied in a regulation square knot or double knot, leaving a small loop below the knot. Then the ring is placed on the rope and another double knot is tied a few inches above it. The ends of the rope are held by two persons as shown in Fig. 96.

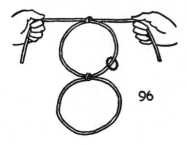

96

It is impossible to remove the ring from the rope, and the knots prevent it from falling from the upper loop to the lower. The handkerchief is thrown over the knots, and it hides the ring and the loops; but the ends of the rope are still in view.

The performer reaches beneath the handkerchief, raising one side so that he can see beneath. In a few moments the handkerchief is removed. The ring is on the lower rope loop, apparently having passed through the solid double knot! See Fig. 97.

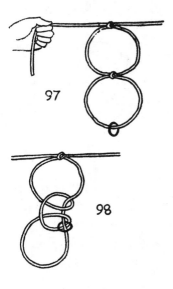

97

98

The secret of this trick is simple; yet the method of its accomplishment is never suspected.

The double knot between the loops is not tied tightly. You loosen it under cover of the handkerchief, and you can push the ring along the string and right through the knots, on to the loop below. See Fig. 98. Then draw the knots as tight as possible, and remove the handkerchief.

With a little practice, this can be performed very rapidly. Everything may be examined and the result is very puzzling.

WHOLESALE RING REMOVAL

Any number of harness rings and a two foot length of rope are passed for examination. After having convinced the spectators that the articles are perfectly free from deception, the rope is doubled over and the resulting loop is threaded through one of the rings as in Fig. 99. The ends of the rope are then pulled through

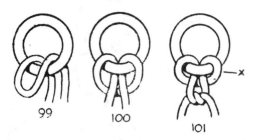

99 100 101

the loop thus formed as shown in Fig. 100. In order to further convince the audience of the ring's security, the two ends of the rope are tied together in a knot which will naturally slide down nearly to the ring, but the knot should not be allowed to run within more than an inch from the ring. The reason for this will be obvious later.

The remaining harness rings are threaded on the doubled rope and the ends given to a spectator to hold. Suddenly the rings drop free and fall into your hands.

This trick is very surprising and will cause much speculation. Neither the rings nor the rope are secretly prepared in any way in advance.

The secret of this pleasing little effect is extremely simple but need not be discredited on that account. Under cover of your hands, the loop marked "X" (Fig. 101) is slipped over and off the ring, the rings will then all immediately fall from the rope.

A personal touch may be given the trick by borrowing and using a number of finger rings.

Any number of knots may be tied with the ends of the rope after the first ring has been threaded and they will remain on the rope after the rings have been released, thus creating a most convincing effect.

CHARLES LEEDY'S ROPO RINGO

A new and novel application of familiar principles, resulting in a showy and convincing trick.

Two spectators each hold one end of a nine foot length of rope. The center of the rope is covered with a handkerchief. You borrow a finger ring and place it beneath the handkerchief where its form is plainly visible. Suddenly whisk the handkerchief away from the rope disclosing a ball of cord wrapped around the rope at its center. Taking the end of the cord you quickly unwind the ball while the assistants hold the rope taut. When cord is all off, ring is found tightly knotted to rope, from which it is cut with scissors or may be, less effectively, untied.

Secret: In preparing for the trick in advance, the cord is wrapped round the center of the rope to form a ball but a round tube is left extending to center so that the center of rope may be drawn out through it. The loop pulled out is placed over the end of the projecting tube which holds it in place. Tube must be large enough to permit the ring to be pulled through it. The rope is placed on your table with a handkerchief covering the ball at center.

Presentation. Pick up the rope. Give one end to each of two spectators. Borrow a ring. Reach beneath the handkerchief and slip the loop of rope that protrudes through the tube over the ring as pictured in Fig. 100. After the ring is looped on and pulled in, you extract the tube and hold one end under the handkerchief to simulate the ring. Quickly pull the handkerchief away to reveal the ball of cord on the rope. Handkerchief may be placed in pocket to leave your hands free to unwind cord. When handkerchief is removed later, the tube is left behind. Tell volunteers to pull tightly on the rope as you remove the cord. This pulls the ring more securely to center of ball and tightens the knot. Would suggest concluding the trick by returning the borrowed ring.

CHARLES T. JORDAN'S PSYCHIC RING RELEASE

A single piece of soft rope is examined, and anyone runs it through an ordinary curtain ring, securing the latter at the line's center with a single knot. The performer removes his coat and runs an end of the cord down either sleeve—the tied ring remaining in full sight. Two spectators hold the cord ends, and under cover of the coat the performer removes the ring, which may be secretly marked to obviate exchange. Then all is examined.

This is the height of perfection in misdirection, the method employed being absurdly simple, yet practically indetectible. The only requisites are the soft rope and two wooden curtain rings, one being placed beforehand in the inner breast pocket of the coat.

The tying is absolutely fair, and the rope ends are run through the sleeves with no deception whatever. As the two parties seize the rope ends, the performer's only move is to secretly hunch the coat shoulders toward one another, so that not many inches of the rope can be seen when the inside of the coat is shown. The coat is suspended by the rope with its back to the company.

To show the ring, the wizard gives the coat a half turn to his right, which slackens the rope somewhat. When he turns the coat back again, and his assistants are drawing the rope taut, he indetectibly slides the coat slightly to his right along the rope, causing the ring to enter the coat's right arm unsuspected by any one. A couple of trials will teach the moves better than a page of print can.

The performer steps aside a moment, then goes to the coat again. Reaching inside it he secretly takes the second ring from its breast pocket, and with the other hand again swings the coat around. Holding the ring against the rope, it naturally appears to be the one tied thereon, as it is the only ring in sight. Holding the coat by its collar with one hand, he apparently yanks the ring free with the other.

Requesting his assistants to release their hold of the rope ends, he carries the coat to the table, laying it there on its back. With the ring still in view in his right hand, he seizes with the same hand the end of the rope protruding from the LEFT coat sleeve, and with the left hand he secretly seizes the ring inside the RIGHT coat sleeve, through the fabric.

The need of a soft rope becomes apparent. If the ring is smooth, and the knot not too tight, the act of pulling one end of the rope automatically unties it. The rope pulled free, the right hand, holding the duplicate ring, enters the right coat sleeve for the purpose of putting the coat on. But on the way it drops THAT RING into the pocket whence it came, and emerges from the lower end of the sleeve with the original one, picked up on the way. The coat on, the ring and rope are passed for examination.

EDDIE JOSEPH'S RINGED

A length of a rope and a ring are given out for examination. While these two articles are with the audience, two persons are invited on the stage. Each of the assistants is now asked to take hold of one end of the rope, performer taking the ring. Performer now explains that he will pass the ring on the rope while both ends are held by them. The center of the rope is now passed behind a screen and after a very short interval the screen is removed revealing the ring—not only threaded on the rope but also knotted thereon by means of a double knot. Performer now asks one of the gentlemen to unknot the first knot and so satisfy himself of its genuineness. As soon as this is done there now remains only one knot clearly seen by every one.

Performer continues "Since it was possible to pass the ring on the rope while the ends were in keeping of the gentlemen you may be thinking that it is equally possible to remove it the same way. Will someone kindly try to do so?" This cannot be done for the simple reason that there is a genuine knot that must be untied in the usual manner in order to release the ring. The rope and ring are now taken to the audience and someone asked to undo the knot.

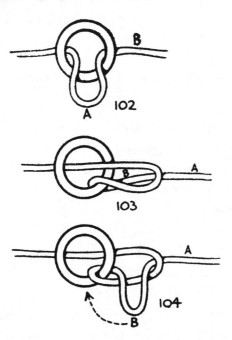

Secret: In Fig. 102, A represents the center of the rope drawn through the ring in order to form a loop. B is at the performer's right.

Loop A is next placed against B as indicated in Fig. 103.

Refer to the final moves in Fig. 104. B is pulled through A to form a new loop which is slipped over ring from underneath as suggested by the arrow. The rope is pulled tight on top of ring to appear as a double knot.

An explanation of only one point is now necessary. After the ring is shown on the rope, tied apparently by means of a double knot, performer must ask the assistant ON HIS LEFT to undo the first knot. While he is untying the knot, the other assistant on the right must not let go of his end of the rope.

As soon as the first knot is undone, a genuine knot will be automatically formed around the ring. Try it and I am sure you will like it.

GRAHAM ADAMS ROPE AND RING EXPERIMENT

The effect of this experiment is that a solid metal ring which has been passed on to a thin rope, the rope being passed around the body of an assistant, and tied once in view of the audience, is pulled free of both ring and assistant leaving the knot intact.

Secret: The ring is of solid brass and measures three inches over all. The rope is of cotton variety and is one quarter inch thick and about twelve feet long. There is no preparation.

Presentation: The method of tying will first be described and then an additional tip that will assist in the performance.

As both the right and left hands have their work to do in this tie it would be well to study the accompanying drawings with a rope and ring in your hands. For experimental purposes use the back of a chair on which to do the tying.

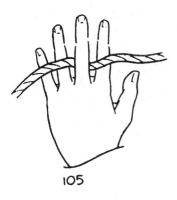

105

Holding the rope in the left hand as in Fig. 105, the right and left hands are extended while exhibiting the rope. The right hand holds the rope between the finger and thumb. Drop your hold on the rope with your right hand and pick up the ring. Thread it on the rope and resume your hold with the right hand.

Stand behind your assistant, hold the rope first over his head, then in front of him and then behind him, arms being extended all the while.

The left hand is now moved behind the back of the assistant out of sight of the audience, while the right hand proceeds to wrap the rope around him.

FOLLOW THIS VERY CLOSELY: When the right hand with its portion of the rope reaches the left hand, the finger and thumb of left hand grasp the rope. The right hand leaves its hold and travels to the back of the assistant.

The finger and thumb of the right hand are placed through the metal ring, travel under the portion of rope in the thumb of the left hand, grasp the loose end of the rope, and pull it through the metal ring.

The loop thus formed by the portion marked A in Fig. 106 is then slipped over the ring, the two loose ends

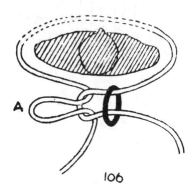

106

of the rope are pulled tightly, tied with one knot at the front of the assistant and the ends are given to him to hold.

You may then explain the situation. "A solid metal ring has been threaded on a rope. The rope has been passed around the body of my assistant and tied in front. The problem is to remove the ring and pass the rope through the assistant, leaving the knot intact."

To remove the ring, all that is necessary is to slip the loop, the ring will come away, and the two assistants, pulling quickly on the rope at both ends, the rope will appear to pass through your volunteer.

This was experimented with and found to work nicely, but after a few performances another idea came along.

When the loop was slipped off the ring to make the release, if the loop was tied once around the rope the ring could be handed to the volunteer, the rope pulled to show it was still firmly tied, the knot at the back slipped, and the rope pulled again, when the assistant was left with the ring in his hands, and the rope free in front of him.

THE ROPE THROUGH THE STICK

A rope is wrapped around the wand, a knife inserted about the center of the wand, the rope looped around the knife, wrapped several times more around the wand, and the ends tied.

You grasp the knot, a spectator removes the knife, and the rope apparently penetrates the wand.

Have any one hold the wand. Grasp one end of the rope in each hand. Place the rope on top of the

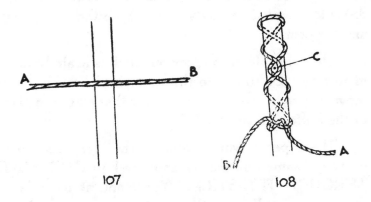

107   108

wand as in Fig. 107. Place both ends beneath the wand and transfer them to the opposite hands. Be sure that A is next the wand and B crosses on top of it. Fig. 108.

The ends are brought to the top of the wand, A still next the stick and B crossing it. A knife is inserted in the stick at C. The ropes again cross A underneath and B on top. They are crossed in the same manner on the under side of the wand, brought to the top and the ends tied. As soon as the knife is removed, the rope will pull free.

The rope may be crossed back and forth, above and below the wand, as many times as you wish but it must cross the same number of times on each side of the knife as each turn around the wand on one side of the knife cancels a turn on the other side. Fig. 108 should make the method of winding the rope perfectly clear.

U. F. GRANT'S WITCH'S BROOM

A girl stands against a broom or post. A single rope is wrapped back and forth around both her and the post and the ends of the rope are tied at her ankles. At a word of command she walks forward. The rope drops to the floor perfectly free of both the young lady and the post.

The principle of the previous trick is again brought in to play. Unknown to the audience, there is a removable peg at the back of the post that takes the place of the knife at C in Fig. 108.

The rope is wound around the girl and post using the same routine as explained in THE ROPE THROUGH THE STICK. You stand at the side of the post and pull away the peg as you command the girl to walk forward.

CUTTING A WOMAN IN HALF

This simplified presentation still retains the appearance of an illusion.

A girl holds a large dagger with the point pressed against her waist. A long rope is passed over the knife, then twice around the girl's waist and crossed in front of her. The ends of the rope are held by two spectators. At command, they pull on the rope and it passes clear through the girl's body.

A rope about eight feet long and an ordinary table knife will do. Have the girl stand and hold the knife pressed against her waist. Lay the rope over the knife —the ends hanging down on each side. Stand in front of the girl and grasp one end of the rope in each hand.

Pass the ends around the girl's waist and cross the end in the right hand over that in the left, then bring the ends to the front. Cross the rope ends UNDER the knife, the end in the left hand passing over that in the right hand. Bring both ends up over the knife and cross the end in the right hand over that in the left.

Once more pass the ends around the girl's waist and cross the end in the left hand over that in the right. Bring the ends to the front and cross them once more. Place a spectator on each side of the girl and give each of them one end of the rope to hold.

The manner in which the rope has been passed around the girl conceals the fact that its middle is really doubled in front of the girl, the two loops being held by the point of the knife. When you order the two volunteers to pull, all the girl has to do is move the knife point an inch or so away from her waist and the rope pulls clear and appears to have passed right through her waist.

CHAPTER 4
CUT AND RESTORED CORD

Chapter 4. CUT AND RESTORED CORD

THE FAMOUS KELLAR STRING TRICK

This is one of the most wonderful of all cut and restored string tricks and has puzzled not only laymen but many magicians as well, chiefly through the very simpleness of the procedure. Only one string is used, and magicians are always looking for a switch, substitution or fake cut.

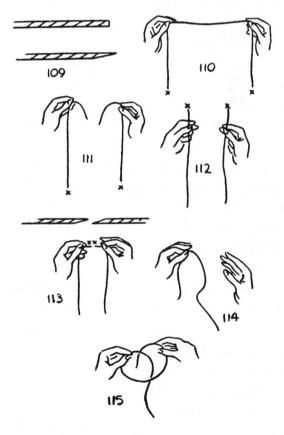

PREPARATION: Procure an ordinary piece of twine and a small cake of "magician's wax," or beeswax. Taper each end of the twine to a point with sharp scissors. Figure 109 shows how the twine will look both before and after this treatment. Wax well the two ends of the twine.

PRESENTATION: Exhibit the string (for those having an insight into magic, same may be measured, but this is unnecessary for a lay audience) holding first by one end and then the other; showing that there is nothing concealed in the hands.

Now, hold the string as in Figure 110 and allow a spectator to cut it near the center. In this, and the three succeeding illustrations, the waxed ends of the string are marked with an X.

Show that it is actually cut into two pieces, holding one piece in each hand as in Figure 111, and also holding by first one end and then the other, so that you finally end with the waxed ends uppermost as in Figure 112.

Bring the waxed ends together and overlap them as in Figure 113. The string is now passed to the left hand as in Figure 114 where the ends are tightly squeezed and rolled between the forefinger and thumb which causes the wax to cement them together.

The attention of your audience is diverted from this action by first tying and then untying a single knot by forming a loop and passing the end through as in Figure 115.

You explain that the ordinary individual would attempt to restore the string to usefulness by tying the ends together with a knot but a magician would actually restore the cord.

KARL GERMAINE'S STRING RESTORATION

PREPARATION: Taper and wax the ends of a piece of cord as in the Kellar method. Join the ends together so that you have an apparently endless loop as in Figure 116. Again the waxed ends are indicated in the illustration with an X.

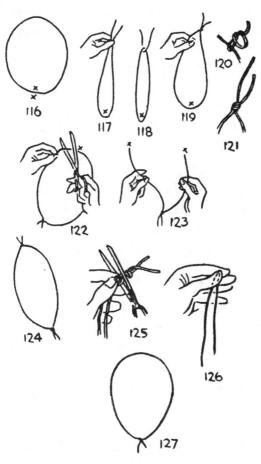

A shorter piece of cord is looped through the circle as in Figure 118. When the string is held as in Figure 117, it appears to be in one piece with the ends projecting above the thumb and forefinger. The string is held in this manner as you commence the trick.

PRESENTATION: Tie the ends together so that the loop appears as in Figure 119. Figure 120 illustrates that it is a weaver's knot that is made. It is drawn up tightly, as in Figure 121, before your audience is allowed to see it.

When you make the cut, hold the cord as in Figure 122 and snip right through where the ends are held together with the wax.

The ends are held far apart to show them actually separated, Figure 123, and a small portion of string clipped from each end. This prevents anyone finding any trace of the wax when the cord is examined later.

Tie these ends together with a weaver's knot to resemble as closely as possible the fake knot you tied at the beginning. The cord now looks like Figure 124. Rotate the loop between your fingers so that your audience loses track of which knot you just tied and the one made at the start. Now, cut away the fake knot, Figure 125.

It is well to keep the apparently resulting two ends, really the doubled center of the loop, concealed for a moment or two between the thumb and forefinger, Figure 126, before revealing the cord restored, Figure 127.

This knot is genuine and may be untied and the string given to a spectator as a souvenir.

JOE BERG'S JAPANESE PAPER STRING RESTORATION

EFFECT: Performer shows a paper-twisted string between his thumb and first finger, the two ends visibly protruding from the tips of the fingers. Spectator is requested to light the string at the center.

After the fire has burned the center of the string apart, attention is called to the fact that it is specially imported Japanese rice paper string and, although it is separated into two equal pieces, the paper may be restored immediately to its original state by merely joining two ends.

A spectator is allowed to hold two of the four ends. Performer covers the remaining two ends with his empty right hand and with a slight rubbing motion causes the ends to become joined and restored. Both hands are perfectly empty and the string is passed for examination.

SECRET: The principle used in this trick is new and has never been applied to any other cut and restored effect.

The two ends that the spectators see protruding from the finger tips are really the center of the string, Figure 128. The center part of the string is twisted

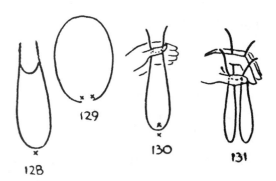

tightly "U" shape so that it appears to be two ends. The real ends of the string are twisted together to make the center, Figure 129.

Hold the string as in Figure 130. Have a spectator light the center (?) thus burning away the evidence. Immediately put the fire out and even up the burned ends by trimming them with scissors. Bring the ends up between first and second fingers and show the four ends, Figure 131. All ends appear to be the same.

Ask the spectator to hold two ends, one in each hand. Of course you give him the two ends between first and second fingers (real ends) while you place your other hand over the two twisted ends (center) and with a slight rubbing motion, pulling the string towards your body, cause the twisted ends to unwind and the string apparently restore.

Spectator is requested to let go of one end and pull the string through your fist. This completes the straightening out of the twisted center of string. Show your hand empty and pass the string for examination.

NOTE: It does not require any special paper, any strip of tissue paper will work. Do not twist it too tightly in the center, the twisted ends will not stay twisted and expose the secret if you do. The string thus prepared may be placed on the table out of sight of the spectators and picked up when ready.

FIGURE "8" STRING RESTORATION

This very old trick has sometimes been called Tying An Invisible Knot With The Teeth.

EFFECT: The ends of a length of string are tied together in order to make a large loop. This is folded so that you have a double loop half the size of the original. A cut is made through both strings of the doubled loop and the resulting ends are placed in your mouth. After a certain amount of facial contortions, during which you are supposed to be tying the invisible knot with your teeth, the string is drawn from the mouth restored.

SECRET: The doubled loop is not as innocent as it appears. The actual formation is as in Figure 132,

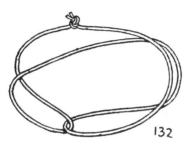

132

with the two loops linked together at some portion of its circumference.

If you are sufficiently interested to try this out, you will probably develop your own move for bringing this state of affairs about. As simple a procedure as most is to hold the loop horizontally in front of you between your extended hands.

The back of the left hand and the palm of the right hand are uppermost. The fingers encircle the cord. Bring the two hands together and take the cord in the left hand only but, as the hands approach each other, you give the left hand a half turn away from you so that the palm is uppermost and the right hand makes a half turn toward you so that the back of the hand is uppermost. These combined moves form the link at that part of the cord most distant from your left hand.

Rotate the cord through your left hand until the link comes under your thumb where it is concealed by it and your first finger.

Cut through the doubled loop a short distance from where you are holding it. This apparently separates the cord into three parts as six ends are visible but the ends that you are holding at the tips of your fingers belong to a very short piece.

It is these ends, and a small portion of the cord itself, that are placed in the mouth. The short piece is shoved by the tongue to the side of the mouth. The cord is grasped at either side of the mouth and slowly pulled forth restored.

Instead of placing the cord in the mouth, the short piece could be tied, Figures 120 and 121, and cut away, Figure 125.

SIMPLE STRING RESTORATION

The magician uses a piece of thin, pliable string. He holds the string in the left hand and lets the spectators gauge the length of it.

Then he holds the string between his hands, and it is fairly cut in the center. In fact, both pieces of string are shown quite separate.

The ends of the strings are brought together and the string is rolled up between the fingers. A moment later the magician draws out the string, and it is completely restored to its original length and condition.

Just one piece of string is used, and it is about eighteen inches long. Before showing the trick the magician winds about six inches of the string around the tip of his left second finger, so that just a few inches of string hang from his left hand. He then exhibits the string, his left forefinger hiding the loops that encircle the second finger. The string appears to be about a foot long.

Taking the long end of the string in his right fingers, the magician lets a spectator cut it in the center. He then appears to have two pieces of string, each about six inches long. In reality the piece in his left hand measures twelve inches.

In bringing the ends together, and rolling up the string, the magician pokes the short piece into his left hand, slips the loops from his finger, and draws out a string twelve inches long!

The short piece of string is either dropped on the floor or hidden at the base of the left thumb. To the spectators, the original string has been cut and restored.

TWYNO

EFFECT: A fairly stiff piece of cord about three feet long is used. Show your hands to be otherwise perfectly empty and then hold the cord in your right hand about fourteen inches from one end. Next seize hold of the short end with your left hand thumb and forefinger with your right hand held above your left. Your right hand next draws the cord back over your

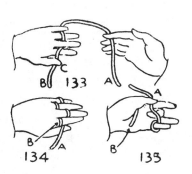

left forefinger, and under your second left finger as shown in Figure 133.

Your right hand now brings the cord back over your left hand little finger, under your third finger, over your second, and under your first, the cord on its return trip being made to pass across the center joints of your left hand fingers; the long end of the cord you permit to hang free over your left thumb. Figure 134 illustrates just how your left hand now looks.

A member of the company is requested, at this point, to cut the string where it passes over the back of your left hand second finger, Figure 134, a pair of scissors being used for the purpose.

Then without covering your left hand with anything, or permitting your right to approach it, move your left hand slowly in the air, with its back toward your friends. Suddenly the severed ends of the cord leap together and reunite in full view of all! You unwind the cord with your right hand and pass it out for examination.

SECRET: The trick lies in what happens on the return trip of the cord as it is brought back from the little finger of the left hand to the left thumb. Arrange the cord just as shown in Figure 133. When you pass it up and around your little finger, you secretly seize the short end, B, C, Figure 133, of the cord with the thumb and forefinger of your right hand and secretly draw this short end up over your second finger. The long end, A, accordingly does not appear on the back of the left hand at all, but crosses on the underside of your left fingers, directly to your left thumb over which it is permitted to hang. The short end, B, C, is just long enough to permit its being held between your left thumb and left forefinger.

When that portion of the string passing over your left second finger, Figure 134, is cut as previously described, you face your friends and, as you slowly wave your left hand back and forth, bend your left second finger inwards towards its palm and insert its end, Figure 135, underneath the long portion of the string.

Immediately straighten out these fingers and at the same moment slightly spread apart your other left hand fingers. This movement will cause the short end of cord to slide clear by your second finger. The short piece remaining in your left hand is clipped between your thumb and forefinger at their roots. The spectators actually seem to see the cord reunite itself.

When you remove the cord from your left hand fingers, get the short, cut piece between your right thumb and forefinger and hold it concealed there while you exhibit your empty left hand and the restored (?) string.

IMPROMPTU STRING RESTORATION

EFFECT: A string is cut into two nearly equal parts. The ends are tied together but the knot dissolves and the string is as good as it ever was.

SECRET: Hold the string as shown in Figure 136. Right hand brings its end up, Figure 137, and places it between the tips of first finger and thumb of left hand, Figure 138.

Let the cord drop from your left hand. Spectators can clearly see that center of cord is just about where you are holding it with right hand.

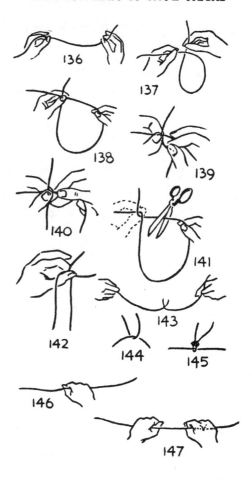

Again grasp the string as in Figure 136 and bring up the right hand end as before, Figures 137 and 138.

Ask a spectator to cut the cord just about at the middle. As he reaches for the knife or scissors, you alter the position of the cord without changing its appearance to the volunteer. This is accomplished by dropping the cord from between your right hand fingers, grasping the cord just beneath the left thumb, Figure 139, and raising it to the position formerly occupied by that portion of the cord you dropped. The dropped cord takes up the position just vacated by that part of the cord you now hold in your right hand, Figure 140.

Figure 141 shows that the spectator really cuts a short piece of the end instead of cutting through the cord's center. After the cut, the ends are dropped so that it appears that the cord is in two nearly equal parts, Figure 142.

The short piece, apparently the ends, is knotted, Figures 144 and 145, and two spectators given the cord to hold, Figure 143.

Conceal the knot by closing the right hand over it, Figure 146. Slide the right hand along the cord to the right carrying the concealed knot with it. Left hand is closed around cord where knot was, Figure 147. It appears that you covered the knot with the right hand, changed your mind, and then covered it with the left.

Ask the spectator on your right to grasp the cord a little closer to the center. You keep the cord from dropping as the spectator changes the position of his hand. This alteration of position is all that you require in order to slip the knot off the end of the cord from where it may be readily disposed of in many ways.

EDDIE JOSEPH'S RESTORED STRING

A length of twine is handed to a spectator with the instructions that the same be measured, cut and knotted in the usual manner. The performer, after showing both hands empty, takes string from party and winds it around his left index finger. Please remember (as the magic catalogue would say) the actual cut string is wound around the finger.

The right hand is shown empty and a few passes made with it over the index finger. A spectator is told to grasp one end of the string and pull it off your finger. When this is done, the string is found restored.

The performer shows both hands empty, and they really are empty.

SECRET: After reading the effect you will naturally conclude that the string has been exchanged after the cut, but at the moment we are more concerned with the method employed to effect the change.

A hollow finger is made to fit over your own left index finger. It reaches to the second joint. I had mine made of silver by a jeweler and it is painted flesh color with nail and other details complete. When this is slipped over my real finger and the hand kept slightly in motion, it is absolutely indetectible at close range. So much for the apparatus—now for using it.

Before commencing the trick, wind a piece of duplicate twine around your real index finger and slip the hollow finger over this.

After the twine has been cut and knotted by a spectator, show both hands empty and then wind the twine around the index finger—really over the false finger.

Show right hand empty and then make a few passes over the finger by moving right hand up and down. On the third or fourth pass, clip the false finger by bending the second and third finger and pull it away from over the index finger. In other words, the false finger is finger palmed in the right hand. This is one continuous move and done under pretense of a pass. Audience has nothing to suspect as the duplicate twine on finger is exposed and believed by them to be the one wound in their presence.

As soon as the false finger is carried away by right hand, suddenly bend forward and ask spectator to pull twine off the finger. Simultaneously with this bending, the right hand gets rid of false finger by dropping it in the pochette or slipping it under the vest.

The right hand is now ready to be shown empty before the string is completely unwound off the index finger.

OVETTE'S SUPREME STRING MYSTERY

This variation of the previous trick is said to be, in Mr. Ovette's opinion, the finest cut and restored string effect ever evolved.

The requirements for the stunt are simply a length of wrapping twine and a thumb tip which fits loosely over your right thumb. Cut a long length of twine into two equal parts. Wrap one of the pieces around the right thumb, rather tightly, and the thumb tip is slipped over the string to conceal its presence.

PRESENTATION: Take the duplicate string in the right hand. Hand string and scissors to a spectator who is requested to cut it into two or three pieces. The cut cord is then tied by the spectator into one length. Take the string in this tied condition and have spectator retain one end. Wrap the twine around your thumb. As you do this the spectator is naturally drawn toward you as the string gets shorter. There need be no fear of detection as the spectator approaches for by this time the thumb tip should be well covered. Make a slight turn away from the spectator toward the audience and, as you make the turn simultaneously slip off the string-covered thumb tip. Nothing different in appearance will be noticed since the removal of the thumb tip brings the second piece of string into view. Turn back to the assisting spectator and, as you do so, bring your hands apart. Request the volunteer to again grasp the end of the string and draw it off the thumb. As he does this, your other hand with thumb tip palmed goes into the pocket and leaves all the evidence.

If this appears a bit bold, you may go into the pocket and bring forth some small object which is supposed to possess mystic power (a Chinese Coin is ideal), touch the string with the coin, and then have the spectator remove the duplicate string as explained. The twine is found fully restored.

LOUIS F. CHRISTIANER'S FAVORITE STRING TRICK

A length of string is cut into small pieces, which are then placed in a glass of water. Using a pencil the performer takes out the wet pieces, and places them in the left hand, holding them between the thumb and first finger. Then squeezing the water out of the pieces, he immediately draws them out, the strings being fully restored.

SECRET: Very little preparation is required for this fine method. A duplicate length of string must be wrapped around the end of the pencil rather loosely. This is then placed in the left vest pocket, or other place where the performer carries his pencil.

Cut up the length of string, and drop the pieces into the glass of water. Now with the right hand remove the pencil and holding it by the end with the string, he fishes out the wet pieces with the other end. The pencil is now transferred to the left hand with the thumb and first finger of same concealing the string around the end. The right hand takes off the wet pieces, squeezes out the water and pretends to place them between the thumb and first finger of the left hand, really retaining them in the right, which at once takes the pencil, while the duplicate piece is exposed.

The pencil is placed in the pocket, pieces with it, while the other length of string is drawn out, apparently the original restored.

A little practice is required to get the moves, but after once mastered, it is very fine indeed.

THE MASTER CUT AND RESTORED STRING

The method used to produce the following effect is so little known that the proper presentation of the trick admits of no satisfactory solution to the beholder.

An ordinary piece of string is measured by some-one of the group and found, say, to be thirty-two inches in length. This string is then folded in the middle and held in the performer's left hand, the loop end projecting three or four inches above his thumb and forefinger. The loop is now cut and the resulting ends lighted with a match. The burning ends are finally extinguished, squeezed together and a few magic passes made over them by the performer's right hand when, behold, the string is found to have been mysteriously restored and still to measure exactly thirty-two inches in length.

SECRET: The secret lies in the fact that the measured string is not cut at all. The conjurer, unknown to the spectators, makes use of a bit of accessory apparatus consisting of a loop of string made from a similar piece of string and to the knotted ends of which is securely tied a length of black silk-cord elastic, Figure 148.

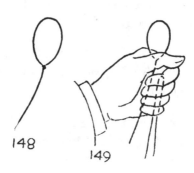

The other end of the elastic is attached by means of a safety pin to the back of the performer's vest, near the top. The small loop of string is tucked into the left vest (watch) pocket and held in place by a pin so placed that the performer's left hand fingers can instantly detach the loop when wanted. In this same vest pocket must be a small pair of scissors or a pen knife.

Equipped as described you are ready to present the trick. The string having been measured, divide it in the middle and hold it in your right hand. At this moment you remember that you need a knife. You reach into your left vest pocket for the knife previously placed there and at the same time secretly get possession of the small loop of string. Immediately pass the knife into your right hand in exchange for the doubled end of the long string. You next apparently pull the looped or doubled end of the long string up through your left hand, but in reality you hold it concealed and draw up the loop attached to the elastic instead, Figure 149.

This visible, fake loop is now cut and lighted. As soon as the burning ends are extinguished and pressed together, and a few magic passes made with your right hand to heighten the effect, the elastic is permitted to draw the small loop secretly beneath your coat. There-upon you triumphantly exhibit the restored string.

A stiff, tough wrapping cord will prove the most satisfactory. While holding the fake loop, keep your left hand in such a position that the black elastic will be concealed against that side of your left wrist which is next to your body thus preventing anyone from catching a glimpse of it. A little practice will enable you to make all the required moves in a perfectly natural manner, without fumbling.

S. B. BLODGETT'S DOUBLE RESTORATION

EFFECT: Two strings are examined. They are of stiff wrapping cord or braided fish line and are each eighteen inches long. The performer holds the strings so that a spectator may cut through the center of both simultaneously. The cut strings are held wide apart— two separate halves in each hand. All four pieces are now placed in the left hand, spectator grasps two ends and pulls them away from the magician. Both strings are restored.

SECRET: An extra piece is tied in a loop about one and a half inches in diameter. Make a tight knot and trim the ends up close. Clip this loop between the first and second fingers of the right hand so that the loop stays open.

After the strings are examined, take them back in the left hand. Grasp both ends near the top and place them in the right hand. As you do so, it is easy to push the ends right through the loop and grasp them between the first finger and thumb of the right hand as they emerge on the other side. It is almost like threading a needle. Grasp the ends in left hand and pull them up so that loop is about at center.

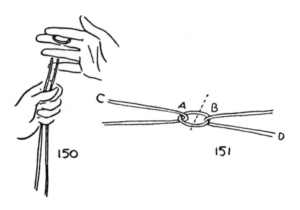

Figure 150 shows just how the strings and loop are held at the start of this move.

Now take one string in one hand and the other string in the other hand with the loop stretched between, Figure 151. The strings are held at A and B with the thumbs and first fingers. The dotted line indicates where spectator cuts thinking he is dividing the two strings at the centers.

Hold your hands at a distance apart with what appears to be two halves of the strings in each. They are then passed to the left hand during which action C and D ends are shifted to opposite sides. As the spectator takes two ends and draws the strings away, you palm off the two short pieces of what remains of the loop.

L. W. PACKAGE CORD MYSTERY

This little experiment is briefly prefaced, as follows:

No matter how smoothly we go through life, there are some problems that all of us must face, and one of them is this: when we get a package, shall we cut the cord off to get the package open quicker, or shall we try to untie it so as to have the cord in case we should want it again? Everyone worries about this save the magician. He does both. I will show you how. Here I have a piece of heavy package cord. I haven't any package to go with it, but you will have to imagine that. We will suppose that the cord is around the package, and that I want to get it off. I will merely take a pair of scissors, and snip it through the center, thus; cutting it, in fact, wherever necessary in order to get it off the package in the shortest possible space of time. So far, so good. But suppose later I wish to use the cord? I merely blow upon it, and lo, it is as good as new, and can be used for tying up anything I wish!"

The working of this experiment is perfectly simple. On the outside of one of the blades of the scissors is soldered a small tube, which has a bottom. In this tube is an extra piece, looped, of the same kind of cord as is used, Figure 152.

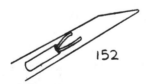

152

The performer first shows the cord, and then doubles it, grasping it by the looped center in his left hand, which is closed into a fist. He makes a half turn, so that his right side is to the audience. The right hand takes the scissors from the table, keeping the side on which the tube is soldered away from the audience. Now, with the same hand, still holding the scissors, he apparently draws the looped center of the cord up out of the left fist. Actually the left hand merely grips the extra loop, which is drawn out of the tube into view. The movement appears perfectly regular.

The supposed center of the cord is now cut. With the aid of the right hand the whole cord is then looped up into the left hand, in a number of irregular loops, tangled together. As the performer remarks that he "cuts the cord wherever necessary to get it off the package in the shortest possible space of time" he apparently slashes into this looped cord at different places with the tips of the scissor blades, and small pieces clipped off fall to the floor. Actually he cuts nothing except the extra piece, which is cut away, leaving the cord whole, but due to the intricate position of the cord the performer appears to be cutting into the cord at different spots more or less at random. In this particular experiment at least, this is a much better excuse for the disposing of the extra loop than cutting a piece openly from each end, as many will believe that the cord has been cut a number of times. The scissors are laid aside; the performer blows upon the cord and then opens it out to show it restored.

This method of working the experiment is very easy, but the magician must take care to keep the faked side of the scissors from the view of the audience. A very thick package cord must be employed to get the best effect.

LE-ROY'S HINDOO YARN MYSTERY

EFFECT: A piece of RED YARN about thirty inches long is used. It is BROKEN at about the center and the pieces held wide apart, one in each hand. The broken ends are placed together and the yarn becomes restored.

Aside from the fact that it is broken instead of cut, this method is a distinct novelty in that absolutely nothing is used but the one piece of unprepared yarn.

SECRET: Break the yarn and show that it is actually in two pieces. Place the two broken ends together so that they overlap each other about a quarter of an inch. Touch the left thumb and forefinger to the lips, to moisten them, and with these you gently but firmly roll the ends over and over TOWARDS YOU. The right hand momentarily lifts the other two ends of the yarn to lead the attention of the audience away from the movement of the left hand fingers.

Left hand now releases the yarn while the right hand holds it up by one extreme end. It appears to be completely restored. A little practice will render the "mending" process easy and it will deceive perfectly at only a few feet distant.

About the best way to conclude this trick is to roll the yarn into a small ball, hold it between the thumb and second finger of the left hand, apparently take it in the right hand, really executing the French drop, and toss it (?) to a spectator.

ELLIS STANYON'S STRING RESTORATION

EFFECT: An envelope is sealed and the ends cut off in order to form a paper tube. This paper tube is threaded on a cord. Performer snips envelope in two with a pair of scissors but when the two halves of the envelope are separated, the string is found to be as good as ever.

SECRET: The envelope is secretly prepared. A vertical slit has been made across the address side. This is best accomplished by inserting a piece of cardboard in the envelope and making a slit with the corner of a sharp razor blade. Discard the cardboard and insert this prepared envelope in a package of ordinary ones. In presenting the trick, you remove your prepared envelope, seal it, cut off the ends and thread the cord through it, being careful at all times to conceal the slit from your audience.

Hold the envelope up in front of you with the left hand. Prepared side is toward you. Insert one point of the scissors into the bottom of the slit in the envelope. Push the scissors up under the cord and out through the top end of the slit. Now when you cut, the envelope will be separated but the cord will be unharmed.

If a tiny triangle of paper is cut away at each end of the slit, it will facilitate the insertion of the point of the scissors. The envelope should be separated with one continuous cut.

T. PAGE WRIGHT'S VARIATION

The effect is the same but the proper position for the scissors, in only apparently cutting the cord, is located far more readily. The very careless and easy manner in which the cut is made improves the presentation considerably.

The only difference is that TWO vertical and parallel cuts, about half an inch apart, are made. The string goes in the end of the envelope, out the first slit, in the second slit, and on out the other end of the envelope. This is easily accomplished if the narrow strip of paper, formed by the two slits, is so creased that its tendency is to curve away from the address side of envelope when you bulge your impromptu tube and lower the end of the cord vertically through it.

There is a half an inch of cord now on the outside of the envelope toward you under which the point of the scissors find their way almost automatically.

RUPERT SLATER'S VARIATION

A cut is made across one side of a packet of cigarettes. The cigarettes are replaced and the packet carried in your vest pocket.

PRESENTATION: Take the packet from your pocket and empty the cigarettes on the table. Cut the bottom off the packet with a pair of scissors. The result is a kind of endless broad band. Pass a cord through this band, then take the ends of the cord, one in each hand, and twirl so that the packet revolves on the cord. This indirectly proves all fair, as the cut will not be noticed. It also proves that the cord really passes through the packet. Drop the whole lot on the table taking care that the prepared side of the packet is undermost. Now move the packet along the cord so that it is nearly—but not quite—in the center. It only remains to cut through the packet as in the other methods, the spectator thinking you have cut through the cord. Do not, at this point, separate the two halves of the packet. Ask the spectators just which of the two pieces of the cord they believe to be the longest.

When guesses have been made, separate the packet and great will be the surprise of the audience to find the cord whole. The spectators will have been expecting an optical illusion, especially if you prefix the experiment with demonstrations of that type.

BAFFLING STRING RESTORATION

This is still another variation of the original Stanyon method. The very puzzling addition in this version is that, under pretense of showing the envelope that is used to be perfectly empty, the spectators who might be familiar with the original or might otherwise suspect previous preparation later, are convinced that the envelope is free from slits.

This clever idea is an adaptation of Charles T. Jordan's Bisected Queen Mystery.

SECRET: The envelope IS prepared by cutting a vertical slit in the center of the address side and inserting an address side, including the flap, cut from a second envelope. The flaps are then stuck together. By concealing the slit with the fingers, this envelope may be shown both sides AND FREELY INSIDE.

PRESENTATION: Envelope is proven empty. It is sealed and the ends clipped off. The cord is now inserted but in the back compartment of envelope. Envelope, now a tube, is shown from both sides while fingers conceal the slit. It is then turned slit side down.

One end of envelope is held in left hand. The right hand picks up the scissors with the narrowest pointed blade down. You now apparently cut the envelope and cord squarely in two but in the cutting the lower blade of the scissors goes ABOVE the cord instead of below, only the two upper thicknesses of the envelope being cut. The lower thickness was cut before you began. This cut should coincide with the cut on lower side. Thus, when completed, the envelope is in two pieces and on drawing them off the ends and crumpling them up, the card is found unhurt. The illusion, if deliberately worked, is perfect.

WISENHEIMER STRING RESTORATION

EFFECT: Two volunteers hold a three or four foot string horizontally between them. A letter-size envelope is freely displayed and the gummed flap is sealed over the string. The performer now cuts the envelope in half but the string is uninjured. Both halves of the envelope may be slid back and forth along the string as they are actually threaded thereon.

The envelope is not double, it does not bear a slit either front or back, and both string and scissors are ordinary.

SECRET: Nevertheless there is a slit in the envelope. This slit is made with a razor blade directly in the center of the fold beneath the flap.

PRESENTATION: Have the volunteers hold the cord as described. The envelope is shown quite carelessly. Seal the flap over the string at about the center. Grasp the envelope in the tips of the right thumb on the side nearest you and the first and second fingers nearest audience, just at the slit. Ask the volunteers to release the ends of the string momentarily. Revolve the envelope for one complete turn between your fingers so that audience sees it from all sides. You will end up with the envelope gripped in the same manner in which you started.

Request the volunteers to again hold the ends of the string and, just before they take them, you turn the envelope parallel with the floor and with your thumb on the under side. It is now that you steal a little slack. Slide your thumb toward you and a loop of string will be drawn through the slit and concealed by your first and second fingers.

Slide your thumb away from you again and this loop will be transferred to the under side of the envelope. Pass the envelope to the left hand, thumb on top and second finger beneath holding loop pressed against envelope. Pick up scissors with right hand, slip point of under blade through loop, cut, and the string will be unharmed.

JOSEPH KOLAR'S STRAW AND STRING TRICK

EFFECT No. 1: A box of soda straws are offered to a spectator from which he chooses one. He is now given a length of string and asked to thread it through the straw as in Figure 153. The spectator may use his own string if desired.

The straw is actually cut by the spectator himself but the string is immediately shown fully restored.

There is only one straw and one string used. No twists or pieces to trim away. It may be performed while surrounded on all sides.

SECRET: With a razor blade, you make a two inch slit in the center of the straw, Figure 153. After spectator has threaded the string through the straw, you take them and pull the string back and forth as if to center it, but really to enable you to locate the slot. Next grip the straw and string in the middle of the slot

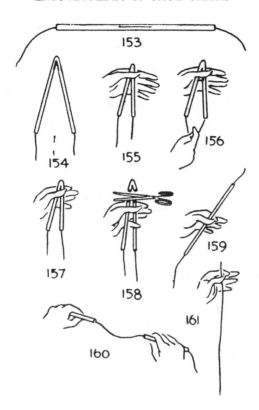

and bend as in Figure 154. Straw is then held so that top of bend is flush with the first finger as in Figure 155. Fingers MUST be held close together to conceal next move. You now pull on either one or both ends of string as if trying to get both ends even and in doing this you pull string down through slit, Figure 156.

Before pulling string, be sure that thumb conceals space where string will stop, Figure 157. Straw can then be pushed up above tops of fingers—spread apart a bit and shown freely from both sides. Now you can wrap a small rubber band about the straw as if to keep it from spreading, but really to conceal the string—in other words the rubber band now takes the place of your thumb and fingers in covering string. In this fashion you are perfectly safe in handing the straw to the spectator and asking him to cut the straw close to the rubber band. If you lack confidence, the rubber band can be dispensed with and you can hold the straw yourself. The straw is snipped by the spectator, Figure 158. Everyone is thoroughly convinced that the string as well as the straw is fairly cut in two.

You now hold two pieces of straw, Figure 158. Bring the straws together, Figure 195. If spectator holds straws, you, of course, move straws together while he holds them as if to show him what to do. Now pull string back and forth as at beginning of trick and finally remove first one and then the other half of the straw, Figure 160. Show the string restored, Figure 161.

EFFECT No. 2: Using a large darning needle you can thread a red, a white, and a blue piece of silk thread through the straw. Chosen color is pulled down using the same tactics as have been already described, and when straw is cut, it is discovered that the two other colors were cut along with the straw but the freely chosen strand is unharmed. How two can be cut without injuring the third appears to be nothing short of marvelous.

EFFECT No. 3: Use a light chain and a pair of light tinner's snips for effect and you can cut and restore a chain. A light flexible wire will work equally as well.

EFFECT No. 4: Make a tube from stiff paper about two and one-half inches long and one inch in diameter. Cut a slit in the center about three inches long. Make a needle by forming a loop on the end of a stiff wire which you use in threading a ribbon through the tube. Instead of snipping off tube as in string effect, cut right through tube where it is bent—this will leave two ends sticking up.

If you glue a piece of ribbon three inches long directly opposite slit inside of tube, this fake will show, after the cut, and appear as part of the ribbon. Cut pieces of tube off right below the fake pieces and then proceed to do the restoring. Fake, however, is not necessary.

EFFECT No. 5: Use the same kind of tube—pass a rope through it and proceed as in the ribbon effect, cutting tube right through the bend. This leaves two distinct ends projecting one and one-half inches above your fingers and looks very convincing. Because the rope naturally spreads a gap in the tube, you twist each tube as if twisting it about the cut ends of the rope, but really to conceal the gap. In this fashion you can easily conceal the rope with the thumb as in the string effect and walk right into the audience and show tube and hands from both sides and nothing more convincing has ever been produced. You now clip off a portion of the opposite ends of the rope to show lack of preparation. Then clip off the twisted ends of the tube—proceed as in the string trick—throw the rope to the audience—also the pieces of tube if you wish and you have performed a remarkable restoration.

NELSON HAHNE'S VERSION

When doing the Kolar Straw and String Trick there is frequently someone in the audience who has a vague idea as to how it is done. It is well known to every performer the value of knowing two entirely different methods to bring about the same effect. Kolar's Straw and String Trick combined with the following method with baffle any audience.

PREPARATION: Thread a string through an unprepared straw. Tie the ends together, trim the ends to make the knot as small as possible and draw this knot in to about the center of the straw. Tie a short piece around the real center of the cord. Actually the cord is prepared exactly as in the Germaine method with the exception that the ends are tied together, and concealed by the straw, instead of being stuck together.

PRESENTATION: Untie the small piece of cord, apparently the ends of the long piece, and retain hold on the ends (?) as you give the straw, which is supposed to have the center of the string in it, to the spectator. In reality, unknown to the spectator, the two ends of the string are in the straw and the performer is holding the center of the string.

The spectator is requested to bend the straw double and to cut off about one-half inch from the doubled center. This small piece of straw that is cut off contains the joined real ends; it falls to the floor, and all the evidence is practically destroyed.

You now take the two cut ends in your right hand and slide the two halves of the straw to the center of the strings. After pattering a bit, slide them on up close to your left hand where you are holding the actual center of string. Place the ends of the straws together, as in Figure 159, and the string is pulled out fully restored. Pieces of straw are dropped to the floor and the small piece of string (imitation ends) is easily disposed of.

It is suggested that this method be used only after having worked Kolar's.

GEORGE WRIGHT'S VERSION

EFFECT: A length of ordinary, white wrapping cord is threaded through an examined straw. The straw, and apparently the string, is snipped in two with a pair of scissors but again the string escapes mutilation. There is no preliminary bending of the straw and it may be cut through whatever portion is indicated by a spectator.

SECRET: Straw and string are quite unprepared although the latter should be a silk thread or soft cord. The solution lies in the fact that the blades of the scissors are blunted. It is impossible to cut through the string with them; it is merely drawn up between the blades. But the same scissors cut the straw quite readily. You have only to try it once to realize that here is a trick that practically works itself—and a very good trick.

FLOYD THAYER'S WIZZO

REQUIRED: A fairly stiff piece of paper, like the stock of a magazine cover, creased into three folds lengthwise.

A length of rather heavy ordinary cotton wrapping twine. Also have a pair of scissors handy, with rather slim points.

PRESENTATION: First show the paper, which you open up, and hold in the left hand as in Figure 162.

With the right hand lay the string along the length of the paper, in left side fold as at C, Figure 162 of the

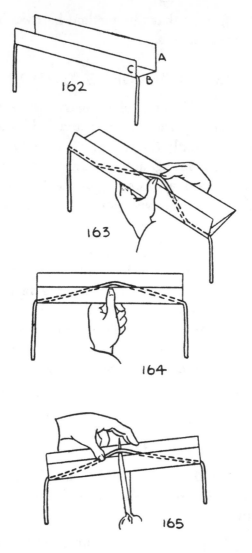

162

163

164

165

drawing. Now with right thumb fold over the side A, and immediately follow by folding over side C, on top of fold A, with the left thumb.

Meanwhile as you start to fold C, with the tip of your right thumb, slightly draw the center portion of the string to the right, so that it forms a sort of loop which overlaps between the folds A and C of the paper, Figure 163.

Now, as you hold the folded paper firmly between the fingers and thumb of the left hand at the center, casually show the paper on both sides, and which may be done, for as yet the loop lies hidden between the two folds of the paper, and is retained so by pressure of the left thumb.

Next, turn the paper to the position in Figure 164, with front facing audience, and slightly pull down, first one end of the string and then the other several times, remarking that it is necessary to have the string about evenly centered in the paper.

The reason for doing this is to really cause the loop to emerge slightly above the edge of the fold, Figure 164.

By a slight upward pressure by the tip of the left thumb as you pull the string back and forth, you will find that the string assumes this position quite readily.

When the loop of string thus becomes visible, change the position of the left hand as shown at Figure 165 and with the right pick up the scissors and inserting the point of one blade between string and paper, Figure 165, sharply snip the folded paper in two.

Still retaining the two halves of the paper after making the cut, grasp an end of the string with the right hand, and draw it completely forth, showing that it is not cut at all, and let the two portions of the paper float gracefully to the floor, or pass all for examination as your fancy may indicate.

L. W. RESTORING THE STRING

In this method only an ordinary pen knife and a piece of string are used. It really adds to the effect in this case to measure the string. If no yard stick is handy a simple method of measuring is to stretch it along a table, say, or some similar piece of furniture of proper length, when simply stretching it along the table at the finish proves the length to be the same without the necessity of fussing with a tape or ruler.

An extra piece of string is placed in the pen knife, in the opening for the blade, and then the blade is closed in on it, holding it securely in place to be carried in the pocket as long as desired. The two ends of string are permitted to project slightly at the end, so that they may be easily grasped. The knife is carried in a pocket on the right side.

The string having been measured is doubled and held by the center between the left forefinger and thumb. The right hand dives into the pocket and brings out the knife; as it does the hands are brought momentarily together and the steal of the extra loop made from the knife. The false loop is now pulled into view and the cutting is done. This leaves four ends visible. Have a spectator knot the two projecting ends. They really belong to your short added piece. Dispose of this extra piece when you replace the knife in your pocket, show the string restored and measure it again to prove that it is the original length.

A pen knife only is suitable for this effect, the blade of a jack knife being too heavy for the loop to slip easily out from under while it is still closed down in the knife handle.

CHAPTER 5
CUT AND RESTORED ROPE
(Impromptu)

Chapter 5. CUT AND RESTORED ROPE
(Impromptu)

FIGURE "8" ROPE RESTORATION

The previous chapter was included in this book primarily to show the evolution of the cut and restored rope from its earlier cousin the cut and restored string, and permit comparison of the necessarily similar principles involved.

Some of those first methods have been altered almost beyond recognition but if you turn back to the Figure "8" String Restoration you will find that the moves there described will work equally well with a rope. It is suggested, however, that you follow the presentation outlined in the final paragraph of instructions.

THE "HINDOO" ROPE RESTORATION

EFFECT: A soft rope about ten feet long is used. The performer places the approximate center of the rope in his mouth while he holds his hands raised, palms toward the audience, displaying them to be perfectly empty. He now grasps the right hand end in his right hand about three inches from the end. The left hand does the same with the opposite end. These ends are brought up alongside the mouth, backs of hands to audience, ends of rope pressed against the inside of the center of the rope with the thumbs. The rope is now lifted away from the mouth and will be found in the position illustrated in Figure 166. The thumbs have

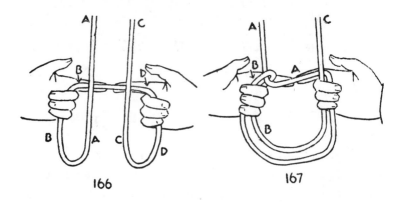

166

167

been lifted to reveal how the ends are placed. Actually they would be pressed at the positions indicated by the arrows at B and D. This is, of course, the state of affairs as would be seen by you.

A spectator cuts the rope between your first fingers. The cut ends are tied in a knot, the knot is trimmed smaller and smaller, and finally the knot is cut away entirely to reveal the rope restored.

SECRET: Everything is just as described until you ask the spectator to cut the rope. The scissors are on a table to your left. You indicate where they are by a motion toward them with both hands. At the same time, you drop D-D from your second, third and little finger and grasp A-A, just below the actual center of the rope, so that when your right hand returns to its former position you now have the arrangement depicted in Figure 167. The other fingers have not been inactive. The right thumb and first finger have retained a grip on C-C just above the center of the rope. The left hand second, third and little fingers have opened out, gripped the center of the rope and pulled it down to the position indicated by the arrow, marked B, in Figure 167. The action of opening out these left hand fingers also shoves the rope A-A out into the proper position to be taken in the right hand fingers.

It will now be seen, Figure 167, that when the rope is cut between the fingers that instead of separating it at the center, merely a short piece is snipped off one end.

Try these moves with a piece of rope in hand and you will find that they may be easily and quickly accomplished, not nearly as complicated as they sound in print.

BLUEY-BLUEY'S METHOD

EFFECT: The method to which this clever carnival performer's name has been associated, is very similar to the last described.

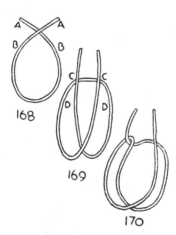

The rope is first held as shown in Figure 168. It is held at A-A by the first fingers and thumbs, the right hand end in the left hand and the left hand end in the right hand. The little fingers curl around the rope at B-B.

The center of the rope is rested on the right knee and the knee raised so that the rope may be taken and held as in Figure 169. The first fingers and thumbs hold the rope at C-C and the second, third and little fingers curl around it at D-D.

This position is the same as Figure 166 BUT instead of the two hanging loops being side by side, one hangs in front of the other.

The rope is again cut between the hands and eventually shown restored.

SECRET: Again a move is made secretly while indicating to the spectator to pick up the scissors and it is the same move as in the "Hindoo" Restoration. The subtle fact, that makes this presentation different from the one just previously explained, is that there is no perceptible difference in the appearance of the loops. One still hangs in front of the other, Figure 170, and the rope is cut near one end instead of through the center as it appears.

ERIC IMPEYS' IMPROMPTU METHOD

The rope is held in the right hand as shown in Figure 171, with about six inches protruding above the thumb. The second, third and fourth fingers are now closed, and the free hand gathers up the rope as shown in Figure 172. The free hand now takes up the loop, and holds it as shown in Figure 173 (this is as seen by the spectators), Y being the center of the whole rope. This part needs a little practice. After one or two trials you will find it quite simple to drape the rope so that the center comes in the correct position. Having got this far, the magician indicates that Y is actually the

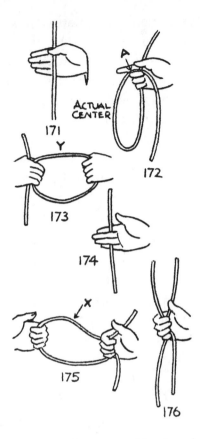

center of the rope, and opens his hands showing it clearly.

Having convinced the spectators, the magician hands out a pair of scissors for examination, at the same time dropping the rope so that it is in position Figure 171 again. While he is holding the rope in this way, he apparently closes his fingers over it as before, but in actual fact what happens is this: He lets the rope swing slightly, and as he closes his fingers, it swings into the position in Figure 174 (the rope passing behind the 2nd and 3rd fingers). You will now appreciate that when the second, third and fourth fingers are closed, you are apparently back at position Figure 172 once more. During the whole of this manipulation the palm of the hand faces the audience. Th rope is now draped over the hand, completing (apparently) the position shown in Figure 172, and now the free hand goes to take up the loop at A, Figure 172, but under cover of the hand, the right thumb presses A into its palm, the other hand taking hold of the piece of rope behind the hand, which the little finger releases. The right hand now slides along the rope, giving it the appearance of Figure 173 again, while in fact the position is shown in Figure 175.

The rope is cut at X, which is apparently the center, and the forefinger of the right hand presses the end upwards, leaving the rope as shown in Figure 176. The cut piece can now either be tied through or over the main part. This is then cut away and the rope restored —and is thrown out for examination.

DR. ERVIN'S ROPE RESTORATION

Dr. Ervin claims to be the originator of this method and claims that he first used it to restore a ribbon.

The rope is first doubled with the ends upward, the loop end hanging down, Figure 177. The loop end is brought up and placed against the actual ends, Figure 178.

This formation is held by the thumb and forefinger and shown freely. You reach for your scissors but in doing so you "accidentally" drop an end of the loop, making it necessary to arrange the rope again.

This second time, in bringing up the loop, a different procedure is followed. Even at close range this new formation looks no different from the first.

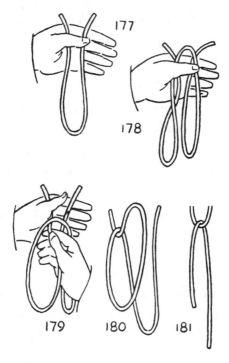

This time the loop stops at the juncture of the thumb and fingers and is held there. Then a short loop, which is a doubled continuation of the left hand end, is pulled above the fingers to simulate the actual center. This move is shown in Figure 179 and the resulting arrangement is pictured in Figure 180.

This is accomplished with one smooth, continued movement. With very little practice it may be executed indetectibly—even with the palm of the left hand toward the spectators.

In presenting, get a spectator for an assistant. Hand him the scissors. "If I were to ask you to cut this rope so that we would have two pieces about the same length, where would you cut it?"

The reply is invariably, "At the loop."

"Do you prefer to cut it just as I am holding it? Perhaps you would like me to make some slight change?"

The reply is also invariably, "Just as it is."

"Very well. Seeing that it's you, go ahead." He cuts the rope through the protruding loop.

"How many pieces did you say there are now?— Two? Correct. Suppose we cut it in a few more pieces."

Take the scissors and cut across the four protruding ends, snipping off about one-third their length. Count them as they fall. "—She loves me, she loves me not.—" Cut across the remainder of the ends, counting them also. At this time grasp the rope below the fist and pull it into the hand a little, causing the remaining short pieces to drop to the floor with the others.

Your assistant is requested to pull one end of the rope and at the end you and the spectator are holding it between you.

THE SHORT AND LONG ROPE MYSTERY
(Harold Sterling)

A trick with two boys from the audience, and great comedy possibilities. The essential part of the trick: After a rope is cut exactly in half, one piece becomes longer than the other, when one rope is cut off evenly with the other rope it is found to be longer, and so on until the two pieces finally become joined together.

Although this trick uses an old move in a cut and restored rope I am sure that you will find the shortening and lengthening to be new. This is not an armchair version but a real trick. I have used it in almost a hundred shows and still can't figure out why it gets so many laughs. I usually present this after I have finished my regular cut and restored rope routine, but it is good enough to be presented as a trick in itself.

Now, for the working, patter in quotation marks. One boy on your left; one on the right. On the table, a pair of scissors and a clothesline. The longer the clothesline the better. I usually start with a bundle of a hundred feet. The rope should not have too much starch in it. The rope is handed to the boy on your left. He is told to measure off five feet. As he starts unwinding the rope, whisper to him to keep on unwinding. Then say 'Are you sure you know how much five feet is? How tall are you?' Quickly whisper to him to say nine feet. When he says it there is a laugh and you say: 'Well, I see I will have to measure it myself.' Pick up your scissors and cut off about five feet. Whisper to him to put the rest of the rope in his pocket as you walk over and hand one end of the five foot piece of rope to the other boy. As soon as you see the boy on your left has the rope fairly well stuffed in his pocket walk over and pull it out of his pocket with a glare (a good laugh) as you hand him the other end of the five foot rope. Dispose of the bundle of rope. Now tell the boys to examine the rope thoroughly and then tell them to pull and see if the rope is strong. Let them pull and usually you will have a tug of war. While the boys are examining the rope you can say, 'Examine it thoroughly as every person in this audience is depending on your word as to whether this is a plain piece of clothesline or not.' Now take the rope from them and have the boys stand one on each side close to you, facing the audience.

Hold the rope, one end in each hand and then say: 'Over in Egypt,' and swing your right hand out in front of the boy on your right. As five or six inches of the rope is held in front of him the boy reaches for it. Just as he does, swing your hand back in front of you. The boy feels sheepish as he realizes he was not intended to take the rope. Then swing the left hand out in front of the boy at your left. Say, 'The Egyptian Magician' boy at left makes a grab for the rope and you pull it back. You need not look at boys, you can see their hands from the corner of your eye. To make sure the boys reach for the rope, just as you swing your hand in front of them, whisper 'take it.' (Right now might be a good time to tell you, that when you first get your boys up and are placing them whisper to them that if they want to stay up they will have to do everything you tell them. Also whisper to them never to stand in front of you. I have seen a lot of magicians that need this advice as they let their assistants obscure them from the audience's view.) You can keep up this grabbing as long as you think the laughs are good, and you will get plenty. Finally say 'All right, if you want this rope, I'll give you each half of it.' Hold the rope as in Figure 177: Two ends held in left hand clipped between thumb and index finger, back of hand to audience, ends extending about two or three inches above left hand. Now reach down with the right hand and pick up loop and bring it up in left hand as in Figure 178 and swing the palm of left hand to audience. Point with right index finger at loop and say, while looking at the boys: 'If I cut the rope here you will each get exactly half. Is that right?' You accidentally let the loop fall, retaining the two ends.

The rope will now be held as in Figure 177. Quickly reach down with right hand and pick up loop and bring it up exactly as you did the first time (back of left hand now toward the audience) but as loop reaches palm of left hand, right hand picks up rope on left side, through the loop, with thumb and middle finger and draws it up to form a loop, Figures 179 and 180, with the original loop lying in palm of left hand. The rope will now appear as in Figure 178, the left thumb covering the crossing of the ropes. Now take the scissors and cut the loop. There will be four ends projecting above your left hand: two ends of the short piece and two ends of the long piece of rope. Let the two ends of the long piece drop. To the audience it appears as though there are two pieces held by the one end of each rope. In reality you are holding both ends of the short piece and the long piece is looped through this as in Figure 181. You will find that one end hangs down about six inches longer than the other. Without looking at the rope say, 'Now we have two pieces of rope exactly the same length.' Audience will snicker or one of the boys will be apt to point at rope calling your attention to it, or you can cue boy to point at rope. You turn to boy and say, 'You told me that would divide it in half.' With right hand pick up the two ends that are hanging down and hold the rope horizontally in front of you, Figure 182. You cheat a little by letting the longer end project about three inches beyond the other end of the rope instead of the six inches that it should. Have the boy on the right of you take the scissors and cut off this three inches and say, 'Save that piece of rope for good luck.' You can introduce some comedy at this point, that is, just as boy is about to cut the rope, by saying 'cut the rope. Notice this is my

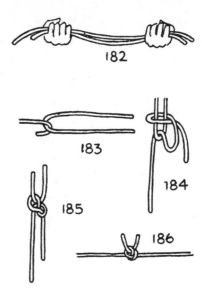

finger (wriggle finger) and this is the rope (pointing at rope.)' Now let go with right hand, still retaining rope in left hand. Once more rope hangs as in Figure 181.

Always remember to keep loop in left hand concealed so that to all appearances you have just two pieces of rope, held each by one end, hanging from your left hand. 'Now they are the same length.' Keep looking at the top ends and boy again points to bottom ends, and the audience laughs. Once more grab rope near the bottom ends and have boy cut off this extra three inches, rope being held horizontally. While the boy is cutting the rope, with your left thumb and forefinger work the short piece of rope through the loop a few inches, Figure 183. Tell the boy to pick up the piece he has just cut off and take it home to his little sister for good luck. If he says he has no little sister, say 'Well, just take it home to your big sister.' If he has no big sister, say, your little brother or if he has no little brother, your big brother, uncle, etc., until you have exhausted his relatives, or say angrily 'Well, keep it yourself!'

Now hold the rope again vertically, hanging from the left hand. Point with right forefinger to bottom ends. 'Now they are even.' The audience will laugh as boy points to top ends which are not even. Have him cut off the extra length and to do this swing your left hand over in front of him. This will cause your arms to be in a crossed-position as the rope is held horizontally. With the right hand, which is partially concealed from the audience's view by your left arm, pull down on one of the long ends until you have worked out a few inches of the rope. Once more hold the ropes vertically and one rope appears so much longer that you will get a good laugh. (It may be that the audience suspects you are in a predicament as you are having so much trouble getting both ropes the same length.) Have the boy cut off the extra length. As the boy is cutting off the extra length you can again pull on the short rope as before and again one rope appears longer than the other. While this is being cut off you can pull out the longer rope and so on until there is very little rope remaining.

Now say 'I will just tie these two ends together and stop all of this.' Continue holding the two ends in your left hand. With the right hand gather up rope hanging on the right a few inches below your left hand and throw a half hitch over the two ends that are projecting from the top of your left hand, Figure 184. Work this half-hitch down over the ends to just below where the ropes are looped together. The rope will appear as in Figure 185. For the first time you will be able to move the left hand away from the rope as the knot now hides the loop. Now hold the rope in front of you and once more one rope will appear longer than the other, owing to the fact that the half-hitch has taken up some of the rope. Again have boy cut off the extra length. You can give this to one of the boys or throw it out in the audience.

If you do throw it out, after the scramble you can say 'And anyone getting that piece of good luck rope will be sure to be married by the first of June.' Now have the boys hold the ends of the rope, Figure 186. Say 'now hold tightly.' They will start to pull. Quickly say, 'But do not pull. If this knot (pointing at knot) should come untied, you (pointing at boy on right) would be sitting back there (pointing behind him and looking in that direction) (as you stand there pointing, the boy will unconsciously look around) holding this piece of rope; (pointing at rope to right of knot) and you (pointing to boy on left) would be sitting over here (pointing behind him).' Now trim off the ends of the knot, in reality the short piece of rope, until it is entirely cut away. Keep the knot covered with the left hand as you do the cutting.

Give these pieces to the boy also and by now he should be fairly well loaded down with rope. 'Now boys, these ropes are so short I am sure you would not want them, so I'll use my magic power to join them together.' Turn to the boy on your left and say that you want him to repeat ancient Egyptian words that will create the miracle. Tell him to say loudly and distinctly, 'Rubber buggy bumper.' Boy will stutter on these and get them tangled, so tell him once more and more quickly, 'Rubber buggy bumper.' You will be surprised at the laughs you get on this and here is a word of warning: Practice these words yourself until you can say them quickly three times in succession. As boy repeats the magic words, your left hand straightens out the half-hitch. The boys now pull and the rope is restored to one piece.

Most of the laughs depend on the trick itself. I do not condone too many gags that have no direct bearing on the trick but here is one that is very funny. Most of the boys now wear sweater vests that have a zipper up the front. When you get a boy that has one of these on walk over to him and zip it open and whisper to him to zip it up again. Turn away as he zips it up. Quickly turn back and zip it open again. Whisper to him to close it up again. This is good for three or four times, and gets many laughs.

R. W. HULL'S STRETCHING ROPE

This routine is most effective. The rope is cut in two uneven lengths and the short one stretched until it is the same length as the long one and then before it is hardly realized the two pieces of rope are seen to have joined themselves together again.

Start the routine by telling the spectators you propose to show them how a piece of rope can be stretched. Hand the rope to some one to look at and see that it has no appreciable "stretch." Then take it back and hold it by the ends, Figure 187. The rope is held in the left hand and the right hand runs down to the bottom of the rope and stretches it taut. While these moves are being made, the patter runs as follows: "Over in India, sometimes they double the rope like this and find the center of it. Strange to say, in India, they always

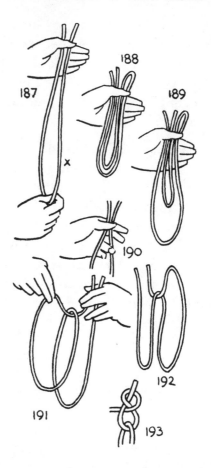

find the center somewhere near the middle. Then the fakir displays the rope like this, Figure 188, and two large loops of equal size are thus formed. (You indicate these by the index finger of right hand being inserted in these loops at the bottom). Now if the rope were to be cut at this upper loop (small loop above thumb and fingers of left hand) it naturally would be cut in two equal lengths." As these remarks are made, you reach for the scissors and with same in right hand and with points spread you take hold of the upper small loop with the scissors, and let go of the rope with the left hand, and it drops, held clipped between the points of the scissors and is shown in two equal sections. The rope is NOT cut at this point, but merely the suggestion is made, that IF the rope WERE cut. Placing the scissors aside and taking hold of the rope again as at first, Figure 187, the patter continues: "But if instead of taking hold of the rope in the exact center, it would be caught a little off center (the right hand takes hold of the rope this time at the point marked "X" in Figure 187) and it is doubled exactly the same as before, then the two loops will again be made (Figure 189), but one of them will be much larger than the other (indicate with right hand pointing to the two lower loops) and now (reach for the scissors again) if we should cut the rope at this upper loop (above the left thumb and fingers) instead of two equal pieces of rope, you see the rope would be in two UNEVEN lengths, one being much longer than the other." As these comments have been made the points of the scissors held in the right hand have again been inserted in the upper loop and the rope allowed to drop as before and it will appear that you are holding the rope at a point, that if you were to cut it (which you do NOT do yet) it would be in two unequal pieces. For misdirection you emphasize the large loops being equal the first time, and unequal the second time.

All this has been mere "by play" and is excellent misdirection, for it has led the audience to the exact point where you want them. They have followed the explanation and would be wearied slightly were you to continue it further and they are just off guard now, and thus the "dirty work" is done and never detected.

Lay the scissors aside and for the third time take the rope in position in left hand, Figure 187, and apparently you again make the two loops as shown in Figure 189, but in reality this time it is just a little bit different. You do not reach down and catch the rope in the right hand OFF CENTER but you catch it exactly IN THE CENTER (as the first time) but this is under misdirection, for just before you do this, you say to the spectator standing beside you: "You take the scissors and cut the rope." It is just as he reaches for the scissors and all eyes are on him that you form the rope into what looks like Figure 189 but in reality is what appears in Figure 192. The following will briefly describe the exact moves. The third and fourth fingers of the left hand separate slightly and allow the rope to pass between them and the first and second fingers as shown in Figure 190. The rope is doubled up with the right hand as before, until it is nearly to the left hand when the right thumb and first two fingers of the right hand slip under the rope they are holding, and take hold of the other portion of the rope just where it emerges from between the second and third fingers of the left hand. The rope is carried right on up and placed in left hand and it looks exactly like Figure 189 to an onlooker, but in reality Figures 191 and 192 show what takes place and if the left thumb were removed, what looks like Figure 189 would then be seen to be like Figure 192. The thumb hides the loop,

Needless to say, all that has been described is just one upward motion and is done in a second's time, and while spectator is picking up scissors. When spectators again look at you, you are holding the rope and to all appearances you have merely made the formation shown in Figure 189, over again, but thanks to the misdirection they do not realize what has really taken place.

Again you mention that you have created the large loop and the small loop (calling attention to the two loops below the hand) and that you desire that spectator cut through the small loop above left fingers so as to cut the rope in two uneven pieces.

The moment he cuts, you allow the outer strand of rope to fall and also the inner strand, transferring to right hand, the two center strands of the rope, concealing, of course, by finger and thumb, the fact that you have merely a short piece of rope and another long piece looped in it.

But as the two ends drop down, you call attention to the fact that the rope has been cut so that one piece is almost double in length that of the other piece. Remark that over in India they always like to keep the rope in a circle, the magic circle, so you apparently proceed to tie the two upper ends (?) together. What you really do is to tie the small piece around the long piece, but to the spectators it looks as though you tied two ends together for they are unaware of the real condition of the rope. You first slide this small piece of rope so that one end of it is longer than the other, and then you tie the long end right around the short end, exactly as shown in Figure 193. This is a very unique knot, and leaves much shorter ends (a distinct advantage later) than any other way of tying a short piece of rope around a long piece. As you tie this small piece around the long piece, make a sliding motion toward the short end of the long piece of rope. This you can easily do and it will make it appear that one end of the rope is even shorter and the other longer. Drop this fake knot and call attention to the fact that the rope has been cut so that one piece is nearly double that of the other in length. Gather up the other two ends and tie them together by what was described in Chapter One as the Vanishing Square Knot. When you have done this, the rope is now in a circle with the sliding piece on the side near the bottom.

The rope is now held in the left hand, just below the Vanishing Knot, and the right hand slides down the short piece (?) of rope two or three times, pretending to stretch the rope. Hold securely at the top so that all may be sure the rope is not slipping there. When the bottom part of the hand reaches the fake knot it slides it down an inch or so, and then as the hand (right one) is turned over a little to allow the knot to pass into the hand, and when the finger tips come again to the knot, they slide it another inch or so. This is repeated two or three times, by starting again at the top of the rope and sliding down it. To all appearances the rope is actually stretching longer and longer before the very eyes of the spectators. The illusion is perfect. Finally, when the knot is clear to the bottom, you say: "There you are! I have stretched the short piece of rope until it is exactly the same length as the long one!"

The rope is shown with both pieces apparently the same length. You say: "Let me prove it to you—I will untie this first knot." (Merely blow on the upper vanishing knot, sliding the loose end out, and it is gone). Take both ends and hold up and again move the sliding knot a little so that it will occupy the exact center of the rope. "More than that, I will untie the other knot and place the strips side by side that you may see that I have really stretched the short piece of rope, but just one moment before I do that. Over in India they wrap the rope around the hand like this (start wrapping the rope around the left hand with the right one) and leaving the knot in the center of the hand, the remainder of the rope is wound around the hand." You do all this except that you do not leave the knot in the left hand. It is slid off with the right hand, and thanks to the short ends of the fake knot, due to the special manner in which it was tied, you easily palm it in right hand and spectators think it is in the center of the rope on the inside of the left hand.

Now you continue the patter as follows: "You see, over in India, the performer always carries a little goofer powder in his pocket (here you reach in a pocket with the right hand, apparently to get some goofer powder, but in reality to leave the small knot) and would you believe it, you must have a hole in your pocket or you can't carry goofer powder. Here it is, a very small portion, absolutely invisible to the naked eye (act as if you are displaying some between the thumb and fingers of the right hand), and now I sprinkle a little of it on the rope, and whether or not you believe it, it really performs wonders, for now it is unnecessary to untie the rope—see (you exclaim), as you gradually allow the rope to uncoil from the left hand, the goofer powder causes the knot to literally melt away, and here is the rope—fully restored again, and doubly strong!" The last part of the trick has been self-explanatory.

S. H. SHARPE'S A ROPE REPAIRED

A rope is borrowed, cut and, by the performer's powers, completely restored. The merit of the experiment rests upon the fact that there is no preparation of any kind.

When the rope is handed to the performer he regards it seriously and then, whatever may be its length, says, "It is much too long for the experiment. A piece about half as long would be about right. Do you mind if I cut it and use but half? No objection being made to this question, the performer doubles the rope in the center and snips it in two. He then takes one of the short pieces, doubles it in the center and cuts through the loop thus, apparently, made. This done, he cuts away the ends, commands a magic wonder to take place, and shows that a restoration has been effected.

The purpose of cutting the long rope in two pieces is to enable the performer to obtain an extra loop to match the rope in use. This is accomplished as follows: Double the rope and grip the doubled portion between the thumb and the base of the forefinger of the left hand. Now, instead of cutting through the loop, as the audience believes he does, he cuts the loop completely off as shown by the dotted line marked A in Figure 194.

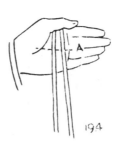

The loop thus obtained is kept thumb palmed in the left hand until one of the short pieces is doubled over. Then it is the false loop that is brought into view and cut. Finally the extra portion is snipped away and the rope is shown to be restored.

JOHN GOODRUM'S SLEIGHT OF HAND METHOD

This is a good method to use as an encore after your regular rope trick.

The trick lies in the way the rope is coiled. First make about three of four loops around your left hand, until about half of the rope is coiled, then start to make another loop. As the right hand comes over, grasp loop A, Figure 195, which was the first loop that was

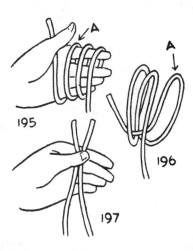

formed, and pull it through the other loops as shown in Figure 196. Make one more loop so that all can see that it is the actual center of the rope, and place it with loop A.

As you turn to the left, to pick up the scissors, you let this last loop drop. Openly cut loop A.

What you have actually done is to cut a small piece off the end of the rope. This piece, about eight inches long, runs through the first three or four loops formed. Grasp the middle of this small piece and the third loop (the loop next to loop A in Figure 196) and let the ends of the rope drop. The appearance is now as in Figure 197.

Bring all four ends together in the hand (left one) and grip one end of short piece and one end of long piece, between the thumb and first finger of the right hand. Let the other real end drop and the rope will appear restored.

GRAHAM ADAMS' CUT AND RESTORED ROPE

EFFECT: The rope is doubled and a spectator cuts through the rope with a pair of scissors. He ties the ends with a double knot. The performer shows this to the audience, saying, "This is just how any ordinary civilized person would join a cut rope." Wrapping the rope around his left hand, he continues, "This is how the Hindu mystic would do it. You all saw that the rope was cut in two equal lengths and joined with a knot, leaving two ends separate, that is, the real center of the rope, and here it is neatly soldered together." The loop of rope is stretched out between the hands and revealed to be completely restored.

The assistant again cuts the rope. Some pieces are cut from the ends of the rope and tossed to the audience for examination. Again the rope is mended as before.

A third time the assistant cuts the rope and more pieces given to the audience. This time the spectator knots the ends together. This being done he is asked to choose one of the knots. The rope is cut through at this point and the knot thrown out for examination. A mystic pass repairs the rope which is also given for examination.

SECRET: There is nothing much to tell as far as secrets are concerned. The whole thing is brought about by showing the audience the position of the cuts in the rope in relation to the knot, which in the first instance is in the middle of the rope.

The first cut is a false one and is the same method as described earlier in this chapter under the title of R. W. Hull's Stretching Rope. When the knot is tied, using the ends of the short piece, it is capable of being moved along the rope to whatever position you desire.

When the performer says, "This is how the Hindu mystic would do it," the real ends of the rope are placed in the curled first and second fingers of the left hand where they are held firmly with the assistance of the thumb. The knot is taken in the right hand and the hands are held as far apart as the rope will allow. The crooked third and fourth fingers of the right hand grip the sliding knot and, as the rope is wrapped around the left hand, the rope is pulled through the knot for about eighteen inches. Hold the left hand out to the audience, still gripping the joint in the first and second fingers and thumb of the left hand and shake the rest of the rope free. The rope hangs as a loop from the left hand and appears restored as you take the bottom of the loop in the right hand and hold the hands wide apart. The fact that the knot is in a new place causes your audience to look in the wrong place for where the rope was originally cut.

The right hand takes a new hold on the rope about four inches from the left hand and the spectator again cuts the rope, between your hands. Hold the ends wide apart, let go with the right hand and let that end of the rope hang. Take hold of the rope with the right hand a couple of inches or so below the left. Have the spectator again cut the rope between your hands.

This leaves you with the rope in the right hand and two small pieces in the left. Throw these for examination.

The audience and the spectator have no time to realize that it would take three cuts to get the two pieces and that only two cuts have been made.

Take the rope by the ends, show the position of the cut in relation to the knot and join it again. This time, instead of pulling the rope through the knot, retain a grip on the knot with your right hand and pull the knot along the rope for about fifteen inches while wrapping the rope around the left hand. Show the rope restored, as before, and have it cut again, as before.

This time you have spectator tie the ends. Give him his choice of either knot. It is better that he select the one he has just tied but it matters little. In any case the genuine knot is given to him and he slips his arm through the circle of rope. Cut off the fake knot and toss it to the audience. The rope is allowed to fall and hang over the spectator's arm where he has perfect freedom to examine it and later give it to the audience.

FERNAND VERHEYDEN'S METHOD

About nine feet of soft rope, that does not go into kinks when it is being manipulated, is required.

The rope is passed for examination. On taking it back, it is held in the left hand, Figure 198. The right hand is placed in the bottom of the loop at point C and raises it; the rope should rest on the back of the hand

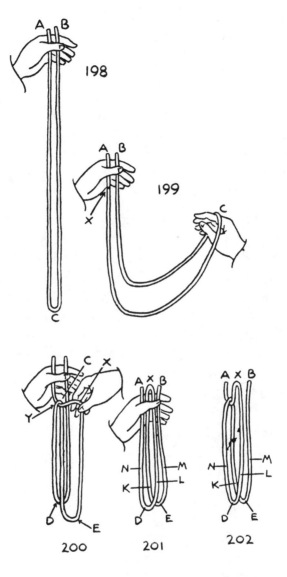

and the fingers should be free; the back of the hand faces the audience, Figure 199. The right hand carries the loop towards the left hand and when the right hand is hidden by the left the thumb and first finger of the right hand catch hold of the rope at point X; at the same time the fingers of the right hand are lowered so that loop C slides off the hand and is held in the left hand Y in Figure 200. The loop formed by taking hold of the end of the rope at X is placed between A and B, Figure 201. These movements must be made without any pause between them. If the reader has followed the directions with a rope in his hands he will see that the rope is now in the position of Figure 201 as the audience sees it. Figure 202 gives the correct position of all parts of the rope in the hand.

The right hand is now placed in the two hanging loops at K and L in such a manner that the ends of the loops, E and D, rest on the back of the hand. The right hand carries the loops up to the left hand, and, when the right hand is hidden by the left, the thumb and first finger catch hold of the parts L and M together at the points V and Z, and exactly the same movement is made; the loops E and D slide off the back of the right hand and the loops V and Z are brought up beside B, Figure 204. All these movements must be made with-

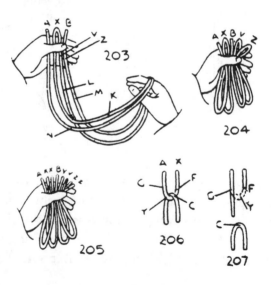

out any pause between them. The loops **X, V** and **Z** are then cut and you have eight ends (Figure 205) and apparently the rope has been cut in four pieces.

As further convincing proof that the rope is really cut, you tell them you will cut a small piece from each of the eight ends. You really cut the rope at **F** and squeeze the next piece **G** between the scissors. Figures 206 and 207. To the audience you appear to have cut off two ends. The other ends are cut in the same way and then you have no "little piece" to get rid of at the end of the trick. All the performer has to do is to throw the rope into the air and the audience sees it perfectly restored.

HARLAN TARBELL'S "MANY-CUT" ROPE MYSTERY

EFFECT: You pick up an unprepared piece of rope and fold it over a number of times. Then you cut off a bunch of the rope wholesale, leaving a number of ends. Again and again you cut. Yet in a moment you throw the rope into the air and it is fully restored.

This method allows of speed, considerable cutting, and a brilliant finish. Then, too, no assistants from the audience are necessary.

SECRET: Display a piece of soft rope about six feet in length. Bring the two ends together and hold in left hand, Figure 208. Grasp looped end of rope with right hand and hold, Figure 209. Give rope a slight jerk. calling attention to the strength of the rope. As you do, allow body to turn slightly to the left and left hand goes out of sight behind upper left leg for a moment, Figure 210. Note carefully the position of rope in left hand,

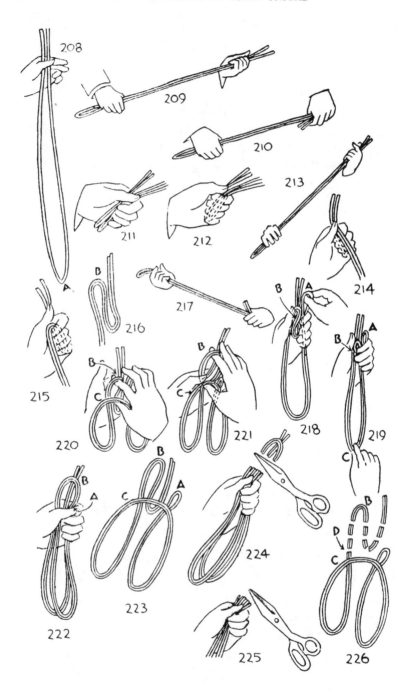

Figures 210 and 211. Quickly open left fingers, allowing the rope to be held doubled over, Figure 212. Now quickly bring the left hand up into the position in drawing, Figure 213. The back of hand should be towards audience. This brings the rope looped once in left hand and coming down over the fingers, Figure 214. Open fingers enough to allow the rope on fingers to come into palm of hand and be covered with fingers, Figure 215. This gives you a double loop of rope concealed in the left hand that the audience is not aware of. Figure 216 shows the type of double loop.

In Figure 217 we have a slightly different method of gaining indetectably the double loop in the left hand. The rope is first held as in Figure 209. Then the hands go to the position shown in Figure 217 which brings the rope into position as in Figure 211. Fingers are opened to get rope inside closed hand. Then when hands are brought into the position, Figure 213, the other loop is made as already described. Give the rope a couple of jerks with the right hand after double loop is concealed in left hand, Figure 215. To audience you appear to hold rope as in Figure 208.

Keep back of left hand toward audience. With right thumb and first fingers grasp loop at point A and bring it up into left hand, Figure 218, allowing A to stick out above hand just a little. Now pick up loop C with right thumb and first finger, Figure 219. Bring it up into hand, Figure 220. The right thumb holds C loop in place while the index finger is inserted into loop B. It is now easy to raise loop B up above left hand, Figure 221, leaving loop C in hand. The left hand closes around the rope, Figure 222. The effect to the audience to date is that the rope has merely been folded.

First, loop A was brought up, then loop C, and to them, loop B is apparently loop C. Figure 223 is a diagram to show the various folds of the rope at this stage. Pick up scissors and cut through loop B as well as the two ends, Figure 224. Keep cutting, Figure 225, until the whole upper loop has been removed. Figure 226 shows the various cuts that may be used until you get to point D. Audience thinks you have cut rope into many pieces, when in reality you have only cut a bit off the two ends. Give the rope in left hand another fold and toss it into the air. Then catch it as it comes down, spread it out, pull upon it to show it restored into one piece and throw it out to the audience for examination.

The "Many-Cut" Rope Mystery is easy to perform, but, like other good tricks, requires a certain amount of practice to perfect.

ZENITH ROPE RESTORATION (METHOD TWO)
(Page Wright and William Larsen)

Apparently the rope is cut into quarters, and the ends trimmed, after which the rope is restored to a single length and may be examined.

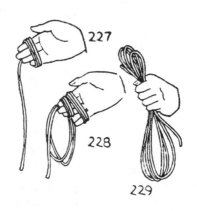

227

228

229

In using this in a program, the magician may bring forward the rope in a length as bought and have a portion cut off by anyone for his use.

Take the rope and calling attention to the fact that it is ordinary begin winding it about the fingers of the right hand, Figure 227. It is wound between the first and second joints of the fingers. The first three loops are made about all four fingers, but thereafter the rope is wound only around the first three fingers, Figure 228. This is apparently merely to show the rope. Now the rope is unwound, but only the portion about the first three fingers is pulled free, three loops still remain about the fingers. At the same time turn right side to audience, holding the right hand so the back of it only is visible, the fingers being doubled out of sight, so that the fact that a portion of the rope remains about them is unknown. Coil the rope into three coils, holding them in the right hand, and calling attention to what you are doing. Now comes the deceptive movement. These coils are apparently shifted to the left hand. As the left hand takes them, the three small coils about the fingers are slid off. Left hand grips junction between large and small coils. Figure 229 shows the state of affairs as they appear to the audience. Actually the three loops which project from above the left hand are not portions of the three large coils, though they appear to be, but the three small loops which were about the fingers.

Call attention to the fact that if you cut through the three coils, you will have eight ends — that is, the rope will be divided into four portions, about equal. Cut through the coils, actually cutting the small loops above left hand. Explaining that you wish to even up the ends, cut at the ends until you have cut them completely away, finally severing the strand of rope which joined large and small coils. This leaves you with a single length of rope, so that you may "restore" the rope with ease, and toss it out for examination.

U. F. GRANT'S 1933 ROPE TRICK

Everything is done in an open and clean cut manner, there are no false moves or sleights. And you perform the impossible by cutting an unprepared rope right in the center and hold the two separate pieces wide apart, then tie them together, trim down the ends, and PRESTO — rope is fully restored and tossed out for examination.

SECRET: Use a piece of soft rope about six feet long. Throw it out for examination, and while rope is in the audience, allow a spectator to cut it into two pieces, then throw the ropes back to you.

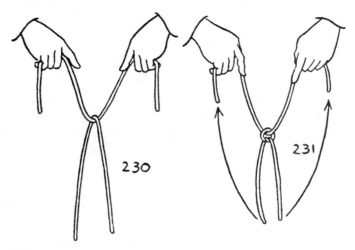

Tie the ropes together, Figures 230 and 231. That is, take hold of the ends of the upper rope and tie a single knot. Draw knot down to center of ropes. Tie another single knot on top of the first. In other words you have tied the two ropes together near the center with a square knot.

Grasp the two ropes on the left side in one hand and the two on the other side in the other hand and pull on knot, Figure 232.

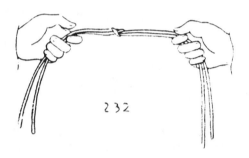

232

Work this in a quick snappy manner and it will not be noticed that you are really picking up the wrong ends. By doing this, you are getting a separate rope at each side of the knot.

State that you will cut the ropes again to be sure

CUT
HERE

233

they are really severed. Cut them as in Figure 233. You apparently have two lengths of rope left, tied together at the top, instead you have one length with a small extra piece tied around it at the center.

Take the two ends of the ropes (?) and pull them out straight. Say that you will endeavor to restore the ropes. All that remains is to coil the rope around the left hand. The right hand, as it does the coiling, slides the little extra piece or fake knot along the rope and off the end keeping it palmed. The left hand tosses the long rope into the air and catches it as it falls to reveal it fully restored and it may be tossed out for examination.

Instead of sliding the little extra knot off the end of the rope and palming it, you may cut away the extra piece as several do when working the restored turban. Personally, we prefer the first method.

We also suggest that this trick be worked in a short, snappy manner. As soon as the two ropes are thrown back to you, tie them, trim off the ends, coil around the hand, throw them in the air, display them restored as they fall and toss to the audience.

CARL BREMA'S KNOTTED ROPE

A rope is cut at the center and the cut ends are tied. Then the two long ends are tied. This makes two ropes and two knots.

Seizing one knot, the performer runs his hand along the rope; both knots disappear leaving a single rope.

The first part of the trick is the same as the "Impromptu String Restoration" explained in Chapter Four and illustrated in Figures 136 and 147 inclusive. The result is actually a single rope with a small piece knotted to the center.

The actual ends of the rope are tied with the "Vanishing Square Knot" explained in Chapter One and illustrated in Figures 17 and 18.

The rope is held by the left hand, near the center. The right hand covers the short bit of knotted rope and slides it to the end. The square knot (?), with which the genuine ends are tied, dissolves and you carry away the tiny bit of knotted rope palmed in the right hand.

U. F. GRANT'S SLEIGHT-OF-HAND ROPE TRICK

EFFECT: A length of soft rope about five feet long is used. This can be passed for examination before and after the trick. The ends of the rope are tied together. The performer states that the rope can be cut and restored in any section of the loop. He cuts the rope three or four inches from the knot and restores it. He again cuts it, through the center this time, and again restores it. Both ends are cut from the rope and passed for examination along with the remaining part of the rope.

SECRET: Both ends are held together in the one hand, Figure 234.

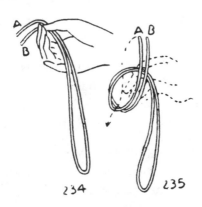

234   235

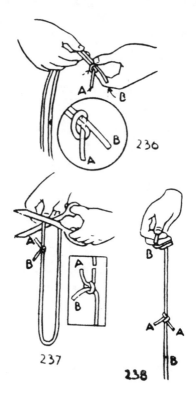

A loop is formed and the ends A and B are apparently pushed through this loop BUT end A only goes through, Figure 235.

Continue pulling the knot taut while at the same time pulling end B so that it is the same length as A, Figure 236.

The rope is cut three or four inches from the knot with scissors. If the cut is made as shown by the enlarged view of the knot, a fake, A, will be made that can be slid back and forth on B, Figure 237.

The B end hanging is now brought up and held under the thumb. At the same time the sliding knot A is pulled down to the center of the loop. This is then brought up and held in the same hand with ends B-B, Figures 238, 239 and 240.

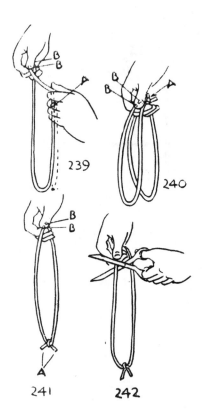

Ends are released and the cut has apparently been restored, Figure 241.

Ends B are still retained under the thumb. The scissors are taken and the rope apparently cut in the center. What really happens, one end of B is dropped as you apparently cut. The rope now appears to be in about two equal lengths. See Figures 242 and 243.

Untie the knot A which brings the ends as illustrated in Figure 244.

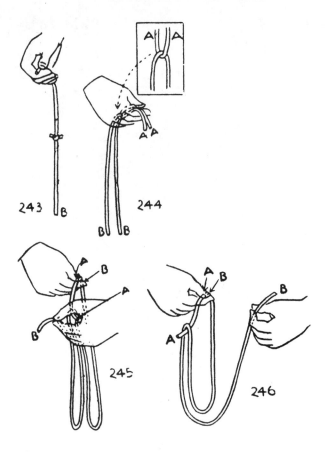

243   244   245   246

The four ends are brought together. Ends A and B are held under the thumb in one hand. The opposite end of B in the other hand, Figure 245.

The actual center of the rope is dropped and the hands are spread apart, Figures 246 and 247.

The two ends are brought together and pieces are cut from each end and passed for examination. The end B is actually cut while the A end is simply dropped, apparently being cut also. The balance of the rope is also passed for examination, Figures 248 and 249.

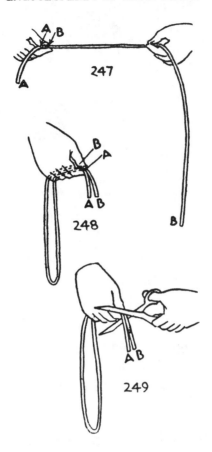

247

248

249

HEISEY'S HINDU ROPE TRICK

There are two ways of starting this trick. If you have had a few seconds to prepare, you will not need to perform these preliminary moves.

Taking the rope you say, "Let me see if this rope is suitable for the purpose. I will test it by tying a few knots." You take the rope, cross the ends and proceed to tie the ends together. But instead of tying the crossed ends in the usual square knot, you simply tie one end of the rope around the other end of the rope, Figure 250.

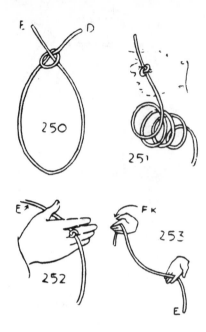

Pull the knot tight and it will look the same as any other knot. In fact, most inexperienced persons when tying the two ends together generally tie this knot, a sort of slip knot, anyway.

Say, "Yes, I believe this rope will probably do. Let me have the shears and I will trim this knot off." Put the shears just under the knot at the left side, Figure 250, taking care that you cut the end that is tied in a knot — and not the other straight end that simply runs through the knot. It is now necessary for you to make one more cut to remove the knot. So you bring the shears up as if to cut the knot off right under the knot at the right side — but what you really do is cut the short end D, quite close to the knot. As this is done under cover of your left hand holding the rope, which shields the actual action from the eyes of your spectators, no one will be the wiser.

Drop the cut-off end, which everyone thinks is the knot removed, in your right coat pocket along with the shears.

This leaves you with a straight piece of rope with a small piece knotted around one end but concealed in the left hand as in Figure 251. This knot will slide up and down the rope.

Turn toward the right side and place the rope in your right hand, Figure 252. The secret knot is concealed behind the fingers of the right hand, Figure 253. Take hold of end E with the left hand, Figure 252, and draw it slowly through the fingers of the right hand, Figure 253, showing both hands empty, palms toward the audience, saying, "The East Indian magicians use just one long piece of solid rope like this, and nothing else, just as you see here." The secret knot slides easily

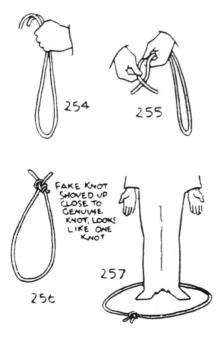

254

255

FAKE KNOT
SHOVED UP
CLOSE TO
GENUINE
KNOT, LOOKS
LIKE ONE
KNOT

257

256

along the rope and remains concealed at the back of the hand. Stop when you get about five inches from the end, and bringing the left hand up and in front of the right, Figure 254, take both ends in your left hand. As you turned toward right side, the left hand covers or conceals the action of taking the rope in left hand so that no one can see the secret knot as it comes from behind the right hand.

Stepping toward one of the spectators, hold the rope ends toward him as in Figure 255 and ask him to "Cross the ends and tie them together, please." Be sure he crosses the ends when tying so that the knot he makes will look like your secret sliding knot.

Take the rope and "test" it by grasping the rope at either side of the knot and jerking it a bit. Quietly slide the little secret knot up against the main knot as you do so. Figure 256. Swing the rope around on the finger and no one can tell there is more than one knot as it all looks like one knot. Say, "The Hindu thus creates a Magic Circle and throwing it down on the ground (throw the rope down on the floor and step inside the circle, Figure 257) he steps within and pronounces the magic sentence "Hindju Galli-Galli, Galli, which means 'This circle shall never be broken.'" This gives you an opportunity to show the rope plainly and your two hands empty in an off-hand manner, Figure 257.

Pick up the rope at the knot with both hands. Move the sliding knot down to the center of the rope under cover of testing the strength of the circle, Figure 260, saying, "Not only can it never be broken with the bare hands but even if severed with cold steel the circle will never remain separated for very long. First I must see if it is really a perfect Magic Circle. I will trim these unsightly ends off." Saying this you bring both hands from the position shown in Figure 260 together as in Figure 259, so you have both real and sliding knots in

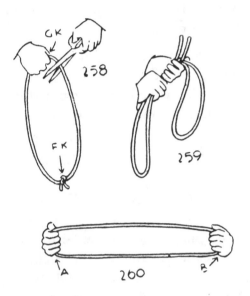

the left hand. Reach into pocket with your right hand and take out the shears. Trim off the ends close to the real knot, so it will look just the same as the sliding knot which has no ends. Drop the sliding knot, allowing it to hang down, saying, "Now it looks a little neater"— and everyone will take this knot to be the one you have just trimmed off.

Naturally, they can think nothing else as they have seen the rope from the beginning when you showed it simply clipped between the fingers, palms empty, Figure 253, on to the time when you showed it again, Figures 256 and 257, all around with hands shown empty. No one can have any suspicion that there is any other knot, for they have seen the rope freely so many times.

Hold the rope as in Figure 258. Hand the shears to someone and ask him to "Cut the rope at about the center," adding, "Where I am holding it, I would judge to be about the center. Just cut it on either side of my hand, and we will thus cut a piece right out of the circle. That will make it doubly hard."

Figure 258 shows the cutting position. The Fake Knot is indicated by "F. K." in the drawing. It appears to be a real knot. The Genuine Knot is concealed by the hand holding the rope, as indicated by the letters "G. K."

When cut, this leaves the real knot in your hand. This you may either pocket along with the shears, or dispose of as follows. Saying, "We will now totally destroy the pieces by making a little rope hash," insert the point of the shears into the center of the knot which will open the knot, or simply clip right through the knot, snip the pieces still smaller and toss aside. This idea gets rid of the second knot neatly.

Take the rope again, tie the freshly cut ends together making a neat small knot closely resembling the Fake Knot. Again "test" the rope as in Figure 260. Bring both hands from this position to Figure 259 with both real and fake knots in the left hand.

Take the shears and again "Trim off the waste ends," Figure 259. This time, Figure 261, bring the

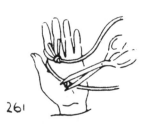

261

shears up and concealed behind back, just snip through the Fake Knot first so that it comes away from the rope center, and immediately cut off the ends of the last tied knot, allowing all the little pieces to be tossed aside together. Thus one cannot be told from the other later on. Your feat is now practically finished.

Hold the rope by the center, let the knotted ends fall as in Figure 258—but this time the real knot hangs where the arrow points to the letters "F. K." You may conclude by having someone hold the rope at either side of your hand, then pass your hand over where the other knot is supposed to be, open it to show the knot gone and the rope mysteriously joined. Or you may have someone untie the knot at the bottom of the circle and have two parties hold the ends while you pass your hand mysteriously up and down the rope, causing the knot to dissolve and the rope to become whole again.

Or finally, you may simply roll the rope into a ball between your hands, pronounce the phrase repeated earlier, toss the rope into the lap of a spectator, saying dramatically — "Behold, it is done, by the will of Allah."

CHAPTER 6
CUT AND RESTORED ROPE
(Unprepared Rope)

Chapter 6. CUT AND RESTORED ROPE
(With Unprepared Rope)

Although the rope itself is unprepared, the methods themselves differ from those described in the last chapter inasmuch as a certain amount of preparation is required in each case.

THE L. W. SIMPLICITY ROPE RESTORATION

This has the advantage for stage use over many other methods of being perfectly natural and straightforward, and very easy to follow on the part of the audience.

The performer comes forward carrying a rope stretched between his hands, which are seen otherwise perfectly empty. Then the ends of the rope are brought together, and the performer grasps the center of it with his left hand. With the other hand he takes a pair of scissors and cuts the rope at the center, trimming off the ends. The rope is thrown into the air, and upon being caught is again stretched out between the hands, and shown to be restored.

This feat resolves itself simply into the addition of an extra loop of rope, which is cut, but the moves utilized for this purpose are perhaps the most subtle yet suggested. The hands are shown clearly empty save for the rope. In spite of this the extra piece is in the hands from the beginning, being concealed by the very simple method of having it in full view.

The usual type of soft twisted rope is employed. The rope proper is a couple of yards long, the extra piece is six inches long.

At the start the rope appears to be held between the thumb and first finger of each hand, about six inches from either end. Actually the right hand holds the extreme end of the rope, and also one end of the extra piece, the thumb and finger hiding the join so that this extra piece appears to be part of the rope proper. Palms of the hands are toward the audience, so that it is clear that they are otherwise empty.

Remarking: "We must locate the exact center of this rope!" the performer brings the ends together so that the rope hangs down in a loop. Figure 262. As

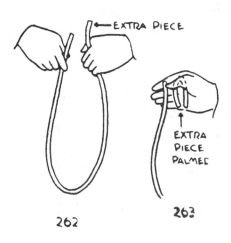

262

263

the hands are thus brought together the extra piece is doubled into a loop, which is thumb palmed by the left hand. Figure 263. Both ends are then shifted to the right hand, being held evenly. The left hand forms into a fist about the rope; the right hand draws the rope through the left until the center is reached, and then drops the ends, the left hand grasping the rope by the center. The right thumb and forefinger are now plunged into the left hand, and apparently draw up the center of the rope into view. Actually it is the fake loop. This series of moves requires but a few seconds to perform, and is absolutely natural.

With the aid of the right hand the position of the rope is now shifted until it is held between the tips of the first and second fingers of the left hand, and the ball of the left thumb. These form plenty of cover to conceal the join between real loop and extra piece, and enable the left hand to be casually turned palm toward the audience also.

The right hand now gets a pair of scissors from the table or pocket. In bringing them up the hand should again be turned about, without apparent intention, so that it can be seen that there is nothing concealed. The extra loop is then cut, apparently dividing the rope in the middle. Calling attention to the fact that there are now four ends, the performer remarks that he will clip a piece from each A small piece is cut from each of the real ends, but the fake piece is cut completely away. The cutting of the actual ends serves to misdirect attention from the purpose of this maneuver. The rope is gathered up into the left hand. The scissors are laid down; the rope is thrown into the air and as it comes down the hands catch it by the ends and hold it stretched out between them, demonstrating the restoration. It is then tossed into the audience, as convincing proof of its genuineness.

If the performer does not like the method of cutting away the short ends, he may easily palm them away in the right hand, and dispose of them via the pocket or table when he puts down the scissors.

Since nothing is required save the rope and the scissors, the experiment may be performed practically impromptu, but it is also useful for the stage.

L. W. TUG O'WAR

The performer picks up an eight-foot length of rope and, after showing it, puts it around his neck — letting the ends hang down in front of him. He then selects two boys from the audience. The boys are chosen for their brawn — "big boys with sound muscles, strong backs and belligerent natures."

Each boy is requested to grasp one end of the rope, which the performer has removed from around his neck. The performer retains a good hold on the center of the rope. The boys are requested to pull hard — HARD! "But wait," says the performer. "First let us cut the rope in the center and then pull hard. This is the most unkind cut of all. Pull harder! When I count three, I will let go!" The boys, visioning a fall over backwards, will not pull so enthusiastically. The performer goads them on. At the count of three he releases the rope — which is found to be restored.

We have merely suggested the fun that may be had with the two boys. The performer who wishes to work out the feat may insure to himself many a wave of hearty laughter over the antics of the boys.

How is the rope restored? Well, again the performer only cuts an extra loop. But where does he get the loop? Oh, that was tucked in his collar, rather between the collar and the back of the neck. When the rope was removed from the neck, he merely carried the extra loop along with it.

L. W. VINCULUM

"Amiel has said, my friends, 'In every union there is a mystery — a certain invisible bond that must not be disturbed.' I shall prove the statement with a length of rope. I lay it across my hand, so, and ask you to cut it there. But, though you have cut the material substance of the rope, the invisible bond remains intact. See! Even now it is restored."

Use for this experiment a length of rope about five feet long. A three-inch length is also required. In the beginning the short piece rests alongside, in back, of the long piece. Pick up the ropes in the right hand, the hand completely covering the short piece. This piece is grasped at one end by the base of the thumb and at the other end between the third and fourth fingers, near the palm. This arrangement can be made while the left hand is taking the long piece of rope from the right.

The long piece is then laid over the right hand, one end allowed to drape down between the thumb and forefinger; the other between the third and fourth fingers. The second and third fingers of the left hand are bent in toward the palm. These fingers pull the long piece of rope back a couple of inches toward the right wrist. The first and fourth fingers of the left hand cover the crotch at the base of the right thumb and the third and fourth fingers, respectively. Thus only the short

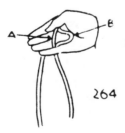

264

piece remains in view. The excuse for the position is the apparent pointing out to the spectator the place to cut. Actually only the short piece is destroyed.

ENCYCLOPEDIA OF ROPE TRICKS

Now the left hand grasps the long piece of rope and pulls it free from the right hand, through the fingers. The cut pieces remain and are pocketed while the rope is being shown to be fully restored.

A reference to Figure 264 should help to make the position of the ropes and hand clear. In any event, if you will follow the description with ropes in hand, you will readily discern the theory of the effect and rapidly be able to put it into actual practice.

In Figure 264, A is the short piece of rope and B is the actual center of the long piece.

THE L. W. GLOVED DECEPTION

Whether this one came to us after seeing Cardini we do not remember. But, the magician does wear gloves.

We need a six-foot length of rope and a five-inch length. Put on a pair of leather gloves. Double the five-inch piece over to form a loop. Stick this loop up inside the left glove, between the glove and the left palm. Allow the two ends of the loop to project a little.

Pick up the six-foot rope. Double it over and hold the loop thus formed between the thumb and fingers of the right hand. The left hand approaches the right, apparently to pull a little more of the rope into view. Actually the right hand pulls the extra loop free from the left glove.

Cut the extra loop entirely away with the shears. After sufficient "presentation" show the rope to be restored.

L. W. RESTORING THE ROPE

This is the result of our experimenting with the various cut and restored methods to find one that would be particularly suitable to our entertainment; what we wanted was one simple, clean cut, easy to make ready and without false or unnecessary moves, always bearing in mind the fact that it was to be presented as part of a program under normal performing conditions.

Since the effect is so simple, the patter is necessarily simple and rather brief:

"Perhaps you have heard it said, if you believe a thing strongly enough it will come true. Do you believe that? Because if you do, it must come true. I've had only fair success; I tried taking this rope in my hands and believing it was a million dollars, but I could never quite convince myself. Yet sometimes it will work. For example, here I have a piece of rope, as you can see. Do you believe that I can make that into two pieces of rope? I do — and because I believe it, it will be so."

Taking a knife, the rope is cut in two, thereby fulfilling the performer's word.

"You see, I believed it and it was so. Do you believe I can make those two pieces of rope into one? I do. All I need do is tie them together and I have one rope, though divided in the middle. Let us try something harder. Do you believe that I can make this knotted rope into one piece of rope again — a single piece as long as it was in the first place? That is impossible, since it has been cut in the center, but if you will believe it perhaps I can. Everyone believe very hard. I feel as though someone were doubting. No, now everyone believe it — and you see, it has been done."

The restored rope is thrown out to the audience, a conclusive proof, even to those that did not examine it, that it must be ordinary.

From the standpoint of method our problem was, not to find a new principle, but to find a way of working that would eliminate all false and unnecessary moves. Consequently we have adopted a variation of the oldest and simplest cut and restored method of all.

The secret lies in the knife. This is like a kitchen knife, with a rather long blade and a fairly long wooden handle. The handle is hollow, open at the end. In preparing it, it is best to completely remove the handle from the knife, and cut off a portion of the blade that is sunk into the handle, as the blade can be fastened rigidly to the handle without extending so far down into it, thus leaving more space in the interior of the handle. A new handle can now be prepared and fitted onto the blade. The handle of an ordinary size kitchen type knife is four or five inches long. The hollow portion should be at least three inches deep, or rather of sufficient size to permit the insertion of a loop of rope three inches long.

To prepare for performing, a piece of rope six inches long is cut off the end of the rope you are to use, which should be around six feet in length. The short piece is doubled and placed in the hollow handle of the knife, which is laid on the table, handle to the back. The rope used is ordinary sash cord.

We will give the moves somewhat in detail, as it is only in their smoothness that the virtue of the feat lies.

The performer begins by picking up the rope and showing it, casually demonstrating at the same time that his hands are otherwise empty. The rope could be measured, but it is hardly worth the trouble; the performer may, however, casually measure it along his body. Now the rope is doubled, and held by the center in the left fist. The obvious reason for this is to leave the right hand free to pick up the knife to cut the rope. Since the right hand hereafter holds the knife, it is natural that the rope — particularly when it is apparently divided into two pieces—should be held in the left hand throughout. The principle of cutting a false loop only fails to be perfectly convincing when the ends of the rope are held in a manner that would make it more natural for the two pieces of rope to be held separate. With this false point eliminated, there is no reason for the audience to suspect the genuineness of the cut, particularly as the handling is so clean.

As the right hand reaches for the knife, the performer stands to the left side of the table, with his left side toward the audience. Now as he takes the knife, he makes a half turn, placing his right side to the audience. In making the half turn, the hands naturally come together for a second, and the left hand obtains the false loop from the handle, holding it projecting its full length from the left fist. The cutting is now done. This leaves four ends visible. Now, with the right hand still holding the knife as before, the ends projecting from the left fist are tied together in a knot or two. With pieces of the length we have described this is not unduly difficult; the left thumb helps. The left fist is held throughout with the front of hand toward audience. The pieces having been knotted, the right fingers apparently push the knot down into the left fist.

Really the short knotted pieces are carried away by the right fingers — as the right still holds the knife nothing suspicious is visible. The left hand is turned over, back of hand to audience, and as this is done, and keeping the eyes on it, the right deposits the knife on the table, and incidentally disposes of the short piece of rope behind something. The feat is now done, but the performer does not at once show this. Rather he advances slowly forward; if in a club, or if he has a run down, right down to the spectators and he throws out the ends of the rope for two people to catch. They are invited to slowly pull it out — and as they do so it is seen to be restored. If on a stage, the performer advances to the footlights, and catching one end of the rope in his right hand — with the very tips of the fingers — he slowly pulls it out, and it may be held up to show it is the same length as originally.

This method is not restricted to stage or club use. In the home nothing could be more natural than that the magician leaving the room to get a rope with which to show an experiment should bring back a kitchen knife with which to cut it. Even better for the married magician, his wife brings in rope and knife, gives him the rope and stands by holding the knife until the moment he wants it, in which case the feat may be worked very close. The knotting done, the magician, to dispose of the knife, drops it into his side coat pocket, handle down, leaving the blade sticking out, while he restores the rope.

BERT DOUGLAS' MAGIC SKIPPING ROPE

Simplicity is the keynote of this version of the cut and restored rope trick. The effect is baffling to the audience and provides plenty of scope for comedy.

EFFECT: The performer introduces an ordinary skipping rope and invites two members of the audience to come forward and assist in the experiment. The rope is thoroughly examined, then cut through the center, and the two pieces are tied together leaving a knot in the middle of the skipping rope. The rope is then held by the volunteer assistants, one holding each end, and at the command of the performer the knot in the center VISIBLY disappears. The rope is instantly tossed out for examination — it is completely restored.

REQUIREMENTS AND PREPARATION: An ordinary skipping rope, and a piece of similar rope about seven inches long. A pair of ordinary scissors and a duplicate pair which has been prepared by having the handles spot welded together so that it is impossible to open them. Rope cement is also recommended although not absolutely essential.

Take the short piece of rope, form it into a circle, and join the ends together with cement, or, if preferred, simply sew the ends together. The cement, of course, makes the cleanest and most perfect join. Place this loop in the left trouser pocket. The ordinary pair of scissors is placed in the upper vest pocket on the left side and the prepared scissors and skipping rope are placed in view on the performer's table.

PRESENTATION: Walk forward with the skipping rope and invite two spectators to come forward and assist in the experiment. Have your two volunteer assistants pull hard on the rope and thoroughly examine same so that everyone will be convinced that the rope is quite ordinary and without preparation of any kind.

Next hand the skipping rope to one of your assistants and request him to cut it through the center, at the same time giving him the prepared scissors for this purpose. The vain attempts of your assistant is a riot of fun, and finally in apparent desperation you give the rope and scissors to the other gentleman, and his fruitless efforts to cut the rope will have the audience in an uproar.

Meanwhile secure the loop from the trouser pocket and hold it concealed in the left hand. Take the scissors from your assistant and drop same in your left vest pocket at the same time drawing the ordinary scissors up into view so that they can readily be withdrawn from the pocket. The audience will of course be unaware that any exchange has been made.

Take the rope from your assistant, grasping it at the center with the right hand, and immediately pass it directly into the left hand. Remove the scissors from the vest pocket with the right hand and proceed to apparently cut the rope through the center, in reality of course it is the small loop or circle protruding from the left hand that is cut and which the audience believe to be the actual center of the rope.

The performer then twists the short piece of rope around the center of the skipping rope and exhibits the rope in this condition. Figure 266. One end of the short piece is then allowed to unwind, as shown in Figure 267, but this is masked by the hands, and the fake knot is quickly tied in the following manner. The short piece and the center of the rope are gripped with the right hand, and slightly to the left of this the rope is twisted around the forefinger of the left hand, Figure 268, and short piece and center of rope are pushed entirely through this loop and it is drawn up tight to form the fake knot. Figure 269.

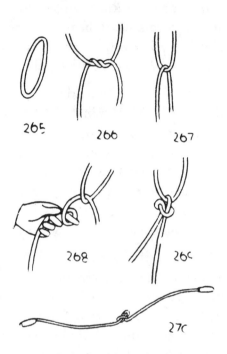

This knot differs from any other that I am aware of inasmuch as it will instantly and visibly vanish without having to be covered and worked loose with the hands. It takes but a second to tie this knot and the audience imagines that the performer has merely tied the two halves of the rope together with a double knot.

Performer exhibits the rope, then taking the scissors in his right hand he proceeds to trim the ends of the knot, actually the short piece of rope is trimmed off entirely leaving only the fake knot. Figure 270.

Each of your assistants is then given an end of the rope to hold, but they must not be permitted to pull on the rope until instructed to do so. The performer then steps right back from the rope, the knot is clearly seen in the center, yet on commanding the assistants to pull hard on the rope the knot will visibly melt away. The performer immediately takes the rope and tosses it to the audience for inspection, or it may be presented to the Chairman, or President of the club, as a souvenir.

SUGGESTION: The comedy business with the prepared scissors may be eliminated if desired and the straight cut and restored rope trick presented, but, apart from the fun created, the fact that both gentlemen freely handled the rope and were apparently given an opportunity to cut same, makes a great impression on the audience, and the fact that the assistants really had no chance to cut the rope does not occur to them.

CHALLENGE: If the reader is already featuring one of the many cut and restored rope tricks in his program I would recommend that an extra loop, Figure 265, be carried in the pocket as a Safety First measure, then should he at any time be challenged to repeat his miracle rope trick he will be in a position to take the same rope back from the audience and repeat the cut and restored rope trick by introducing the foregoing method.

RINGING THE BULL

The magician requests the assistance of two gentlemen from the audience, they are first given a length of rope to examine, also a number of steel rings. When everything has been pronounced genuine the magician threads one ring onto the center of the rope, secures this with a knot, and then slides the remaining rings down over the doubled rope so that they are retained by the first ring and cannot be removed. The puzzle now is to remove the rings while an end of the rope is held by each assistant. Both assistants admit the feat is impossible, but the performer soon solves the problem by taking a scissors and cutting the rope through the center. This immediately releases the threaded ring thereby allowing the other rings to drop right off and scatter on the floor. The performer then completes the miracle by magically restoring the rope and immediately the rope and rings can be passed out for examination.

HOW IT IS DONE: This is a novel adaptation of the ropes and rings and the cut and restored rope, some subtle moves are introduced and it forms an ideal item for the club performer.

A length of rope about eight feet long is required, also seven or eight steel rings, small linking rings will answer the purpose admirably. Both rope and rings are genuine, but unknown to the audience one ring is prepared as follows: Take a short piece of rope and prepare the ends with rope cement, then form it into a loop around the ring by rolling the cemented ends together. Figure 271. This prepared ring may be sus-

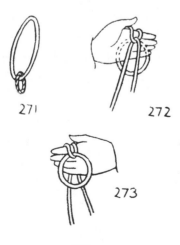

271   272

273

pended under the coat on the left side, or it may be on the table concealed by a handkerchief.

Briefly the working is as follows: Have two spectators come forward and assist in the experiment, one standing at your left and the other on your right. Give each a few of the steel rings to examine and when pronounced O. K. take the rings back and hand the rope for inspection. Meanwhile obtain the prepared ring from under the coat holding it with the other rings in the left hand, then place all the rings on the table with the exception of one (the prepared ring) which is kept in the left hand. If the prepared ring was originally concealed on the table then lay the bunch of rings down on the table and later pick up one, really the prepared ring. Care must be taken to keep the loop of rope concealed in the fingers. Now take back the rope and proceed to thread same through the steel ring, actually under cover of the left hand thread the rope through the loop.

Ring and portion of the loop is allowed to hang over the left hand as you grasp ends of rope and quickly tie a knot, this knot being actually tied close up against the loop, the audience of course are not aware of the presence of the loop as same has been kept concealed behind the left hand. Figure 272 shows the state of affairs, as you see it, just before the knot is tied. The appearance to the audience is as Figure 273.

The rope may now be quite freely shown with the ring apparently securely threaded and knotted thereon. Grasping the two ends of the rope the performer next slides all the rings down onto the threaded ring.

Each assistant then takes one end of the rope and the puzzle is to remove the rings while the rope is thus held. Accordingly the performer takes the scissors and cuts the rope at the center (really the loop) when all the rings are released and fall to the floor.

The rope now has a small portion of the short piece within the knot as in most cut and restored rope effects. Trim this short piece away entirely with the scissors.

Knot is then dissolved in the usual manner and the rope is completely restored and together with the rings may be given out for thorough inspection.

I cannot too strongly urge the reader to refer to The Tale of a Bull by Stanley Collins as this excellent patter scheme with minor alterations will be found ideal for this problem, and it is splendid for club work.

R. M. JAMISON'S SEVERED ROPE

A snappy little rope cutting item, quick and easy to do, and a fine introduction to further versions of this effect, using one rope. The moves are natural, well covered, and while not original or new, there is a different twist to this routine, that puts it in the "new" class.

The effect is that two lengths of rope, of about three feet in length each, are shown, doubled in the center and cut by the spectator, and later restored of course.

Just a little previous preparation is required, and that is, to make a loop of the same rope, from a five inch piece. This makes a loop about an inch and a half in diameter. Either cement the ends, or use as I do, adhesive tape, smudged up to the shade of the rope. I make up these loops about a dozen at a time.

Some may prefer to hold the loop in the palm, as the two ropes are shown, but I prefer to have the loop already on the ropes, it being about eight inches from the rope ends, and in picking up the ropes, this loop is pushed well down into the crotch between first and second fingers, the loop except for the part which overlaps the ropes, this being covered by the thumb tip, hanging on the back of the hand, on the knuckles.

With palm of hand to audience, thumb tip on loop junction, ropes are shown as two separate ropes, right hand pulling each to even up the ends.

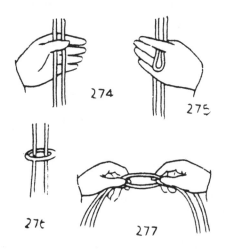

Figure 276 shows how the ropes are prepared. Figure 274 shows how the ropes appear to the audience and Figure 275 discloses how the loop projects at the back of the hand.

The right hand finger tips reach up to rope ends, projecting above the left hand, and pull them on up until the centers are reached. The ends are next released, and right next reaches to left hand, looping one rope in the fake loop. Pulling fake loop from between left fingers, until junction of fake loop and rope is reached, this is now grasped by right finger tips, pulling a little more until loop is free. Then this end of fake loop and rope are grasped by left finger tips. Figure 277.

Now still holding the rope in this manner, bring hands down in front of you, and have a spectator cut the ropes in the three inch space between your finger tips. Several cuttings are better as less evidence is left to get rid of. Ropes are now shown in each hand, as two separate, and four ends each. Rope ends are now balled up in the hand and re-appear restored. My getaway of the cut fake loop ends is by having an Oriental looking salt shaker in the pocket. This shaker supposedly contains a restoring powder. The small pieces from the fake loop are left in the pocket when procuring the shaker.

The reader has but to give this routine a tryout to realize just how nicely it works out, the open handed moves, the minimum of covering and above all, every move is a natural one. The fake loop on the back of the hand is so small that it is surprising at what wide angles this routine can be shown.

BAFFLESO!

Baffles Brush has seen so many rope tricks in the last two years that he decided it was up to him to add his name to the long list of perspiring inventors of village cut up fame. Here is one you will use.

A coil of rope is picked up from the table and tossed out into a straight line. It is about eight feet long.

Next it is taken by the center and held by the thumb and palm of the left hand with two ends hanging down to the floor. Figure 278.

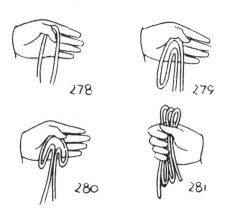

One piece is grasped at the middle where it is brought up to the thumb and palm and held. Now the other piece is handled in the same manner leaving the two ends still hanging down and the rope formed into three loops at the top. Figure 279 and Figure 280. The rope is now passed to the right hand and a spectator allowed to cut through the three loops extending above the fist. Again the rope is placed in the left hand and a short piece snipped from each of the six ends just made.

Either one of the ends hanging down is now held while the remainder of the rope is tossed out in a straight line. The rope is seen to be restored and may be passed out for examination if you desire to be generous and give it away.

METHOD: A small piece of rope about eight inches long is coiled into three loops and the ends sewn together. Thread is also used to tack the loops together so they will not come undone. If you have enough thread left, or use catgut, make a loop big enough to go over your left thumb so that the tri-coil will hang from there back of the left hand. In picking up the coiled piece of eight feet, you slip this over your left thumb.

Toss the rope to let the large coil unwind and the right hand slips the rope between the first and second fingers of the left hand. It is pulled back to about half way and then the middle is clipped between the left thumb and palm allowing the two ends to hang down about four feet on each side.

You now take each half, one at a time, about two feet from the bottom end and bring it up under the left thumb so that three loops are held in the left hand and two loops and two ends hang down.

By this time the left hand is pretty full and the left hand has closed some to hold the rope in position. Up to this time the performer has been standing with his right side more or less to the audience. He now makes a turn so that his left side is toward the audience and at the same time transfers the rope to his right hand. The loop back of the left hand is also taken. This is allowed to protrude above the fist and it is this fake that is now cut.

If you can manipulate the scissors sufficiently well with the left hand, the rope need not be transferred back to the left hand to trim off the ends. During this trimming, the tri-coil fake is completely cut away.

All that remains is to take one of the hanging ends and toss the rope out into a straight line and then to the audience and another MIRACLE has been performed.

U. F. GRANT'S STAGE ROPE RESTORATION

Here is a snappy method of presenting the cut and restored rope mystery.

The rope is tossed to the audience for examination. The performer takes it back, loops the center up through his left fist, an assistant cuts it, one half of the rope is held in each hand, the ends are placed together, the rope shown restored, and again tossed to the audience for examination.

METHOD: A black fiber tube, about 2½" long, is used. This tube is of a size to just slide nicely over the rope you will use.

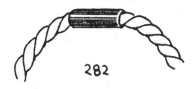

282

Tube is concealed in the left hand. On taking back the rope, one end of the rope is passed through the tube as you take it in the left hand. You grasp this end with the right hand and pull the rope through the left fist, and the tube, until you have the center of the rope at your fist. Drop the end you are holding in your right hand and allow the doubled center of the rope to project above the closed left hand.

Your assistant steps forward with the scissors but only PRETENDS to cut the rope. As soon as the rope is apparently cut, you shove the loop back down in the fist to conceal the fact that the rope is uninjured.

Now grasp the rope at one end of the fiber tube, about two or three inches from it, in the right hand thumb and forefinger. Do the same with the left hand. The fiber tube in front of your dark suit produces a black art effect and the rope seems to be in two separate and distinct pieces.

Again take the black tube in your closed left hand. It will appear that you have two ends of the rope concealed in your fist. Grasp either one of the hanging ends and draw the rope through your left fist, and out of the tube, and again toss for examination.

SCOTTY LANG'S SUCKER ROPE TRICK

A spectator takes a rope in his own hands, cuts it at the middle, two ends are tied in a knot, and then the rope is rolled into a ball. A touch with the magic wand to restore the rope proves successful. However, spectators notice that in your hurry to get a duplicate rope from your right coat pocket, you have left the original cut rope protruding from the pocket for two or three inches, apparently being drawn out of the pocket by mistake with a genuine rope which is supposed to be restored.

With perfect acting and showmanship you have performed a miracle. But when your attention is drawn to the rope protruding from the pocket, yank it out and throw it on the floor in disgust. However, to cover it up, say, "Some magicians get away with stunts like that, and I am one of them; however, on this occasion I have been unfortunate. Nevertheless, magicians can restore a rope by putting you off the scent. But, don't forget, I cannot restore this rope any more than the best magician alive, yet if I can take your attention off this rope with what I say, and apparently restore the rope by getting another one unnoticed, well, more power to me!"

Proceed to roll the rope up into the hand with one hand, telling the story about the Scotchman who was treating his wife to a dinner at a hotel, I mean a quick lunch counter, and the waitress was very much alarmed to see that the Scotch woman had not started to eat, and the Scotchman was nearly finished. "Is there anything wrong, lady?" inquired the waitress. "No" was the reply. "Then why are you not taking your dinner?" "Well, I won't be long. John's nearly finished. He has the teeth just now."

Meanwhile the audience will be trying to watch you exchange the rope which you roll up with your left hand into a ball, back of hand to audience, and leave the two ends hanging an inch or two so that they can always be seen.

Pull on one end and show restored, with palm of hands facing audience, and finish with restored rope held with the forefingers and thumbs at the ends. Address the audience with this statement: "While I took your attention off the rope for a second or two, I did the trick. And here is the cut rope up my sleeve." Display it.

REQUIREMENTS: Four pieces of fine cord, string, rope or shoe laces. Anything to be original. Four pieces all the same length as follows.

1st PIECE in right coat pocket, and in the small pocket of that pocket. (Most pockets have one; can be worked without, but preferred. Or, a piece of cardboard in pocket to make a division). A short piece is tied about the center to give it the appearance of two ropes tied together.

2ND PIECE of rope in right hand corner of right coat pocket. A piece without a knot.

3RD PIECE is up the left sleeve under the armband and within reach from the bottom of the sleeve. It may be held by a safety pin if desired. This piece of rope has a double knot in the center with the ends trimmed very close. It must resemble the rope that is supposed to be exchanged.

4TH PIECE is the one cut in the middle by the spectator.

WORKING: Rope No. 4 is cut, tied in a knot with ends from knot about two inches long, and rolled up in right hand in that condition until it can be held comfortably in the right hand.

Left hand reaches for wand on table which is on your right. At the same time right hand changes rope No. 4 for rope No. 2, and, in bringing same from pocket, brings rope No. 1 with it, which is left protruding from the pocket. (Not too much to make it suspicious looking.)

The next move is made in disgust. Pull rope No. 1 from pocket and patter.

Rope No. 1 is trimmed until short piece is cut away and falls to the floor. Use apparent strength as if to tighten a knot, but just give that impression. Rope No. 1 is now drawn up by left hand only. Proceed until it is all in the hand except two ends about three or four inches long, meanwhile misdirecting audience after telling what was going to take place.

Show the rope restored and then pull rope No. 3 from the sleeve, showing how a magician takes their attention away.

THE L. W. LOST CHORD

"I seek," says the magician, "the Lost Chord. Perhaps it is somewhere hereabouts — AH! There it is. But look! The Lost Cord is cut in three pieces." So saying, the performer picks up three pieces of rope, each about two feet long, from the table. Something must be done. The Lost Cord, the **famous** Lost Cord, can't be left in such a condition. What would the people say? Especially the musicians? So he drops the three pieces into a plush bag which he has shown empty. A hat is also shown empty, and the magician commands the ropes to pass from the bag to the hat and be restored.

He reaches into the hat and pulls out the ropes, but, though they have come together they are in no wise restored. They are merely knotted together in one six-foot length. He replaces the knotted pieces back into the hat. Immediately the hat is shown empty. He walks over to the bag, reaches therein and pulls out the rope —rather, three ropes, STILL KNOTTED.

"Such nonsense. I might have known these ropes would not obey me if I let them out of my possession. Come, I'll take a hand to them." So saying, he passes his hand along the rope and the knots dissolve, leaving the rope fully restored.

You will require for the effect the following:
A large size plush changing bag.
A Brunel White changing hat.
Three two-foot lengths of rope.
Three two-foot lengths of rope knotted together to form one length.

A six-foot length of rope prepared as follows: Two feet from one end of the rope tie another piece of rope of the same kind around the center. Cut the ends of this knot short. Do the same two feet from the other end. Thus there are two fake knots on the long piece of rope. These knots should be loose enough so that they may be easily slipped off, but not so loose that they will fall off of their own weight. Figure 284.

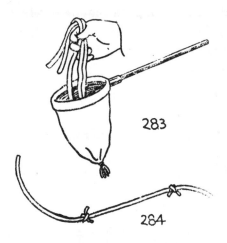

283

284

This six-foot length, so prepared, is placed in the changing bag and the handle twisted to conceal it.

The three pieces which are knotted together are placed in the hat, under the fake bottom.

The three separate pieces are in the beginning lying behind some piece of apparatus on the table.

Presentation: Place the three separate pieces in the changing bag, Figure 283, and command that they pass to the hat, restored. Reach in the hat and draw out the knotted pieces from under the fake. These, after being shown, are replaced, still knotted, in the hat. The hat is then shown empty. Pick up the changing bag, bringing the side bearing the long rope to the front, reach therein and remove the long piece.

Pass the right hand along the rope and carry the fake knots with it. Thus is the rope apparently restored.

WILL BREMA'S CONVINCING ROPE TRICK

A length of rope approximately six feet long is cut and the ends tied. This is repeated. Audience sees rope in three pieces joined by two separate knots. Rope is restored to one piece.

The advantage of this method is the fact that no special rope is necessary, there is no advance preparation of the rope and it is a perfect trick to climax any other rope trick. At the same time, as an individual effect it is 100 per cent effective from an audience point of view.

285

First examine Figure 285 which shows the construction of the special Brema made fake. The open end faces toward audience when in use. TO HOLD, curl the fingers lightly around the fake, hook pointing to little finger. When hooking fake to the clothing, move thumb forward to hold fake at the open end. Draw second, third and fourth fingers away.

Fake is hooked to body according to conditions under which you are performing. The regular position is on the pants or coat just beyond the coat pocket. For bad working conditions, fake is placed at same position under coat out of sight.

With fake in position, face audience. Hold one end of rope in left hand as right hand moves along rope as in Figure 286.

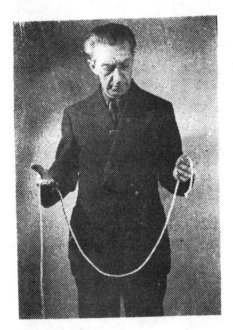

286

Right hand turns in, bringing it up to position as in Figure 287.

Carefully note the position of the three extended fingers of the left hand. With the rope resting on these fingers, the end of rope out of sight in the picture falls on the floor, Figure 287. The left thumb and first finger holding end of rope do not move as the three extended fingers curl around rope and pull it in towards palm. The right hand moves down in the direction of the body and the three fingers are straightened out so that two

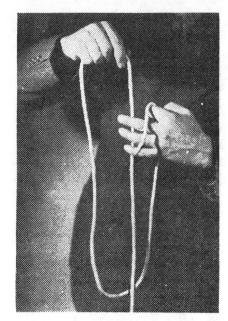

287

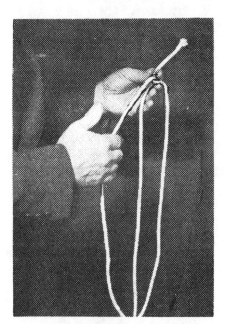

288

portions of rope now rest on the open fingers of left hand. Figure 288.

Right hand is moved away to secure scissors. Draw back first left hand finger so that this hand holds rope as in Figure 289. The foregoing moves take no more than three seconds to accomplish.

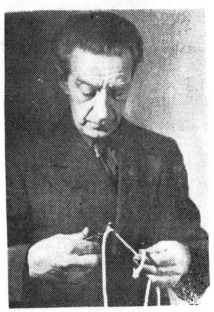

289

Rope is cut and the short piece tied around the rope proper. The end of rope nearest knob is dropped to the floor and the same procedure gone through with the opposite end. Rope is then held as in Figure 290. Knots do not show up prominently in the photo but their position in photo is less than one half inch from the elbow. Figure 290 also shows the position of the left hand getting ready to secure the fake. In actual working, the position of the body is right side more toward audience, as in Figure 292.

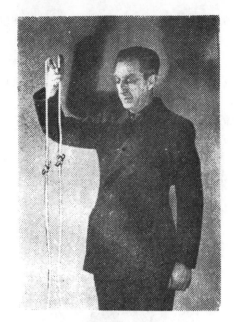

290

291

The left hand is brought up as in Figure 291. Rope is placed over left hand momentarily to permit right hand to secure one end of rope. The balance of the rope is allowed to fall to the floor. The rope is then drawn through the left hand (through fake) and coiled as in Figure 291.

292

The knots are automatically left in the fake. As right hand raises coiled up rope, the left drops to hook fake to clothing. Figure 292. A continuous sweeping movement is all that is necessary to hook fake, the left hand not being long enough out of sight to arouse suspicion.

NOTE: Moves Fig. 286, 287, 288 and 289 are all blended into one continuous move. The rope should be handled lightly and a certain amount of swaying movement with the rope will make the moves all the easier.

SECOND METHOD FINISH. Draw the rope through the hand as in Figure 291 but don't coil the rope. When the rope is pulled through the hand leaving the knots in the fake, retain fake in hand as you hold up rope stretched between both hands (hands about 18" apart), the ends of the rope hanging down, backs of both hands toward audience. Accidentally drop the rope (?). As you reach to pick it up, hook the fake on the body.

Again hold the rope between both hands and then permit the audience to see that the hands hold only the rope. Fake is easily secured and dropped into pocket or put to one side.

The cutting of the rope may be repeated as the fake has a capacity for more than two knots. The hole in fake is for magicians who prefer a "pull" fake to that of a hook.

Fasten elastic through hole and opposite end to a safety pin. Engage pin on back of vest. Bring fake around the left side of body, allow elastic to run through slot of fake and engage hook in the vest near the lower pocket. Fake can be secured in the left hand in the action of looking for shears, etc. The rest should be obvious.

THE ALADDIN ORIENTAL GIMMICK BY WINSTON FREER

The gimmick is a small tube of thin white rubber, which is to be rolled onto the rope, over the joint to be spliced, in the manner described in the following directions. It depends upon the principle of the old "Japanese Thumb Cuff" to securely fasten the rope ends to-

gether by contracting tightly upon them as they are being pulled upon.

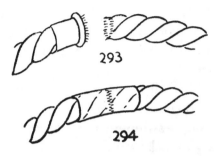

Figure 293 shows the gimmick as it appears on the
rope, with the slight fray on the rope preventing it
from rolling completely off the end. In Figure 294 is
illustrated the manner in which the rubber forces the
little frays on the ropes to fill in between the rope ends
as the gimmick holds them together. Note also that the
weave of the rope will show through the rubber, making
it look like the rope itself.

Preparation: The rope used is HARD WOVEN
SASH CORD. Besides the rubber tubing, you will require a dowel stick of a size to fit in the tubing, a pencil
from which the eraser has been removed and a sharp
knife.

(Always keep the rubber tubing wrapped in black
paper when not in use as light causes it to deteriorate
if not so protected.)

Thrust the stick for about an inch into the rubber
tubing. Roll the tubing back on itself towards the same
end of the stick by pressing directly on the end of the
tube with the thumb and first two fingers of the right
hand, while the stick passes between the first and second fingers. In actual use, the tubing is always rolled

in just this manner, which is the easiest way to get the roll started.

Continue to roll the rubber back and forth until it is stretched for about half an inch and is loose upon the stick. Now cut off ⅝" from this stretched end. Roll this short piece upon the stick until it has stretched as much as it will. Roll it from the stick onto the pencil, and continue to roll and stretch it upon the pencil until the ends curl up as though starting to roll by themselves. The gimmick is now ready to roll onto a rope which you insert into the pencil cap. Allow it to unroll half way, and then cut the rope close up to the roll. Fray the rope a little to prevent the roll from unrolling.

Be certain to keep your gimmick stretched until it is very soft, or it will not operate when your hands are nervous and moist. Keep your fingers as dry as possible, and you should have no trouble. In an emergency, should the gimmick be hard to roll, you can always proceed with the trick as in the second part of Tarbell's favorite method of performing the Rope Mystery, explained in Chapter Seven, as the gimmick will have served its purpose in the first part of the trick.

Method of Cutting and Restoring a Borrowed Rope

In your pocket you have a 10" piece of rope with a gimmick on one end and another 10" piece rolled up, ready to palm.

As you have specified HARD WOVEN SASH CORD, the spectator's MEASURED piece will match your sample. Compare it with your sample (really fastening them together) and give away the palmed piece. You can make this move very natural, with a little practice.

Their rope now has a 10" piece fastened on one end. Apparently tie the ends of the rope together. You really change the gimmick fastening so that it connects the two ends of their rope together and tie the 10" piece around their rope with a slip knot. Slide the knot to a point opposite the gimmick and you are ready to perform the last part of the previously mentioned Tarbell Rope Mystery.

TO CUT AND RESTORE THE ROPE IN THE CENTER: Borrow a rope and prepare as explained. The ends of the rope now appear to be the center and the center appears to be the ends.

Secretly roll the gimmick from right to left so that the two ends are separated again, and immediately put these two ends, which audience believes to be the un-broken center of the rope, in the left hand. (Always roll the gimmick with a push of the three fingers to-ward the other hand.)

Cut the rope end on which there is no gimmick about 2" from the end. Exchange the cut end for the gimmicked end in the left hand, leaving you in a posi-tion to roll the two ends back together again, steal away the short piece, and show the rope restored.

The short piece of rope shows as you roll the ends, of the rope proper, together and leads the audience to think that nothing has happened yet. The ends to be fastened should always be cut off square at a hard place in the rope.

K. W. LIDDLE'S PHENOMENAL ROPE TRICK

Effect: A length of ordinary rope seven to ten feet in length is thoroughly examined by the audience. Two spectators hold the ends of the rope while it is being cut into THREE pieces. The performer holds two ends in his right hand and two in his left. The rope is then sensationally restored and is again passed for examination.

Any thickness of cotton or flax rope can be used—string, cord, or rope up to 1 inch in thickness. The more the cut ends fray—the better the effect. The rope is the same length at the conclusion of the trick as in the beginning.

No preliminary tying of the ends together. No cement or fasteners used. The rope is absolutely genuine and unfaked. The ends of the rope are firmly held by the spectators throughout the trick.

Apparatus And Preliminary Preparation. To prepare a gimmick, take a piece of rope twenty inches long, double it in the center and sew the two ends together. Fix a piece of **strong** cord elastic twenty inches long to the doubled joint and sew the rope at this point also.

Place this piece of rope in the right coat sleeve and attach with a safety pin to the back of the vest so that the end of the loop hangs concealed just within the right coat sleeve.

Presentation: Introduce a large coil of rope and have a piece cut off about seven to ten feet in length. While this is being examined, get the loop of rope from the right sleeve with left fingers and it is retained with right fingers curled in toward palm.

Keeping the back of hand to audience, form a loop in center of rope and give an end to spectator on either side. The loop made is a large one.

In bringing the hands apart, preparatory to cutting, the extra loop is withdrawn completely from the right hand to the position indicated in Figure 295.

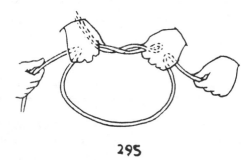

295

The doubled rope is now cut (extra loop) apparently leaving it in three pieces. Hold the ends wide apart and show to the committee. The short ends in right hand are gradually worked into this hand with the left fingers. Hold the right hand about knee level and the back of the hand to the audience. Gradually release the grip on the extra piece in right hand, thus allowing it to be drawn by the elastic up through between the fingers and thumb and into the sleeve. This is a knockout as you immediately open the right hand and show the restoration.

Turn to the committeeman on your left and show him the restored portion. Under cover of this movement, slip the ends in left hand into left coat pocket or, as an alternative method, these ends may be trimmed with a scissors until they are cut away completely. The left hand is suddenly opened and the rope is whole again.

Important Variation: We will imagine that the rope has been cut by the spectator on your left and that you are still holding same with all cut ends exposed.

Remark to the party who did the cutting, "Now, sir, I am going to ask you a very peculiar question. Are you quite sure you have cut the rope?" Whatever the reply you continue, "Fearing that you are not quite sure, I will ask you to cut again. Cut off a piece for a souvenir. Right up close to my left thumb if you please."

With which you give your left hand a quick shake and exclaim, "No, not my thumb, please, just the rope." Thus as he cuts and you give your hand a shake, the short ends fall to the floor and with them you let go the small extra loop end that has been held under cover in your left hand.

This enables you to get rid of this part without any suspicious moves whatever. It leaves you quite free to finish with as much dramatic effect as possible.

L. W. CHASED

We have called this item "Chased." That is what the magician will be after he tries it.

The local magician strolls down Main Street. He stops in front of the Trip Hammer Department Store to exchange pleasantries with the proprietor thereof. "Ah, it is a good morning. Yes indeed. Yes indeed. How is Mrs. Trip Hammer? Excellent. So glad. And how are all the little Trip Hammers? Well, well—glad to hear it. My, what a nice awning you have. Very pretty. Very pretty. Must be a lot of trouble to have an awning like that to put up. Yes indeed. But isn't the awning rope too long. I've never seen such a long awning rope. Here! Let me trim it off a bit. I know I cut a lot off. I did it purposely. What? You didn't want me to? Well, why didn't you tell me? I thought you would like to have it short like that. What? Now when you put the awning down the rope will be drawn away up and you won't be able to reach it? Deuced, positively deuced luck! I never thought of that. Perhaps I can fix it. I will speak to the rope, 'Rope! Pull yourself together.' See! It's all fixed. The rope is as good as new. Well, good day, Mr. Trip Hammer. Drop in and see us sometime. . . . . . .Say! Do you think it was nice to throw that rake at me?

There are two kinds of awning rope commonly used. One is a narrow white braided variety. The other is also a white rope but it is made of two twisted strands. You may run down to the ten cent store and buy a hank of each variety. Or you may wait until it gets dark and then dash out and clip off a few six-inch specimens from the nearest awning ropes available. In any event, you will need some short lengths of awning rope.

These are looped and added to the awning rope proper at the time of the ostensible cutting. Of course, it is the loop which is cut, not the rope itself. In talking with the victim, the performer has ample time to reach in his pocket and get the loop in position to add.

If you like a little fun with your magic—try it!

CHAPTER 7
CUT AND RESTORED ROPE
(Prepared Rope)

Chapter 7. CUT AND RESTORED ROPE
(With Prepared Rope)

L. W. MARKING THE CENTER

We have used this idea in conjunction with the old figure eight rope trick. (See Chapter Five.)

About four or five inches from one end of the rope tie a small piece of colored ribbon, trimming the ends of the knot well away. The ribbon, thus tied on the rope, is concealed by the hand in the course of handling the experiment.

Now request a spectator to tie another piece of ribbon, identical with the one which is being kept concealed around the center of the rope. The ends of this knot are likewise cut away. The rope is then looped up in the usual fashion; the real center grasped in the hand and the end substituted for it.

"You will note that we will cut the ribbon exactly in the center, which place on the rope you yourself marked with the ribbon." The spectator cuts the rope near the end, the cut pieces are dropped, the ribbon carried away, and the rope eventually restored with THE RIBBON STILL MARKING THE CENTER.

In passing, it may be worthy to note that the marking of the center may just as well be done with an ordinary single knot which is tied in the rope. Or, the performer could mark the center by tying a ring on the rope at that point. A switch of knots or rings, according to which idea is used, is fully as easy and practical as the ribbon method.

R. W. HULL'S MARKED ROPE AND THE THUMB TACK

The rope seems to be cut into three pieces and is restored and even the mark that a spectator placed in the center of the rope in the beginning is still there to identify it. No extra ropes are used—nothing but the one piece of rope and a thumb tack—one with a large red head is ideal, for all can see this.

You will obtain best results by following the instructions exactly in regard to the length of rope used etc.

The rope should be 8 feet and 6 inches in length. Exactly 13 inches from one end, place a pencil mark (or mark with a fountain pen if you intend using a fountain pen to mark the rope with later). A straight mark on one side of the rope is nearly always what the spectator will make so you make this kind of a mark on the rope 13 inches from the end as explained. Additionally you insert the sharp point of a pencil a time or so into the rope right close to the mark—within an eighth of an inch or closer to it. This will leave a little perforation and the black from the pencil will make it more noticeable. With a thumb tack available and a pair of scissors, you are ready to perform.

Start the trick by showing the rope, and then tie the two ends together, using the "SQUARE KNOT" already illustrated in Figure 17 and then converting this "SQUARE KNOT" into a Slip Knot. Figure 18. Use just enough rope that the two ends beyond the knot will measure 2 inches. A little experimenting will show you just the way to tie this knot. Then the rope will appear as in Figure 296 and this illustrates the manner in which

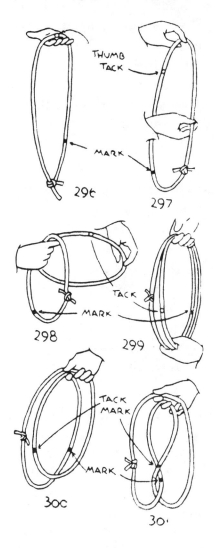

you hold the rope in the right hand. Be sure the secret
mark and pencil dot are on the end of the rope that does
the sliding. The exact center of the rope will be in the
hand, and it is here that you have the spectator place
the mark with the pencil or pen, and then you place
the thumb tack at the exact place where the spectator
marked it, and it will cover the mark. This will be in the

center of the rope, and you emphasize this fact that you are placing the thumb tack in the CENTER so that all may follow it with their eyes and not lose sight of the CENTER. In other words, you explain that if the rope be cut at the place where the thumb tack is inserted, there will be no doubt but what it is cut at the CENTER. This is of course to offset the theory that only the end of the rope is cut off.

Now the left hand comes up and takes hold of the rope just 3 inches below the right index finger. The right hand lets go of the rope and the left hand holds it. The rope thus changes position a little and Figure 297 (ignoring the hand holding rope on side for the moment) will show position rope is held in, with thumb tack now a little ways down the side and the knot that was on the bottom a little up the side. Tell spectators to follow the thumb tack closely as you double the rope over in two loops, as shown in Figures 297, 298 and 299.

To make this double loop, the right hand comes down on the same side of the rope that the knot is on and takes hold of it about the center, or a little below as shown in Figure 297. Right hand turns over and also takes hold of the other side of the rope and as it does so, the left hand, carrying rope, drops to the bottom of the loop as shown in Figure 298 and thus the two loops are brought together as shown in Figure 299 and straightened up by the hold you will have on both the top and bottom of same. Both sets of marks are illustrated in these drawings so you can follow the same exactly and thus be sure of getting this important move just right. Left hand now lets go of the bottom and points to the thumb tack which spectators have followed all the way through. Performer mentions that this thumb tack is at the exact center of the rope, and if the rope now be cut at this point, there is no question but what it will be cut in the center.

Pull the thumb tack from the rope and the mark the spectator first placed on the rope is still there thus locating the center. Place the thumb tack on the table, and call attention of the assistant spectator to the scissors and tell him to cut the rope.

Now the subtle part of the trick has been reached, and again it is under the misdirection occasioned by the spectator reaching for the scissors that the dirty work (if indeed it should be called that) is performed. Your right hand will be holding the rope exactly as shown in Figure 300. Note that the thumb and index finger hold the outer loop and the other loop (the one with the knot in it) is held back in the hand with the three fingers. The move to accomplish the whole sleight is to merely straighten out the second or middle finger (right) against the rope held by the index finger tip and the whole loop will turn over in a beautiful manner as shown in Figure 301. The left thumb is inserted in the center of the loop at the point marked with the "X" and the hand goes right to the bottom thus making what appears in Figure 302. To the spectators nothing has happened except you have taken hold of the rope to hold it taut while it is cut, but a most deceptive sleight has been accomplished, and one of the prettiest sleights in the whole realm of rope magic. Apparently you have the same formation in Figure 302 (note that the writer says APPARENTLY) but in reality, something quite different is the case, for concealed by the fingers of the left hand is a loop which has been most subtly and adroitly—and we might add, instantaneously—made. The appearance of this loop is shown in Figure 303.

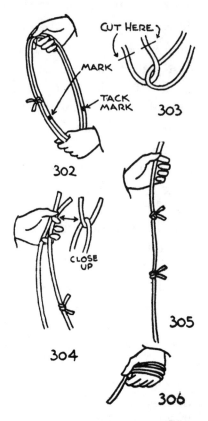

And marvel of marvels—something else has happened. The mark that the spectator placed on the rope has just as quickly vanished and the other mark near the end of the rope (and secretly made when preparing the rope before the performance) is substituted in place of it, even occupying the same position the other one just occupied.

All this is so subtle that the most critical observer cannot follow it. The real mark the spectator placed on the rope is now hidden out of sight by the fingers of the left hand which take hold around the rope as it is held up for the spectator to cut. (This is explained later.)

In Figures 303 and 304 you will notice the inscription "Tack Mark." This has reference to the spot where the thumb tack had been, but after it is pulled out, the mark made by the spectator is still under it, also there is a small perforation left in the rope where the thumb tack has been. This is the reason that at the beginning of this routine it was suggested that the point of the pencil be inserted in the rope at, or very close to, the secret mark placed on the rope, for this small perforation left by the point of the pencil (and darkened just a little) will look exactly like the hole where the thumb tack had been, to a careful observer.

In Figure 302, you will find that the "tack mark" will be down just a little lower than shown in the illustration and the fingers of the left hand will readily conceal it.

By this time the spectator will be ready to cut the rope. You can at this point follow one of two courses. Hold the rope up and have the spectator cut through the place where the mark is (he will think he is cutting the center of the rope where he marked it in the beginning) and then you can prompt him to cut the other rope at the same point. Then you pretend to the audience that he made a mistake and cut both ropes and that you only intended that he should cut one. Of course that is merely "build-up" but you can say that now it would be a problem to restore the rope since it is cut into three pieces.

The other method is to allow the spectator first to cut at the point of the mark (where he thinks the thumb tack had just been) and then say to him: "Oh, well, just cut the other rope also for good measure."

In either case, the moment both ropes are cut you allow the two ends to drop (end with knot on it and other end beside it) and this leaves you with what the audience will take for two pieces of rope held in your left hand as shown in Figure 304. The close up shows what is concealed under the left thumb. Really the spectators will be sure that the rope is in three pieces, for to all appearances there is a third small piece tied on the end of one of the longer pieces hanging from the hand.

Now you comment on the fact that you have three pieces of rope, and some "Goofer Powder" in your pocket that will work wonders. Quickly you tie the upper ends of the two ropes together (?)—but in reality only tying the small loop around the long rope. Again the knot that is used for this is our old favorite, as shown in Figure 193. Really too much cannot be said of this knot. It is easy to tie, it is most natural in appearance (much more so than the usual knot used for such purposes) and again it takes up the extra rope so that no long ends are left dangling around to be exposed a moment later when you desire to get rid of same.

After you have tied this small piece around the long piece as just explained, (which to the spectators looks as though you tied the two ends of the rope together, thanks to the fact that they do not know of the secret loop in the rope) you turn the rope end for end and hold it as in Figure 305. It is held in the left hand at this time.

There is one other subtle piece of trickery performed here. In Figure 305, the knot appears a little further from the end than you will find it in actual practice. Well, here's how that happens. As you bring up this end, you take the knot and apparently tighten it just a little, as though it were not tied securely enough, but what you do is find the actual or proper end, and just slide it down the rope an inch or so. This adds to the appearance and the spectators never notice it. It causes the three pieces (?) to appear a little nearer the same length, by making the short rope on the end appear a little longer.

Next you take the rope in the right hand and start wrapping it around the left hand as shown in Figure 306. As you do this you will slide the first knot another inch or so, and then leave it in the hand and continue wrapping until you come to the second knot about mid way down. Leave it in the palm of left hand also as you wrap. Shortly you will have the rope wrapped around the hand as shown in Figure 306.

Then you tell the spectators you will show them the difference between NOT using the Goofer Powder and USING IT. "Without the Goofer Powder, the rope will remain unchanged for a thousand years!" So you state, as you slowly allow the rope to uncoil showing the two knots, the first one still a little further down on it, thanks to the extra inch or two stolen in wrapping it around the hand.

Quickly wrap the rope around the hand again, just the same as before (apparently) but in reality this time sliding the first knot right down the rope in the right hand until the other knot is reached in the middle of the rope, and from this point on, both knots can be stripped right on down and off the end of the rope in the right hand. The right hand carries them to the right trouser pocket to get the GOOFER POWDER (?) and needless to say leaves them there and comes away with the imaginary "GOOFER POWDER" (absolutely invisible to the naked eye) and a little of this is sprinkled on the rope and it is again allowed to uncoil—and with much dramatics you bring the trick to an end and hand the rope to the spectator who marked it in the beginning. His examination of course only serves to identify it as the original rope. You have seemingly performed a miracle.

U. F. GRANT'S SUPER ROPE TRICK

Effect: Performer calls attention to a length of rope, the ends of which he ties together, forming a loop. Then a spectator is allowed to cut the rope right in the center of the loop.

The two cut ends are held wide apart and shown to be actually separated, with the knot now in the middle of the rope.

Then, by simply passing his hands over the two ends, the performer restores the rope to its original condition and immediately throws it out for examination.

Secret: Take any convenient length of soft rope and tie an extra small piece around one end, as shown at A, Figure 307. Then coil up the rope and lay it behind some object on the table.

When ready to present the trick, pick up the end with the extra piece, concealing this in the hand. Then grasp the free end with the other hand and hold out for inspection. Bring the two ends together and tie, forming a loop. In the act of showing the rope to be apparently solid, slide the hand containing the extra piece down to the bottom, carrying the extra piece with it.

Now grasp rope at top with other hand, **covering** real tied ends as at B, Figure 308. Then place end A also in upper hand. This hand now conceals both **the** real and the fake tied ends, as shown in Figure 309.

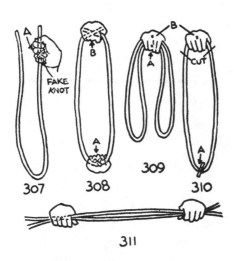

307   308   309   310

311

Next pick up the shears, at the same time **dropping** end A into view, and the audience will naturally think this is the two tied ends of the rope. Figure 310. Now request a spectator to cut both sides of the loop **near** the hand, still holding as in Figure 310 with the **real** knots concealed. After being cut, place the small piece with the real concealed knot in the pocket. Now hold the cut ends wide apart. Next untie the extra piece A and hold rope and loop as in Figure 311.

In restoring the rope, either cut away the **extra** piece or slip it off, and same is left in the pocket while going after a ring to pass over the rope. Show rope **as** one piece and toss out for examination.

The simplicity of this effect makes it really worth while and effective.

WALDO CLARKE'S LITTLE RHODY ROPE TRICK

Most cut and restored rope tricks demand that the performer have some skill in palming and be able to introduce into the trick some "gimmick" and get rid of it when the trick is over. We want a rope trick which has all the ear marks of a professional presentation and yet be capable of performance by one who has not yet become adept in the art of sleight of hand. A year or so ago I saw a rope trick which puzzled me so that I returned to the theatre twice in order to study it, and to this day I am not sure as to the means employed.

So, taking that trick as a basis, I experimented until I could produce the same effects, and whether my method is similar or totally different I don't know, and I don't care now. Some magician friends of mine tell me I have introduced a new principle, and anyhow I consider it my own trick and have named it the Little Rhody for my home State, Rhode Island.

Here it is, and you should be able to present it successfully whether or not you have performed any magic before. It will help a lot if you are a bit of an actor to the extent of being able to hold the attention of an audience while you talk. Talk and "misdirection" play as important a part in its presentation as do the simple finger manipulations, and these are not beyond the powers of any normal handed person.

The equipment is very simple. A piece of soft rope, there is a variety of loosely woven clothesline which will answer fairly well. A four foot length is about right for the performance. Tie a shorter piece of the same rope, five or six inches long, around the long piece tight enough so that it will not slide off of its own weight and loose enough to allow the longer piece to be drawn freely through it. Hold this knot concealed in the left hand and make your entrance drawing the rope back and forth through your hand as if the hand were empty. You need no palming skill for this as your left hand is holding the rope and is partially closed, a perfectly natural position for it.

Bring this sliding knot near the top end of the rope as it hangs down from your hand, leaving proper space at the upper end for tying the two ends of the rope together. Learn by experiment just where to begin the knot so as to make the short ends of it correspond to the short ends of the sliding one, it being important that the two knots look as much alike as possible. See that all ends are trimmed off squarely before starting.

When you tie the ends together use a SQUARE KNOT as in Figure 17, and don't pull it tight. Now bring the knot you have just made to the bottom of the loop by sliding the rope through your left hand and of course, through the false knot which you are holding there. Thus your left thumb is about at the actual center of the rope, and you announce that you are about to cut the rope at that point which will result in your having two short pieces tied together by the knot. This is so manifestly true that no one will argue the point with you, but it's up to you to begin to do a little acting. Pretend to notice some indication of incredulity on the part of your audience and you repeat your assertion, arguing as though you thought they doubted it, meanwhile drawing the rope through your left hand, apparently absent-mindedly, thus causing the knot to travel up the opposite side of the loop toward your left hand and disappear inside it. But it emerges at once at the thumb side of your hand, only this is the fake knot

which the real one has pushed out, and it bears sufficient resemblance to the other to be taken for the one
they have seen you tie.

But it isn't all as easy as this. Here's a bit of trouble that will require some practice. As you feel the real
knot enter your left hand get the short end of B, Figure
17, between the thumb and the fleshy part of the hand,
away up in the crotch where the thumb joins the hand,
and pinch it so as to hold it back while you continue to
pull on the main part of B. Figure 18 discloses the effect that this action has. It converts the square knot into
a slip knot and you will find that the end B will come
free in your hand. Pull cautiously until you have the
end between the tips of the thumb and finger, but don't
be too vigorous and pull it out. Now you have the end
at the finger tips, while the other end is twisted up in
your hand, so you must practice until you can get that
twisted end straightened out and the two ends brought
together between the thumb and finger and enable you
to open your hand for an instant and prove that your
hand is entirely empty except for the continuous piece
of rope they see between the finger and thumb. Don't
make too much display of this open handed business,
but make it appear to be without intent. You must,
with good reason, hold your hand in the manner they
have seen you hold it, partly closed, from now on.

If you are new at this line of endeavor, you will
naturally wonder how a magician can stand up in front
of a lot of people and go through all the manipulations
which these instructions make necessary and yet escape
detection in what he is doing. The most remarkable
things can be done with misdirection. Some writer has
said that misdirection is the back bone of magic, and I
believe it to be the truth. Howard Thurston wrote a

book covering his career in magic. In it he tells of his long association with the late Harry Kellar and tells us of Mr. Kellar's mastery of the art of misdirection, making it cover many defects in his sleight of hand, an art which Kellar never seemed able to master, on account of his clumsy fingers. Yet Kellar's fame as a great magician was international.

Misdirection consists in diverting the attention of an audience by whatever means may be appropriate at the time and for the purpose desired. The attention of an audience is surprisingly easy to sway. They are gathered for the purpose of being entertained and have nothing else to do than watch what you are doing. For the moment they are entirely dependent upon you for something to occupy their minds. If you should stand before them wiggling and twisting your fingers trying to get the ends of the rope to meet between your thumb and finger and nothing was said or done to shift the general attention from your hands, they certainly would notice your struggles and either get some idea of the secret of the trick or wonder what variety of fit you were suffering from.

In the first place NEVER LOOK AT YOUR HANDS when you are doing anything like this. If you look at them, the people out in front will look at them too. You can depend on the majority of the spectators following your gaze. An audience is a mighty handy thing to have around, especially when they have paid admission, but psychologically they are a flock of sheep.

Now, totally oblivious of your hands, if you ask the buxom lady in the front row, looking squarely at her, if she has any objection to your cutting this nice piece of rope squarely in two in the center, the attention of the company will be directed to the lady, and if she replies something to the effect that it isn't her rope and you can go as far as you like, the whole assemblage will be alert to any exchange of trivialities you may be able to manage, leaving you to do about as you like with your hands, provided of course that you use deliberation and not too much energy. Nobody knows that you have the two ends of the rope in your left hand instead of a solid part.

Having the ends straightened out you are able to open your fingers and afford a fleeting glimpse of your empty hand. The sliding knot is near your left thumb where it was pushed by the real knot. You cannot deliberately slide it down to the bottom of the loop as you did the other because it might be noticed that the rope did not move as it must if it were the real knot. To cover this difficulty grasp the knot with your right hand and swing your body around quickly to the right, presenting your left side slightly to the spectators, and slip the knot quickly to the bottom during this turn. This imparts a swaying motion to the rope and covers the fact that it does not move through your hand.

With the knot at the bottom of the loop you now remark that everything is just as it was before and we all seem to be agreed that this is the center of the rope and that cutting it will give us two pieces of rope tied together with a knot. Take your scissors from your right hand coat pocket and cut the rope near your left thumb. The piece cut off will be a half inch or less, and this bit of rope you drop into the curled fingers of the right hand as it holds the scissors. Return the scissors to your pocket and drop the bit of rope there too. Use short scissors, those with rounded points are the best.

They are so short that the right hand is almost directly under the left in the act of cutting.

The rope now hangs down in a straight piece from your left hand, the spectators believe that it is two pieces tied together. Explain that the purpose of this experiment is to dissolve this knot and knit the two ends of the rope as firmly as before it was cut, but before doing so you must create the "magic circle" by tying the ends together again and making a magnetic plane, the two knots serving as poles, one the positive and the other the negative pole. If you know something about electricity, which I do not, you can doubtless rig up some better explanation as to what you are doing. Tie the ends together again, using the same loose square knot, and run the loop of rope rapidly through your hands, stopping with the sliding knot in your left hand. Close your left hand over it and say that you will try to dissolve this one first. After holding it a second or two report that you can feel it dissolving very rapidly. Open your hand a little and take a cautious peek at it and announce that it is getting smaller and smaller. Another peek and the knot is all gone and the ends are knitting together nicely. After another brief interval slide your left hand carefully aside and look anxiously at the spot where the knot was. It's perfectly mended! Look! With your right hand hold it up for inspection while you sweep the left to the extent of the loop. Here your hand encounters the real knot which prevents the sliding one from going any farther and you simply slip your hand along to cover the real knot, leaving the sliding one exposed to view in place of it.

This move is not so open to detection as you may think. You have just worked a miracle by healing the cut place in the rope and the general interest in the mended spot, though fleeting, is enough to bridge over the flash of time that it takes to sweep your hand to the left and cover the knot. But even if some one happened to be watching your left hand instead of the restored spot in the rope, it is a very deceptive move and he would hardly know what had taken place. Of course a person with pre-knowledge, or a shrewd suspicion, as to the method used, would see through it, but don't worry about that. The one who knows the tactics employed in magic will be the first to appreciate and applaud a clever ruse. His viewpoint differs materially from that of the ordinary observer. He is there, not to be puzzled, but to see some good work in a line with which he is familiar. Show your own astonishment at the success of the operation.

Do some acting. And while you proceed methodically to get the short end of the real knot in the crotch of your thumb tell your audience how you yourself are always amazed at the result of this experiment. Address some one and say that as you passed his or her house the other day you noticed one or two knots in the clothesline and offer to step around and fix them. If you are met with an indignant denial that there are any knots to be found, or that they have a line at their house, so much the better. It creates interest and aids you in getting the loose end to the tip of the finger and thumb. It is not necessary at this point to get the ends together and open the hand, but proceed immediately to getting the sliding knot to the bottom of the loop and cutting the rope again, apparently in the center, making the turn to the right and dropping the bit of rope and disposing of it, all in the same manner. Now, holding the upper end of the rope daintily between the finger and thumb, you may open your hand and casually show that it is empty.

Again you have the two short pieces tied together (?), the sliding knot being about half way down the length of the rope. Take the knot in your right hand, releasing the upper end of the cord. Transfer the knot to the left hand and with the two ends hanging down, hold the knot so that most of it shows above the index finger as you hold it between the thumb and finger.

Taking your scissors out, you explain that if you attempt to dissolve two full sized knots at one performance you find that "it takes too much out of you" and to preserve your vital energy you have adopted the practice of trimming the knot to a smaller size.

Begin by cutting off the ends, and gradually all of the rest of it, letting the pieces fall to the floor. The index finger will conceal the fact that the rest of the knot is gone, and at this point say that you are leaving enough to keep the ends of the rope together. Close your hand around the place, and remark that reducing the size of the knot induces quick action. After a second or two, open your hand and show that the rope is in the same condition as when you first showed it although you have cut it in halves twice.

Most stage performers toss the rope to some member of the audience as a souvenir, but as you have cut off only two half inch pieces you can of course use it many times more by attaching a new sliding knot each time.

This is a very simple little trick, but not so simple as to be capable of performance without practice. Go through the routine many times before you venture to show it to a gathering of friends. Perform it as though you were really the marvelous healer of ropes that you are pretending to be. That's acting. And finally, don't tell others the secrets of the tricks you learn and perform from time to time. A veil of mystery over your feats of magic will enhance your reputation, not harm it.

THE TARBELL ROPE MYSTERY

Here are the secrets of the rope trick that set the magic world ablaze explained by Doctor Harlan Tarbell himself as follows:

This mystery has puzzled audiences time and again, and even magicians have found it utterly baffling. Some of the finest newspaper men in the country have seen me perform it and have admitted their complete bewilderment. It has received more comment, perhaps, from the magical fraternity than any other effect in twenty-five years. Thurston, the famous magician, stopped his show in Milwaukee at one time to have me present the rope mystery to his audience. Houdini, Laurant, Reno, and others have done the same thing. Each time it sent the audience away talking about this peculiar Hindu mystery.

I tell you these things because I want you to realize the possibilities you have for creating a sensation with this master mystery. My only regret is that I cannot first present this effect before you and let you puzzle over it for a few weeks before I teach you the secrets of it. You would then appreciate that its very simplicity is what makes it so baffling.

A peculiar thing about this effect is the elusive principles on which it is designed. Even after you have learned how to perform it, if you were to see me present it, you might doubt my having given you the correct method. It is so elusive that some of the finest magicians on the stage to whom I have taught the effect have asked me time and again whether I was sure that the methods I taught them were the methods I use myself. I have gone into every detail of the presentation with them over and over to convince them that I had really given them the true secrets.

I have refused hundreds of dollars for these secrets for I desired to disclose them to the profession as a whole. And now you are getting one of the finest effects ever designed in the whole history of magic. Guard this mystery carefully, for remember that the secret of greatness lies in being able to do something that no one else or but few others can do.

Perform this effect as "A Hindu Miracle," for giving it the Hindu atmosphere permits of fine newspaper publicity and advertising. The fame is widespread of the story of the East Indian Rope Trick, in which a rope is thrown up into the air and is then climbed by a boy. Associating your effect with this one fires the imagination of the audience and permits of a miracle performance. The Orient has always been known for its mystic splendor and thus presenting an Oriental effect gives you an opportunity for background and stage setting that will add romance to your program.

One big advantage of this rope mystery is its versatility. It is simple and may be carried in the pocket for performance at a moment's notice. And yet it is so designed to be made a feature number on a program. It may be done under the most difficult conditions, close to your spectators, or it may be performed at a distance with excellent effect. It is suitable for parlor work and club work, and also the stage. It can be worked at the dinner table and has proved to be a sensation at banquets.

There are several methods for performing this rope mystery. This permits you to vary the effect for different occasions. I want you to learn every method. Then you may select the routine you prefer and rehearse it until you can convince any audience that you are performing an oriental miracle.

Do not present this mystery as you would a pocket trick for that will not bring you the power that this effect brings. Stage it in the proper atmosphere so that you will gain all the credit you can from it. Build an interesting story around it and present it in a convincing, positive manner, working up to the forceful climax.

METHOD A

This is my favorite method because it permits you to repeat the effect and then pass out the rope for examination without exchanging it.

Effect: A piece of fairly soft white clothesline, about seven and a half feet long, is freely shown. The two ends are tied together in a knot to form a "mystic Hindu circle." A spectator is given a pair of scissors and is asked to cut the rope in the center opposite the knotted ends. The rope is cut and the cut ends are held far apart. To make sure that the rope has been cut, a piece is cut from each of the two ends. The two cut ends are placed together, part of the rope wrapped around the left hand, and a magic ring applied to the rope. The rope is then removed from left hand and shown to be completely restored again to the mystic circle, as in the beginning. Performer then states that perhaps there are a few in the audience who do not know how the mystery is done. He asks spectator to cut the rope again in the middle and to cut a piece again from one of the ends to make sure the rope is cut. The two ends are then tied together in a knot. Magician now holds rope with knots at opposite ends. He cuts off one of the knots, then passes his hands over the two ends and touches them with the magic ring. Suddenly the rope is restored. Performer now unties knot at original ends of rope. Two spectators are asked to pull on rope to show it is whole, and then the rope is thrown out to the audience for examination.

Paraphernalia: 1. A piece of soft white clothesline about six or seven feet in length.

2. A piece of similar clothesline about six inches long.

3. A piece of clothesline about ten inches long.

4. A metal or wooden ring, an inch or so in diameter.

5. A pair of scissors, preferably with round ends.

6. Two Special Rope Gimmicks or Fasteners.

A Rope Gimmick consists of two pieces of tubing, corrugated and painted white to resemble the rope. One part of the Gimmick has the positive side of a snap fastener and the other has the negative side. Each part is so made as to screw on to the end of a rope. When they are placed on the rope and then fastened together, they are not visible at a short distance, especially if the rope is swung a little. When the rope is held close for inspection, the fingers cover the Gimmick. These Gimmicks may be used over and over again. Figures 312, 313, 314.

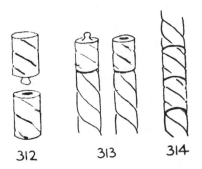

Secret and Patter: How to attach the special Gimmick to the rope. Take the long piece of rope and the six-inch piece and prepare both ends of each piece as follows: Near the end wrap a piece of white thread around several times. Figure 315. With sharp scissors,

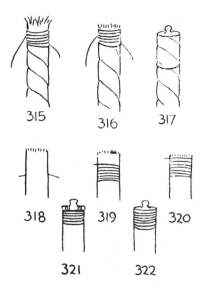

cut end of rope up close to thread. Figure 316. This gives a substantial enough end on which to screw the Gimmick firmly. Cut away any thread that might show on rope outside of Gimmick. Be sure to place a positive part at one end and a negative part of Gimmick at other end of each piece of rope. Figure 317.

The Rope Mystery, as formerly sold, required the use of snap fasteners sewed on to the rope. The method of working the rope trick was the same but it took time and trouble to sew on the fasteners. The new Special Gimmick eliminates all this. It is easily and quickly screwed on to the rope and can be used over and over again.

However, for the benefit of those who still want to sew on snap fasteners, I shall explain the procedure. I want you to know how to do this, though I doubt if any of you will want to go to the trouble, now that the new Gimmick is available.

The fasteners to use are known as ladies' dress fasteners. There are several brands. The one I recommend is the Boye Dress Fastener, Size 3-0.

How to sew on the fasteners: The idea is to sew on opposite parts of the fasteners at the ends of the ropes so that when they are snapped together, the rope looks whole. It is necessary to use care in not drawing the thread too tight or leaving it too loose. Use white cotton thread, about No. 40, and use a fine enough needle to go through the holes in the fasteners. Use about a yard of thread and double it for each part of fastener.

Take end of rope and pull needle through about half an inch from the end, bringing thread through to knot. Figure 318.

Wrap the thread around rope four or five times and run needle through rope again. Figure 319.

This wrapping of thread keeps small strands of rope from unravelling so that you can cut rope off sharply about a sixteenth of an inch above it. Figure 320.

Now take one part of fastener and sew it carefully to end of rope. Figure 321.

Run needle through rope again, then wind enough thread around rope again to even it up. Run needle through rope several times and cut thread close to rope. Figure 322.

A little practice will enable you to make a neat clean-cut job of sewing on the fasteners. The more care used and the neater the work, the better results you will get. Paint the nickel fasteners with a little white Japan paint (it can be purchased in small tubes), which has been thinned with benzine for quick drying. The advantage of using white paint is that less thread can be used in sewing on fasteners and thus the two opposite parts will grip tighter together. As with the Gimmicks, be sure that you have opposite parts of fasteners at each end of each piece of rope.

How to prepare rope: Take the long piece and the six-inch piece of rope which you have prepared with Gimmicks or snap fasteners. Attach the short piece to the long one to form a circle of rope. Figure 323.

Now tie the ten-inch piece of rope around the middle of the rope, opposite to the Gimmicks. This gives the effect that the ends of the rope are tied together where the extra piece of rope is tied on. The real ends of the rope are attached by Gimmicks to the six-inch piece, and as these are invisible, it gives the effect that this is the middle of the rope. The audience knows nothing about the Gimmicks and, of course, is not looking for them. I have never had the Gimmicks detected.

Especially if the rope is swung a little, the Gimmicks are not detectable. Figure 324.

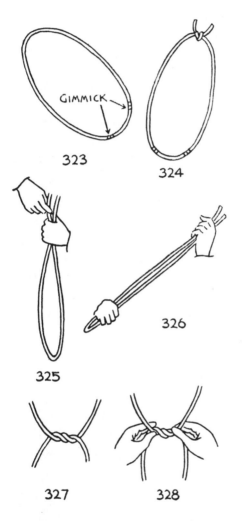

323

324

325

326

327   328

Fold up prepared rope and place in coat pocket or some handy place. Scissors may be in upper left coat pocket. I use the round-end scissors to avoid possibility of accident from sharp points. Place the "magic" ring in right trouser's pocket.

Presentation: Take rope from pocket and open it up. Hold knotted ends up in hands, allowing part with Gimmicks to hang down. Figure 325.

As you talk, untie the knot, and without exposing the short piece of rope, hold long rope between your hands as shown in Figure 326. Right hand covers the Gimmicks and left hand covers joining of long rope with ten-inch piece.

"There is perhaps no magical effect in the world as well known as the great East Indian Rope Trick. You have all heard tell of this trick in which a rope is thrown high in the air and is then climbed by a boy until he gets way up out of sight. There is, however, another rope effect, equally mysterious and, like the East Indian Rope Trick, seldom seen. It is performed by a certain high caste of Hindu magicians. Tourists watching this odd mystery, have been completely baffled. Even magicians who have seen it time and again have been able to offer no solution to the problem. Dr. Harlan Tarbell of Chicago, a prominent American Society magician, discovered the secret, and he in turn baffled magicians as well as lay audiences with it. Until recently, Dr. Tarbell was the only white man who understood the true working of this ingenious mystery. Dr. Tarbell very kindly taught me this peculiar effect and now I want you to see this miracle of magic."

Have two gentlemen come up and have one stand at your right and the other at your left.

"The Hindu magician performs out in the open with the sky as the roof of his theater. He uses a piece of rope about this long and ties the ends together to form a circle."

Drop rope from right hand and grasp the short piece of rope at other end, being careful not to expose it as a separate piece. Wrap one end of short piece around big rope once again and bring it upward as shown in Figures 327 and 328. To the audience it appears that you tied a single knot with ends of the rope.

Now allow this same end of short rope to drop down again and bring it upward so that it is only once around long rope. Drop your hands as you do this and bring them up again to keep audience from detecting what you are doing. Then tie a single knot with two ends of short rope on long rope. Figures 329 and 330.

To the audience it appears that you tied a double knot with the ends of the long rope.

"His effects are based on Hindu philosophy and occultism. It seems that the circle, the square, and the triangle have mystical occult meanings. The Hindu sometimes sits inside his circle of rope and calls it his cycle of life."

Place the rope down in front of you near the floor to illustrate how the Hindu places his circle on the ground. Then bring rope up again.

"He says that all within is physical."

Put right hand and arm through loop of rope to illustrate.

"And that all without is spiritual or psychic."

Wave right hand outside of loop of rope.

"To pass from the material to the spiritual plane, it is necessary to cut the line of life. In which case, we shall just cut the rope."

To gentleman at right: "Would you mind, sir, taking these scissors?"

Remove scissors from upper left coat pocket and give to this spectator.

"Now, will you please cut the rope in the middle?"

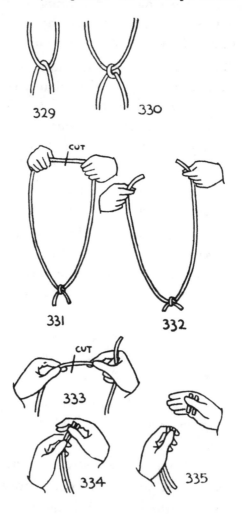

Turn rope around so that Gimmick part is at top between your hands. Keep Gimmick concealed. Figure 331.

"I think this is about the middle of the rope."

Have spectator cut rope. Audience thinks he is cutting whole rope in half, but in reality he is merely cutting short piece in half between the two Gimmicks. Hold the ends far apart. Figure 332.

"Thus the Hindu says he can enter the psychic world. Are you quite sure, sir, that you cut the rope? Just to make doubly sure, cut it again. Cut a piece from this end."

Hold rope as in Figure 333, and have spectator cut a piece from left side of rope within about an inch of the Gimmick, keeping Gimmick concealed. Toss this piece to audience.

"Perhaps you would like a souvenir."

Show cut end to spectator at your left, and say:

"Will you notice the cut end, sir?"

Now to gentleman at right:

"To make positively sure that the rope has been cut, will you kindly cut a piece from this end also?"

Hold rope so that he cuts a few inches from right end of rope rather close to Gimmick. Give him the piece of rope just cut off.

"Please toss it over there to that lady."

You now have an inch-stub of rope attached to each end of the long rope by Gimmicks. While spectator is tossing piece of rope to lady, take ropes in hands as in Figure 334. Grasp the short stubs between thumb and base of first finger of right hand. Figure 334. This view is away from audience.

With a natural movement, pull the Gimmicks loose from long rope. Back of right hand is to audience. Figure 335.

"I should have a magic ring for this."

Reach into right trouser's pocket and leave the short pieces of rope there, bringing out the ring.

"Here it is in my pocket."

To gentleman at left:

"Here, sir, I shall give you the magic ring."

Give him the ring and then hold the two ends of rope far apart in your two hands. Be careful to conceal Gimmicks at ends of rope with your fingers. Figure 336.

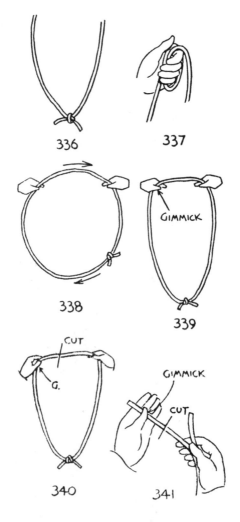

336

337

338

339

GIMMICK

CUT

G.

340

GIMMICK

CUT

341

To gentleman at left:

"I believe you, too, are quite sure that the rope has been cut. No doubt, you wonder why I ask this so many times. I do it because when I get through and you go home, you many wonder whether the rope was really cut. Anyway, the Hindu brings the ends of the rope together for just a second. . . "

Bring the two ends of rope together and under cover of the fingers, snap the Gimmick together. Do this with as little noise as possible.

"And wraps the rope around his hand."

Wrap rope quickly around left hand with the right so that audience can see that rope is already restored. Figure 337.

"Touch it with the magic ring, sir."

Gentleman touches rope with ring.

"The Hindu says, 'Chee-la-wah-la-bong-wah. Watch, for you are about to behold a miracle—a miracle that you will never forget as long as you live.' Then he quickly unwraps the rope from his hand."

Unwrap rope.

"And, of course, the rope has been restored completely to what it was in the beginning."

Show rope by passing it quickly around in a circle through both of your hands. This gives the form of the magic circle and also keeps the Gimmick invisible. Figure 338.

Finally get rope into position so that knot is at bottom and left fingers cover Gimmick. Figure 339.

"I realize that it may be hard for several of you to understand how the Hindu restores his life-line, so perhaps I had better explain it to you all over again."

This usually gets a laugh because there is no one in the audience that knows how to do the trick. The tendency in such an effect is for the audience to want to get the rope and examine it. You forestall this until you are ready to pass out the rope by saying you will do the trick again.

In some effects repetition is not good, but in this rope mystery, repetition strengthens the effect and leaves the audience thoroughly mystified. The two methods of working are different so there is no danger of detection.

To gentleman at right:

"Please cut the rope again."

Have spectator cut the rope about an inch and a half to two inches to the right of the Gimmick in the left hand. Figure 340.

"And to remove all suspicion, cut the rope again."

Grasp left side of rope about four inches below left hand with your right hand and have the rope cut between your two hands. That leaves the long loop of rope entirely free from Gimmicks in your right hand and the short piece of rope with the Gimmick in your left hand. Figure 341.

Casually place left-hand piece with the Gimmick in your left coat pocket. Do this without hesitation as if you were just getting rid of the cut piece of rope. Audience sees nothing suspicious in this.

Now hold both ends of rope far apart and say to gentleman at left:

"Since you are one of the chief inspectors, perhaps you would like to look at this rope a bit closer. Examine the ends."

Allow spectator to examine the ends of the rope closely.

"Since you give your official O. K., I shall now tie the two ends together to form a knot."

Tie the two ends together in a double knot. You now have this real knot and the fake knot at opposite ends of the rope. Figure 342.

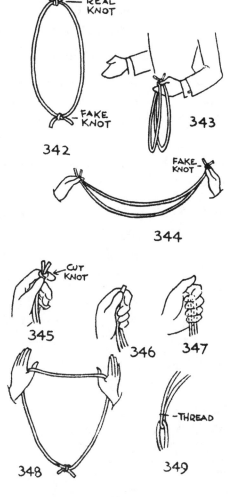

Take scissors from gentleman at right.

"The Hindu says now his troubles begin because the knots are supposed to be knots of trouble in his life-line. One knot of trouble is enough, he says, for any good Hindu. Of course, we can make the knots less conspicuous by trimming them up a bit."

Trim the ends of the knots up to about an inch from each knot. Try to make the knots look alike. Then hold both knots in left hand as you gesture with right. This confuses the two knots so that audience cannot keep track of them separately. Figure 343.

"Of course, we have two knots."

Take a knot in each hand—the fake knot in the right hand and the real knot in the left hand. Show knot in left hand, pretending this is the first knot tied. Figure 344.

"This one we tied originally to make a mystic circle of the rope."

Then show knot in right hand as the second knot tied.

"And this knot is the one tied from the two ends the gentleman just cut. I believe, sir, you cut the rope."

Drop real knot from left hand and bring fake knot in right hand over to left, holding rope from this knot as shown in Figure 345.

With right hand cut knot off, leaving a short piece still around long rope. Figure 346.

"If a knot causes trouble, the solution to the problem is to cut the knot off. This leaves two ends as we had before we tied the knot. Of course, we can even up the ends."

Pull up end of short piece and cut it away, repeating until you have finally cut away the short piece entirely and have the long rope looped in left hand. Figure 347.

"While the life line is cut, the Hindu says he projects his astral body back into the physical again. He wraps the rope around his hand again."

Wrap rope around left hand several times. Then ask spectator who holds ring to touch rope with it.

"Touch it with the magic ring. The Hindu says, 'Chee-la-wah-la-bong-wah. Watch, and you shall behold a miracle. Hoy!'"

Throw hands upward, releasing rope from left hand.

"And the rope is again restored."

Hold rope over your thumbs. Turn palms of hands to audience and spread fingers wide apart. This exhibits the rope well to audience. Figure 348.

"To prove to you that the rope has really been restored. I shall untie the knot, and give one end of the rope to the gentleman here and the other end to the gentleman at the other side."

As you say this, untie knot and give one end to spectator at right and other end to spectator at left. Ask them to pull hard on rope, then take it from them.

"Thank you. You have pulled hard on the rope and have proved that every fiber even unto the thousandth has been fully restored."

Fold rope up a little in your hand to make it easier to throw.

"Now you can prove it yourselves by examining the rope."

Toss the rope into the audience for examination.

This is your finish. Make it as dramatic as possible. Toss the rope high enough to suit the dramatic action. Bow a little. Thank the spectators who assisted you and allow them to go to their seats.

Note: Short piece of rope may be attached in another handy manner. Put it around long rope, then wind a piece of white thread twice around it. This enables you to carry rope prepared in pocket without knotting it in advance. You can also lay rope over your shoulder or over back of chair before it is knotted. The thread is then broken when you tie the knot. Figure 349.

Study every move in this master effect until you can perform it so that audiences will talk about and remember you for many months.

As I have said, this is my favorite manner of presentation which is adapted to your use. There are a number of variations that you can use from time to time. These follow.

Method B

In this method, you start with a straight piece of rope, apparently, without having the rope knotted.

Let A represent the short piece to be tied into a knot—B, the small piece with Gimmicks, which is to be cut—and C, the long piece with Gimmicks. To begin experiment, bring in rope, holding A and B between thumb and fingers of left hand. Back of hand is to audience and they believe you hold one long rope. Figure 350.

Bring up lower end of C with right hand, covering Gimmick. Figure 351.

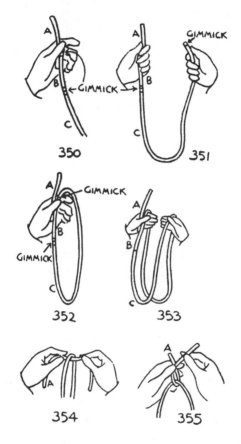

Place this end in left hand, and as you do so, snap Gimmick into top end of B, making a loop of rope. Figure 352.

With right hand, grasp lower end of loop and bring it up to left hand toward short piece A. Figure 353.

With a swing of the hands, grasp free end of A with right fingers and slip loop of rope in right hand over it. Quickly drop rope from left hand and grasp A so that rope hangs down from A as shown in Figure 354. To audience it appears that you have merely tied a single knot with the ends of the rope.

Now tie A once around rope. Audience believes you have now tied a double knot with the ends of the rope, but in reality, you have the fake knot at one end and the Gimmicks at the other end of the loop of rope. Figure 355.

These moves all blend into each other as one continuous movement and the audience does not suspect any trickery. From this point, continue with Method A.

Method C

This is one of the finest of the rope trick methods. In performing, you bring in an apparently unprepared roll of clothesline.

Take either a ball of clothesline cr the regular roll in which it is sold. Figure 356.

Unroll the clothesline and straighten it out. Allowing about ten inches for A, about six inches for B, and six or seven feet for C, attach a Gimmick to the ends of A and B—B and C—C and D. Figure 357.

Roll clothesline back into original form, even to placing a piece of paper around it as shown in Figure 356.

To perform, unwrap the roll of clothesline and unroll it to two or three feet beyond the last Gimmick. Pick up scissors and cut rope an inch or so beyond Gimmick on D. Figure 358.

Place roll of clothesline aside and show piece you have cut off. Bring the two ends together in left hand.

Backs of hands are to audience. Steal off a little piece of D from the Gimmick and pocket it. Figure 359.

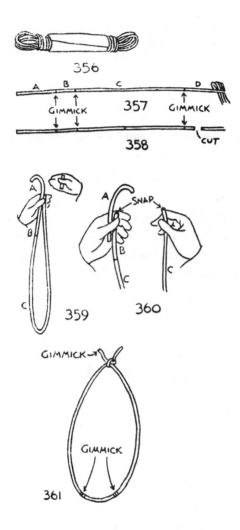

356

357

358

359   360

361

Bring right hand up to left again and pull Gimmick apart between A and B. Now hold A and B in left hand and end of C in right hand. Separate hands a little. Figure 360.

Use routine of Method B to get A tied around long rope and then continue effect by Method A. Figure 361.

To dispose of Gimmick at end of A, just cut the ends of the knot shorter and put the pieces in your pocket.

Method D

Effect: Magician shows a piece of white sash cord about seven and one-half feet long. A spectator is asked to cut the rope in half and the rope is then shown in two pieces. To convince the audience that the rope is actually cut, another spectator is asked to cut a small piece from each of the four ends. Magician then holds an end of each half of the rope and gives the other ends to each of two spectators to hold. Performer now wraps his two ends of the rope around his left hand. He removes a ring from his pocket and asks spectator at right to thread it on the rope. The ring slides down to his left hand. Suddenly he unwraps the rope and it is seen to be completely restored. The ring is then allowed to slide off other end of rope.

Required: 1. Two pieces of soft white clothesline, each about three and a half feet in length.

2. A short piece of clothesline, six inches long.

3. Two Gimmicks.

4. Pair of scissors.

5. A metal or wooden ring, an inch or more in diameter.

Secret and Patter: To Prepare: Half of a Gimmick is placed on one end of each long piece of rope. Half Gimmicks are placed on both ends of the short piece of rope. The Gimmicks must be so arranged as to permit you to fasten the short piece between the long pieces of rope and then remove the short piece and fasten the two long pieces together. Place the short piece between the two long pieces. To the audience it appears that you have one long rope. Figure 362.

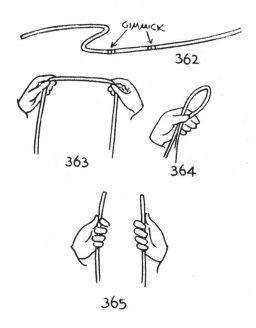

By keeping the rope in motion while performing, the Gimmicks will not be visible.

Place folded rope in right coat pocket, scissors in upper left coat pocket, and the ring in right trousers pocket.

To perform: Have two spectators come up to assist you. Place one of them at your right and a little in front of you and the other one in a similar position on your left. For convenience in explaining, let the man at the right be Smith and the one at the left, Jones.

"All of you, no doubt, have heard of the great East Indian Rope Mystery, in which a rope is thrown high into the air where it remains suspended so that a boy can climb it and vanish into space. Thousands have told about this mystery, but no one except a very few magicians have been able to solve it. Would either of you two gentlemen like to climb up a rope? Well, perhaps, it will not be necessary. India is famous for its rope tricks—and there is another rope mystery which has not only baffled tourists in India, but has baffled every magician who has ever seen it. A few years ago Dr. Harlan Tarbell of Chicago, an eminent American magician, discovered the secret. He first presented the effect in Paris with great success. Only until recently he was perhaps the only white man who understood the working of this peculiar rope mystery. Dr. Tarbell very kindly taught me how to present this ingenious mystery, and I want you now to see this miracle of magic. The Hindu usually performs out in the open air with the sky as the top of his theater. To begin his rope miracle, he takes a piece of rope from his pocket similar to this one."

Remove rope from pocket and unfold it, keeping it slightly in motion.

"A rather short piece of clothesline, but long enough for a Hindu washing."

Start with left end of rope and run it through your hands. Give rope three or four tugs in different places, being careful to pull rope only outside of middle piece. This convinces audience that rope is strong and is in one piece.

Strange to say, the rope has two ends and a middle. The middle should be about here in the center."

Run rope through your fingers until you hold a Gimmick between thumb and fingers of each hand. Figure 363.

Bring two Gimmicks together and hold in left hand while you bring out scissors with right hand. Figure 364.

To Jones, at left:

"Please take these scissors and cut the rope in two pieces of about equal length."

Give him the scissors, then hold rope as shown in Figure 363, and have Jones cut rope between the two Gimmicks. Audience believes he is cutting the rope in half, but he is merely cutting the short middle piece between the two Gimmicks. Separate your hands about two feet so that all can see the separate pieces of rope. Figure 365.

"Are you sure you cut the rope? Would you mind just cutting off an end here for a souvenir?"

Have Jones cut about an inch from the short piece in your right hand.

"Now cut a piece from the other end here."

Jones cuts a piece from the short rope in your left hand.

"Please examine the two ends. Give the scissors to the gentleman here and let him cut off the other two ends."

Bring lower ends up and have Smith cut about an inch from each. As he does this, let him hold the two lower ends, while you retain your hold on the two upper ends in your left hand.

Bring your right hand up to left and palm off the two short pieces from Gimmicks on ends of long ropes. Carry these away between thumb and base of first finger.

When two ends are cut and examined by Smith, reach into right trousers' pocket. Leave the two stubs of rope there and bring out the ring.

"This is a Magic Hindu Ring. Will you, Mr. Smith, look at it closely?"

Hold both ropes apart in your hands, keeping Gimmicks at top covered by fingers.

"By the way, are you sure that you cut the rope in half? I want you to be sure so that afterwards you will not say, 'Well, maybe the rope wasn't cut.' Mr. Smith, will you hold one end, and Mr. Jones, you the other? Now, the Hindu ties these two ends together into a knot."

Bring your two hands together and snap the two ropes together by the Gimmick. Do this noiselessly and under cover of your hands. Keep Gimmick in left hand and wrap rope several times around this hand. This prevents any accidental opening of Gimmick.

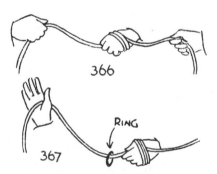

Figure 366 shows your position now in relation to spectators assisting you.

"Mr. Smith, will you please slip the ring on to the rope and let it slide down to my hand?"

As he does this, take hold of his end of rope with your right hand and have him release it. Figure 367.

"It is impossible for the ring to go farther because of my hand. But watch closely, for you are about to see a HINDU MIRACLE. Behold!"

Allow the rope to unwrap from left hand. The rope then straightens out between your right hand and left-hand spectator, and ring slides down to left end of rope.

"The rope becomes whole again!"

Take rope from Jones and allow ring to slide off into your left hand. Place ring in pocket.

Run rope through your hands, keeping it in motion so that Gimmicks will not be detected by assistants. Pull on rope several times to show it is whole, keeping on each side of the Gimmick. Dismiss gentleman assisting you.

Method E

This method is extremely puzzling for it seems that the spectators do the work themselves and allow no opportunity for trickery.

Take a piece of clothesline about seven feet long, and two small pieces about three inches long. Screw a half-Gimmick on each end of the long rope and corresponding half-Gimmicks on one end of each short piece. Fasten the three pieces together. Figure 368.

Place rope in hands of spectator at left. As the Gimmicks are near ends of rope, they hang down and are not noticed. Have this spectator walk over to the spectator at right so that latter can cut the rope in half. Figure 369.

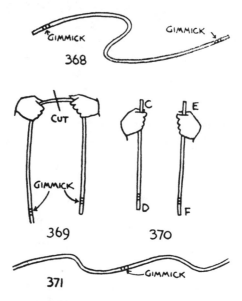

As spectator holds the halves of rope apart, you grasp ropes at D and F with your left hand, covering the Gimmicks. Figure 370.

Ask spectator to drop rope. This brings ends D and F upright in your hand. Cut pieces from D and F so that inch-stubs remain above the Gimmicks. Then give scissors to gentleman at left and have him cut pieces from ends C and E. As he does this, steal the short stubs of rope with right hand. Reach into pocket for magic ring and leave stubs there.

Continue routine as in Method D.

The rope is, of course, restored by snapping the two remaining halves of the Gimmicks together. Figure 371.

Method F

This is a very simple method, requiring no Gimmicks.

The effect is that a piece of rope is tied together to form a loop. It is then cut in the middle, opposite to the knot. Several inches are then cut from one of the cut ends. These ends are tied together. Magician now cuts away one of the knots and the rope is restored.

Take a length of rope and sew the two ends together with white thread. In the middle of the rope, opposite to the sewed ends, tie a small piece of rope to make a fake knot.

Bring rope out prepared as in Figure 372.

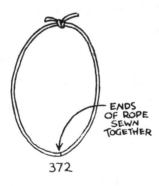

ENDS
OF ROPE
SEWN
TOGETHER

372

Follow routine of second part of Method A to perform this effect.

There you have the real secrets of the Tarbell Rope Mystery. You will find any one of the methods a real hit on your program.

CAPTAIN JONES' ROPE TRICK

The rope trick performed by this magician is exactly the same as Method F, just explained, but the two ends are joined together with adhesive tape instead of sewn.

MINOCHER NOWROJI'S RESTORATION

Effect: The performer displays a giant bead or ball threaded on a rope the ends of which are tied. The problem is to remove the bead without untying the ends of the rope. The magician has an easy solution. He cuts the rope. That is not very magical and so he ties the ends together, trims the knot, and the rope becomes restored.

Secret: The ball is threaded on the rope in advance and the ends of the rope sewn or taped together. See A—A in Figure 373.

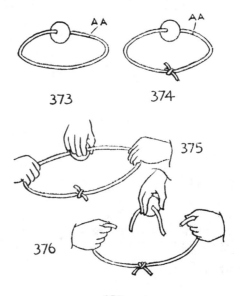

373   374

375

376

A short piece of rope is tied about the large loop to represent the actual ends being knotted. Figure 374. The ball is slid over the joint.

Presentation: As the secret joint is safely hidden in the ball, the rope may be freely displayed at close range. Two volunteers hold the rope. Figure 375.

Slide the ball from one volunteer to the other to show how impossible it would be to remove it without opening the knot. The ball is moved with the right hand and the joint is covered with the left hand as soon as it emerges from cover. This is a natural move to apparently assist you in sliding the ball first to one spectator and then back and across to the second. The left hand must, of course, release and again grasp the joint during the ball's journey across to the second spectator.

The rope is cut after the ball finally rests over the joint and in such a manner that about two inches of the rope projects from each side of the ball. Figure 376.

The ball is disposed of and the ends just cut are knotted together. Conclude as in Method F of the Tarbell Rope Mystery.

BALL THEM UP

Although originally described as a string trick, by Joe Berg and Nelson Hahne, this routine is readily adaptable to rope.

A ball with a hole through the center is displayed threaded on a length of rope. The ball is cut off the rope. Figure 378. The two ropes are tied together by the spectator. The performer ties the other ends of the ropes together. Either of the two tied ends is chosen by the spectator. The performer covers these two ends with a fancy foulard and states that he will replace the ball on the rope. To the spectator, this seems to be very simple; for the performer only has to untie the knot, place the ball on the rope and retie the knot. However, when the performer removes the foulard, the ball is on the rope but the knot is gone. The rope has been restored into one piece!

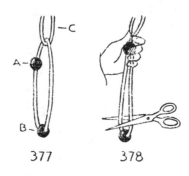

377   378

Secret: Two balls of similar appearance are required. They must be small enough that one can easily be concealed in the hand. The two balls are threaded on the rope and the ends of the rope sewn or taped together. This joint is concealed by sliding one ball over it. The other ball is concealed in the left hand. An extra piece of rope is looped through the main piece of rope to represent the ends. The ball covering the joint is apparently on the center of the rope.

Refer to Figure 377. A is the concealed ball. B is the ball that covers the joining of the actual ends. C is the short piece of rope that represents the ends.

Presentation: Display the ball on the rope and tie the fake ends of the rope together. The spectator is invited to cut the visible ball from the rope by cutting straight across both ropes. Figure 378. The spectator is requested to tie these two newly-made ends together, leaving the ball off the rope.

He is asked to choose one of the knots. If the real ends are chosen, he is allowed to hold them. If the fake ends are chosen, performer states that he will use those ends. These ends are held under the foulard along with the secret ball that is already on the rope.

The right hand places the visible ball under the foulard with the remark that the ball will be placed on the rope. When the right hand is under the foulard, the ball is palmed and the fake ends are untied and removed from the main rope. The short piece of rope is palmed along with the ball. They are disposed of as the foulard is laid aside.

Apparently, the ball has been placed on the rope and the rope restored in the process.

NU-CUT ROPE TRICK BY ELDON NICHOLS

Effect: A length of rope, probably seven feet long, is displayed. The ends are tied together so that a large loop is thus formed. This loop is cut through at any point desired and immediately restored. The effect is immediately repeated.

Secret: The rope is prepared as in Method F of the Tarbell Rope Mystery. However, Mr. Nichols uses rope cement to fasten the ends together. In addition, there is a small circle of rope, the ends of which are also cemented, linked into the large loop. Figure 379.

Presentation: Loop is brought forward with the small circle of rope concealed in the right hand. The large loop is drawn through the right hand, and the circle of rope, in a rotary motion. At any time you stop, pull the small loop up above your fisted right hand and cut it in two. Trim the ends until it is completely cut away and then show that the rope is restored.

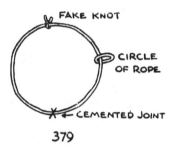

379

The second time you rotate the rope between your hands, you stop at the cemented joint on the large loop. Cut through the joint itself, trim the ends and then knot them. Conclude as suggested for Method F of the Tarbell Rope Mystery.

Variation: Can also be worked by cutting the small circle and tying the resultant piece around the main rope. Now, cut at the joint on the large loop and tie those ends together. The audience think the rope has been cut into three unequal lengths. All you have to do is to trim away the extra rope in the two fake knots, untie the real knot, show the rope to be again in one piece, and toss to the audience.

Another Variation: The Encore Rope Trick is explained later in this chapter. Add the small circle of rope to the large loop used in that trick.

Slowly draw the large loop through your right hand, and circle fake, until told to stop. Cut the rope (really the small fake loop) right at that point. Trim it away and show the rope restored.

Remark that in case some one still doubts that the rope can be restored regardless of where the rope is cut through you will give them the rope in their own hands to cut where they will. Continue with the regular Encore Rope routine.

DOC NIXON'S ROPE MYSTERY

This is not the explanation of a routine but the description of what Doc Nixon used in place of snaps. He used round wooden toothpicks. The ends of the rope were immersed in Clear Lacquer to which was added a portion of White Lacquer. The ends were allowed to dry and were then trimmed off squarely with a razor blade. Using a nail, a small hole was bored quite deeply in the center of each end. A toothpick was then dipped in the lacquer and pushed well into one end. The ends of a short piece of rope were prepared in the same manner. The projecting ends of the toothpicks were shortened to about half an inch and whittled to a sharp point. The short piece of rope could now be attached to the long rope and the two united into a large loop around which another short piece of rope could be tied so as to be all set to work Method A of the Tarbell Rope Mystery.

THE ENCORE ROPE TRICK

Magi shows a length of rope, the ends of which are tied, making a complete circle of about six feet. Magi passes rope to a spectator and asks him to cut the rope anywhere. This is done. The tied end is then cut away. There can be no doubt in the minds of the audience. They have actually seen the rope cut. Now without any tying of ends or without rolling the rope up into a ball or bundle, the rope is seen to be one whole piece and can be given to spectator with your compliments. Just stop and think. Here is a method that does not require intricate twists, snap fasteners, cement or a switch.

Secret: A novel type of rope is used that is extremely easy to cut and handle and the fact that IT IS AN ENDLESS PIECE completely puzzles the wise ones.

A six-inch piece is looped as in Figure 380 and pinched over a portion of the loop. Figure 381. It can be removed quickly and easily by merely pushing or sliding it off the circle of rope.

Presentation: Exhibit rope, tie the ends together while explaining that you have one piece of rope which you are thus forming into a circle. Pass scissors and rope to a spectator and ask him to cut it anywhere he wishes.

There is very little chance of him tampering with faked ends as he is busy finding a place in rope to cut.

After he has cut rope, take from him and hold it so that everyone can see the four ends. Now lay the rope over the open left hand so that the knot section rests on the end of first finger.

Place thumb firmly on knot, then curl fingers around the rope and pull this section of rope away from between thumb and first finger. When this easy move is finished, you should be holding the small piece of rope, by knot, between thumb and first finger and the middle section of long piece in closed left hand, second, third and fourth fingers. Now pick up the ends of short piece in right hand and ask spectator to cut once again —right through the knot. When he does this, allow these two pieces to drop to the floor and with them the very small piece of knot that was left between thumb and first finger in the cutting. Double up ends of rope and hold all between fingers of either hand, say the "Magic Word," open out the rope and show it restored.

Very little ingenuity is needed to work many different methods of presentation with this idea. For instance, this rope material folds up so small that it would be an easy matter to exchange a number of cut pieces for a duplicate in one piece prepared to represent a number of cut pieces and then proceed with the restoring.

ADDITIONAL ENCORE ROPE METHODS BY BERT DOUGLAS

Have the short piece of rope tied to circle of rope and, as you introduce the trick, casually untie the short piece of rope and then hold rope and extra piece in left hand, so that the thumb covers portion of ropes where linked. Figure 382.

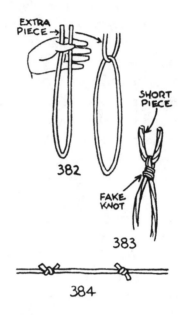

Now right hand grasps long piece of rope just below link, and twists same around second and third fingers of left hand and pushes ends of rope through this loop to apparently form a regular knot. Actually the ends of rope are pushed through one loop only (instead of double loop) and this actually forms a trick knot. The knot is then drawn up tight behind the short piece of rope, and the result is as in Figure 383.

The rope may now be tossed out to the audience and there is absolutely no danger of the short piece of rope becoming prematurely dislodged and thus spoiling the trick. The short piece of rope is held securely in the knot, yet it can easily be withdrawn and disposed of when required.

Have spectator cut the rope anywhere he wishes—99 times out of 100 he will cut through the center directly opposite knot. Now tie the cut ends of the rope together in the usual manner, making the two knots as much alike as possible, then trim the loose ends of both knots so they appear similar. Show the rope quite freely, twisting it around so that no one can keep track of the knots, finally have a spectator select either knot he wishes. If fake knot is selected, immediately cut off the unprepared knot. If unprepared knot is chosen, cut it off. This is really a force and whatever knot is chosen the unprepared one is cut off and the fake knot left.

If desired, two spectators may be allowed to hold the ends of the rope while you proceed to trim down the knot with the scissors. Actually you keep trimming away until the short piece of rope is cut entirely away, leaving only the fake knot. Standing at a distance from the rope, you request the volunteers to pull on the rope when commanded to do so. Ask the audience to keep their eyes on the knot. When the rope is pulled the FAKE KNOT VANISHES VISIBLY—the rope is restored and may be immediately passed out to the audience for thorough inspection.

After working the previous effect several times, the performer will be in possession of several lengths of special rope which cannot again be used for any of the two previous methods of the Encore Rope Trick. Here is a novel routine that can be performed with the straight pieces of rope, and which can only be performed on account of the special soft material of which the rope is made.

In addition to two lengths of the rope material, you will require a tube similar to that used for the color changing handkerchief through the hand. In this case it should be slightly wider than usual, and a cardboard tube is preferable to metal. Take one length of the rope and tie two short pieces of rope thereon in position shown in Figure 384, using the special fake knot explained in the previous method. This prepared rope is pushed into the tube, and the latter is carried in a convenient pocket.

To perform the trick, first show duplicate length of rope and have it cut by a spectator into three pieces, i. e., thirds. Now tie the three pieces together so that this rope will look exactly like the prepared one.

As you place scissors in pocket, steal out the loaded tube and retain in right hand. Take rope from spectator and draw it through the left hand several times (as you do in the color changing silk routine) finally leaving tube in left hand. Push the cut rope therein as you draw out the prepared rope from the bottom of the fist little by little. When rope is fully inside tube, steal the tube on fingers of right hand, and dispose of same while all eyes are directed at rope in left hand. Appear disappointed that your magical powers have failed you as the rope has not been restored. Nobody will suspect that the rope has actually been exchanged.

Two spectators may then be requested to hold the ends of the rope while you make another attempt to work the miracle. You then proceed to trim off the short pieces until only the two fake knots remain and these, of course, vanish visibly on command. The rope is now completely restored and open to unlimited inspection.

NED ASBURY'S VARIATION

At first it may seem that I have stolen Bert Douglas' version where the straight length is used, but it will be found that there is really quite a difference.

Take the straight length of rope that is left from cutting the loop open, and remove from it a short piece four or five inches long. Tie this in a real square knot around the middle of the long piece.

This piece of prepared rope can be left in plain sight on the table, including the knot portion, the rope being arranged so that the two long free ends hang down over the table edge and well apart from each other.

When ready to perform, pick the rope up quite carelessly, making no attempt to conceal the knot Dangle the rope around in your hands during the opening patter and even make a feint of untying the knotted "end", but after getting one knot untied, proceed to think better of it and tie it up again without revealing that they are only fake ends.

Gather up the two dangling ends and deliberately tie them together in any kind of knot, finally exhibiting the rope stretched taut, apparently two pieces tied together at each end.

Now give the spectators their choice of cutting either apart. (No force.) If they choose the fake knot, cut through the knot (really cut off the short piece through its knot but leaving the long piece intact) but just as the knot is about to cut through, bunch up the whole rope in the right hand before they can see that the rope is really a long loop. This is the only point where any concealment is necessary.

Take the scissors from the right hand and place them on the table with the left hand. Pull out the remaining knotted end (the real knot at the actual ends of the rope) and ask if they wouldn't like to have you cut that knot too, to make the trick more difficult. Transfer the balled up rope to the left hand and leave just the knotted end in sight.

Pick up scissors with the right hand and cut the knot off. Replace the scissors on the table, bring the hands together and rub them in a circular motion, gradually show more and more of the rope until it is seen to be restored.

If the spectator chooses the real knot instead, cut it off. Stuff the rope into the left fist until you reach the fake knot. Display the two ends and say that you will see what will happen if you cut this knot too. Cut through knot and, as pieces fall to floor, place the scissors on the table (misdirection from the rope) and right hand immediately goes back to left hand, concealing looped end. As soon as right hand covers loop, begin to pull rope free from left fist as if testing it as you go along. Finally show entire rope restored and toss to audience.

DR. CLYDE CAIRY'S FOLLOW ME ROPE ROUTINE

Effect: The performer and a volunteer each take a rope and cut it into three pieces. The performer restores his rope to one straight unknotted length but the volunteer still has—three pieces. The restored rope is presented to the volunteer as a souvenir.

Secret: The rope (?) that Dr. Cairy uses is really stockinette. This is obtainable from a Packing House and will make a continuous loop some nine to ten feet in circumference. If you are satisfied to use smaller loops, they may be made from the tubular polishing cloth obtainable at auto supply stores.

Of the two ropes that are used, one is an endless loop with a twelve or fifteen inch piece linked through. Figure 385. The other rope is an unprepared, straight

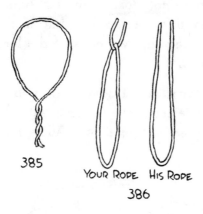

385

YOUR ROPE   HIS ROPE

386

length. Both are on the table with the loops forward and ends away from audience.

Presentation: Pick up unfaked rope and give to a member of the audience. Take other piece, by the looped end, AND LET THE TWO ENDS DANGLE. Due to the nature of the material, it tends to twist and effectively conceals the joint. The rope may even be parted slightly, the lower fake end will remain twisted.

Run rope through your left hand to get the two ends. Hold the secret joint concealed between the left thumb and forefinger. Trim off the ends, ostensibly to show them unprepared, an inch or two at a time, until you get down about two inches from the fake twist.

The member from the audience does the same as the performer is apparently doing.

Both men tie the two ends of the rope together in order to form a loop. In the case of the magician, he has merely tied a short piece around the main rope. Each spread their loop wide apart so that all may see.

Instruct the assistant to take the rope in his two hands with the knot close to the left hand. Figure 387. (It makes no difference to him but it does to you.) Tell him to bring the two ends of the loop together to form two loops.

A fake twist is introduced in your rope in this manner. The secret move is made with the right hand. Hold the loop as in Figure 387. Allow loop to fall onto

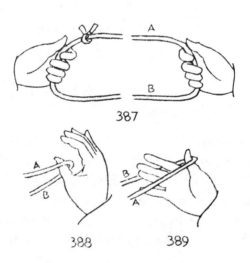

thumb. Figure 388. Turn fingers in toward body and engage strand marked B. Pass fingers up between B and A, as shown in Figure 389, and allow loop to drop into curled fingers as in Figure 387.

This move simply twists the right hand loop a half-turn and is easily accomplished as the hands come together to make the double loop.

If the right hand loop is placed behind (away from audience) the left hand loop, a double loop will be formed with a fake twist in the center. Figure 390.

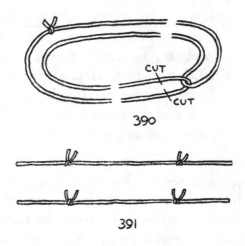

390

391

When stretched tight, this twist cannot be seen. (Stockinette is about the only material that will do this.)

Run the double loop round and around between the hands but keeping it tight. The fake twist can be felt and should be stopped under the left forefinger and thumb. Due to holding the original knot near the left hand, the fake twist should be located across from the knot. Figure 390.

Let the loop fall from the right hand. The knot should be down. Tell the volunteer to hold his loops in the same manner. He is then instructed to cut through both strands about two inches from his left forefinger and thumb. When you do this, you are cutting to within a couple of inches of the fake twist you have made.

Both of you again tie the two ends together. The other ends are let fall. Both ropes are apparently identical, three pieces of rope tied together with two knots. His is actually in that condition but your rope is one long length and bears two fake knots.

This trick would be very poor if one did not have a member of the audience follow him with another rope. The spectators have no way of knowing what results SHOULD be obtained if a rope is tied into a loop, doubled, cut, and the ends tied. In this way the volunteer proves that the correct result is three pieces, tied with two knots, to make one long piece.

Both of you wrap the rope around the left fingers until a knot is reached. One more turn is made to keep the rope from falling when the knot is cut off. The knot is placed in the hand in each case to be trimmed away. It is necessary to make certain that the assistant trims the knot completely away, in which case two cut ends will show up. He is cautioned to keep a finger over these, so the ends will not fall, and you should pretend to do the same as you snip off a fake knot.

The rope is then wound some more, covering the two cut ends again to hold them in place, until the second knot is reached. This is disposed of in the same manner as the first. The rest of the rope is wrapped around the left hand.

The dramatic climax is reached when you stand side by side, wave your hands over the rope as you repeat a mystic phrase, and then unwind the ropes. The volunteer's comes out in three pieces. Yours is restored.

WINSTON FREER'S SUGGESTION

Mr. Freer suggested that the magician could now present the volunteer with the restored rope, which would prove it was O. K., take the spectator's three pieces, tie them together and apparently restore by switching for a duplicate rope.

Dr. Cairy offers this solution. Tie the three pieces together. Wrap them around the hand and tell the assistant to repeat what he did before. Without instruction, he probably will have some difficulty. In order to help him, you put the rolled up rope in your pocket, or on the table, and help the assistant. It is a duplicate that you remove from your pocket or from behind some object on the table. Finish as before.

S. REILLY'S ROPE TRICK

Effect: The ends of a length of rope are tied in order to form a circle. THE ENDS OF THE ROPE ARE A BRIGHT RED. The rope is fairly cut. The cut ends are not tied together. Rope is simply wound around the hand, allowed to uncoil, and is revealed restored. The ends of the rope are still red. The next effect is that of tying the rope around the neck, and instantly releasing neck from the rope. It's a perfect routine—a marvelous rope effect—and the patter story is a dandy. There is no cement or snaps used. So ingenious that it will even fool magicians and it is practical to present it within three feet of an audience.

Preparation. First paint a ¾ inch band of color on both ends of a 6 inch piece of rope.

Then take a 6 foot length of the same rope and paint a ¾ inch band of color about 1 inch from each end. When the paint is dry, slip two white metal tubes or shells on the rope to cover the painted bands. Bring the two ends together and fasten with a piece of adhesive tape to form a circle of rope.

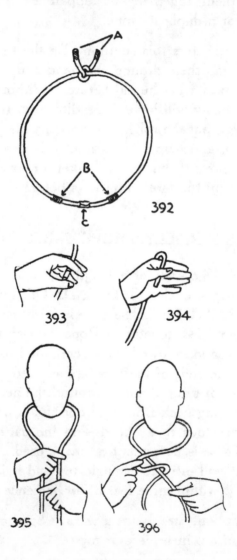

Tie the 6 inch piece of rope, with painted ends, in a single knot, on the large circle of rope directly opposite the adhesive tape.

Refer to Figure 392. A represents the painted ends of the 6 inch piece tied around the main rope. B marks the painted bands, near the actual ends of the main rope, covered with the white metal shells. C indicates the actual ends of the long rope held together with the adhesive tape.

Now make a small circle of rope, using a piece about 4 inches long, and fasten the ends together with adhesive tape.

Place the prepared large circle of rope in the left trouser pocket, the small circle behind the right coat lapel (the pressure of the lapel against the coat will keep the small circle in place), a scissors in the right vest pocket and you are ready to perform.

Although the description of the necessary moves is quite lengthy, if you will take the time and effort to carefully work them out properly, you will be amply repaid by having at your finger tips the greatest of all rope tricks.

Patter: Centuries ago, a Chinese legend tells us, there lived an old high priest called Chow Coon. And he lived in a small Buddhist Temple, surrounded by a bandit infested wilderness, (1) on the banks of the Yangtze River.

It is told that Chow Coon was the proud possessor of a piece of magic rope, which on many occasions was the means of saving his life (2). It seems, that whenever he would tie the ends of the rope together it became a magic circle, and if placed around his neck (3), protected him from all physical harm.

Now one day while strolling through the temple garden, the magic rope about his neck, Chow Coon became tired, so he paused to rest in the shade of a beautiful tree, and fell fast asleep.

Bandits appeared on the scene and saw Chow Coon slumbering peacefully, with the magic rope around his neck. How well the bandits knew the story of the magic rope is told in the legend by their actions (4). Stealthily they crept close to the sleeping old man, (5) cut the rope in two pieces, thereby destroying its magic power. Chow Coon was rudely awakened, easily made a prisoner and was carried away to a secret cave in the mountain side.

(6) Now Chow Coon was crafty, (7) and he knew a thing or two about magic. (8) He cut off a small piece of the rope, (9) and saying the magic words, Mock-a Yey-a, caused it to become a magic charm. (10) He passed the magic charm over the two pieces of rope, (11) then wrapped the pieces around his left hand, (12) a few more passes with the magic charm and instead of two pieces of rope, (13) he now held the rope in its original form, one piece. His safety was now assured, (14) if he could but once again form the rope into a magic circle. (15) He placed the rope around his neck, but before he could tie the ends together, he was seized from behind—he was helpless.

The bandits decreed that Chow Coon should die and they decided to hang him. So that same day he was placed beneath the limb of a very large tree, (16) a loop of rope was thrown around his neck, (17) and several knots were tied.

Now the bandits had expected the old man to cry out in fear, (18) when about to be hanged, but his face was wreathed with a smile for had not the bandits, unconsciously, formed the magic circle when they tied the rope around his neck. Chow Coon became serious, (19) he placed his left hand beneath his chin, raised his head and mysteriously removed the securely tied rope from about his neck.

The bandits were astounded, (20) for who but the Son of Heaven could perform such a miracle. (21) Chow Coon was given his freedom and safely returned to his Temple where, it is told, he spent the remaining years of his life in peace and happiness.

The legend continues. When Chow Coon died and went to his Celestial Kingdom, he was rewarded by the Son of Heaven for his good deeds, and permitted to take his magic rope with him. (22) He spends many hours, (23) showing the rope to his thousands of Celestial Ancestors. (24) He cuts the rope in two pieces, (25) ties the two pieces together, (26) and trims the knots closely. It is still said in some parts of China, when it snows, "Chow Coon is trimming his knots." (27) We would witness a miracle to be remembered all the days of our life if today we could see Chow Coon, tie the two pieces of rope together, (28) pass his hand over the knot, and cause the two pieces to become one. (Throw rope into audience for examination.)

As they say in China, Tie Schen. That means, thank you—good night.

Presentation: (1) Take prepared rope from pocket and slowly untie the fake knot.

(2) At this point you have opened the fake knot, the short piece of rope, so continue patter and tie it again. This action gives the effect that you have tied the ends of a straight piece of rope to form a circle.

(3) Place the circle of rope over your head, fake knot behind neck and large loop over your shoulders, hanging down in front.

(4) Take scissors from pocket.

(5) Cut rope on the right hand side of adhesive tape and as close as possible to the metal shell. Scissors back to pocket.

(6) Both hands go behind neck and grasp rope lightly on either side of the fake knot. Lift rope over your head and bring arms out in front, arms outstretched and pointing toward audience. Slide hands apart so that you are now holding the ropes near the shells.

(7) Release the end of the rope held in the right hand and the left hand holds the opposite end of rope. Figure 393. The first and second finger holding the rope above the shell and adhesive tape and the thumb and third finger holding below.

(8) With scissors cut off the protruding end just above the shell. Cut as close as possible to shell. Scissors back to pocket.

(9) Take the short piece, just cut off, in your right hand between thumb and index finger.

(10) Wave the short piece of rope over the long piece. Use the short piece as if it were a magic wand.

(11) We must now get rid of the shells and fake knot. Still holding the short piece of rope in the right hand, reach over and grasp rope by the shell and take it away from the left hand. Immediately turn back of left hand to audience. Bring rope over the back of left hand so that the shell touches the left palm. Grasp rope

tightly with left thumb, Figure 394, and secretly re-move the shell which remains hidden in the right hand. The exposed red end is hidden in the left palm. Right hand wraps the rope around the left hand. Arriving at fake knot, grasp it in the right hand so that it cannot be seen by audience and as you continue to wrap the rope around left hand, the knot will easily slide toward the end of the rope. When you arrive at the end of the rope, fake knot and shell will come off into your right hand. As this happens, just place second red end of rope into the palm of the left hand which will con-ceal it from the audience.

(12) Once again use short piece of rope as a magic wand.

(13) Allow rope to uncoil and hang down from left hand showing that the rope has been restored. Both ends are red.

(14) Place the short piece of rope, the fake knot and both shells into your right coat pocket.

(15) Place the rope around your neck, the two red ends hanging down in front from over your shoulders.

(16) This is a one rope version of the Strangle Tie, and is accomplished in three moves. In the first move, Figure 395, your right hand goes over the right rope and grasps the left rope, about six inches from the neck, between its thumb and index finger. The left hand goes over the left rope and grasps the right rope between its thumb and index finger, left hand below the right. In the second move, Figure 396, right hand moves to the right and draws the left rope in a small loop over and several inches across the left rope. In

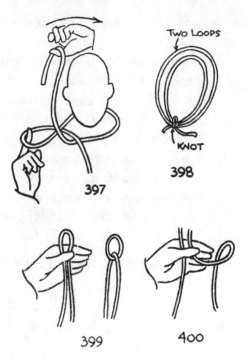

the third move, Figure 397, the right and left hand move in unison. Loop held in right hand is drawn around to the back, at center of neck, and the left hand at the same time, holding right rope, moves up and over the head drawing the right rope around the neck. This leaves the rope, loosely held by a loop, behind the neck. The two red ends hang down in front. One end will be much shorter than the other. These three moves should be made smoothly and blend as one.

(17) Tie the short end around the long end. Use several knots.

18) Hold the long end up as if it were thrown over a tree limb.

(19) Place left hand under chin with back of hand toward audience. Right hand goes up behind left hand

and right index finger goes between the two loops around neck and up behind the top loop. Now turn right palm toward audience and, at the same time, twist a loop of rope around the index finger of right hand. Take hold of lower rope between thumb and index finger. Now, by a strong pull on the loops, the rope comes free from your neck and is in two loops as if it had been fairly tied around your neck. Pass rope from right to left hand and show to audience. Figure 398.

(20) Stand with right hand holding right coat lapel and secretly secure small loop of rope in right hand.

(21) Secretly holding fake loop in right hand, untie the knots in rope. This gives you an opportunity to secretly slip one end of the rope through the fake loop. Release rope from left hand. With back of right hand facing audience, thumb holding hidden fake loop, pull the rope with the left hand through the fake loop until the ends hang down even with each other.

(22) With back of both hands facing audience, pass rope from right hand into the left. Hold rope between the thumb and index finger of the left hand, fake loop extending above the left hand with long ends hanging downward toward floor, the thumb and index finger of the left hand concealing the junction between the fake loop and the length of rope. Figure 399.

(23) Secure scissors.

(24) Cut through fake loop. Put scissors in pocket.

(25) Right hand makes a loop in the right rope about 6 inches from left hand. Figure 400. Turn palm of right hand upward and put this loop over the two short ends in left hand. Grasp the two short ends be-

tween the thumb and index finger of the right hand and pull the loop down with the left fingers, to about a ½ inch below the short piece. Again, as in Figure 399, the left thumb and index finger grasps the junction between fake short piece and long rope. Right fingers tighten loop against short piece and it now looks like a fair knot. It is really a slip knot around the short piece of rope and can be shown to audience. These moves should also blend as one and should impress the audience that you simply tied the two ends of the rope together.

(26) With scissors, cut the fake short piece into small bits and scatter them about. When you have cut away as much of the fake piece as possible, there will be one small piece remaining in the tightened loop. Grasp this short piece of rope with the tips of the scissors and pull it loose. Return scissors to pocket. You now have only a slip knot on the long rope.

(27) Grasp one end of the rope in the left hand. Hold it high in the air.

(28) Put right hand around the "knot" and with a little pressure by the fingers the loop will loosen and the knot disappear.

EDDIE CLEVER'S TRIPLE CUT ROPE ROUTINE

The effect, up to a certain point, is as usual. A rope is knotted to form a circle and a spectator cuts it. The cut ends are tied and one of the knots is selected by a spectator. This knot is untied. The knot in the center is cut away and the rope shown to be restored.

It is again tied in a circle, cut once more and restored. The rope is then thrown to the audience. You perform some other trick. When this trick is finished, you look at the audience and say "There are still some persons out there who don't believe I really cut that rope. I shall show you once more."

Walking into the audience you get the rope and drop it around your neck. Going back to the platform the rope is removed, the middle taken in the left hand and again it is cut and restored, and thrown back to the audience.

Secret: At the start, the real ends of the rope are fastened together with adhesive tape and a short piece is knotted around the actual center of the rope. This preparation is the same as for Captain Jones' Rope Trick described earlier in this chapter.

The supposed middle of the rope is cut, near the tape, and the ends trimmed off to get rid of the tape.

The newly cut ends are tied and a knot selected. Regardless of the choice made, the real knot is untied.

The ends are cut away from the fake knot but the knot is not destroyed. As the right hand comes up it covers the fake knot but the impression is given that the knot is under the left hand. While all eyes watch the left hand, the right hand carries the fake knot to within about four inches of the end of rope. The rope is allowed to hang from the right hand and is shown to be restored.

You are now ready to perform Grant's Super Rope Trick, described earlier in this chapter, at the finish of which the rope is tossed to the audience.

Now for the third cut. This is the L. W. Tug Of War method, described in Chapter Six, with a slightly different dressing.

F. H. JEUDEVINE'S ROPE ROUTINE

Open with the Encore Rope Trick. This was explained in the present chapter. When finished, and using the same length of rope, state that perhaps all were not paying attention so you will repeat the effect.

Cut and restore it this time as you would the Cut And Restored Turban. Refer to The "Hindoo" Rope Restoration or Bluey-Bluey's Method, in Chapter Five.

State that the audience still seems to be a bit skeptical so it will be necessary for you to try again. Use U. F. Grant's Sleight Of Hand Rope Trick routine which permits you to cut the rope two different ways. This was also explained in Chapter Five.

The turban effect is again repeated, only this time I appear to cut off about a foot and tie from each end. You seem to have three lengths of rope tied together with two knots. Slide these knots off under cover of wrapping the rope around the left hand. This time you have apparently joined three pieces of rope back into one long length.

For the final and best applause getter of all, hand the rope to an assistant. He turns his back and finds the exact center of the rope and holds on to it at that point. While this is being done, you obtain a short piece of rope from your left coat pocket. This short length is folded in half.

As he gets the shears, you place the looped end of the long rope in your fisted left hand and draw the short piece into view. He cuts it, thinking he is separating the rope at the center which he has just located.

If you use the Encore Rope, or any very soft rope, it is not necessary to tie the ends each time before restoring as you may hold them at the finger tips and have assistant cut several times until no pieces are left.

This may seem like a lot of "fussing" until you try it out yourself, but as each and every "cut" is so different it completely throws the wise ones off the trail.

As you have cut and restored the rope each time in such a different manner, it does not become tiresome.

Aside from the first method, the rope is totally unprepared. There is no cement and no snaps, nothing but a piece of rope, a pair of sharp shears, and a bit of nerve. If you are a magician, you possess the last.

THE BAKER TAKES A CUT

Effect: A loaf of bread is displayed through which a 3 foot length of rope has been threaded. Figure 401.

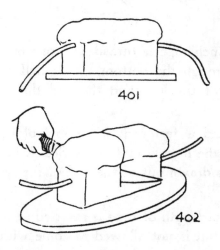

401

402

The Magician saws through the loaf until it is divided into two sections. Figure 402. The pieces of bread are separated, the cut ends of the rope being shown. Then the loaf is squared up and the rope is withdrawn restored and tossed to the audience.

Secret: Three ropes are actually used.

A 10 inch rope is inserted in the loaf at the center. See B in Figure 403.

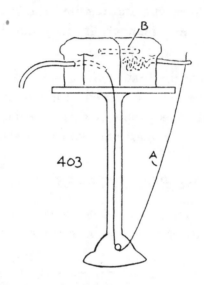

A 16 inch rope is threaded in one end of the loaf and out through the bottom, about half way between the center of the loaf and the end through which it entered.

A thread is fastened to the end of this rope and goes down the hollow table leg. See A in Figure 403. This rope is drawn out of the end of the loaf for about 1 foot.

A 3 foot length of rope is inserted in the other end of the loaf but is not allowed to come within a couple of inches of the center. It is tucked into the loaf so that only 1 foot extends beyond the end. Figure 403.

The thread is passed through the visible end of this rope so that it may be quickly and easily withdrawn when required.

Presentation: Call attention to the loaf and the rope and, in so doing, lift it two or three inches from the table. Remember to leave sufficient slack in the thread to permit you to do this.

Cut completely through the loaf and the 10 inch rope. Separate the halves of the loaf so that the cut ends of the short rope are visible.

In preparing the loaf, it may be necessary to insert a couple of hat pins from the back and through this short rope at each side of the center of the loaf. This is to overcome the fact that the knife sometimes has a tendency to draw the 10 inch rope out of the bread, rather than cut it.

Place the two pieces of bread back together. Hold them steady with the left hand as you grip the end of the 3 foot rope, and thread A, and pull slowly.

As the 3 foot length is withdrawn from the loaf, the thread draws the 16 inch rope down the table leg.

When the rope is fully withdrawn, and shown restored, the mere action of walking away from the table, in order to give the rope to a spectator, pulls the thread clear of the rope.

THE L. W. GREAT DIVIDE

Two blocks are introduced. Each is two and one-half inches square by four inches long. Through the center of each is bored a three-quarter-inch hole. A rope is threaded through the holes—necklace fashion. The blocks are placed together on the table, the ends of the rope projecting. A sharp knife is pressed down between the blocks—the knife being held in the right hand. The left hand reaches down and picks up the two blocks, pressed together. This done, the knife is pushed all the way through, between the blocks, and comes out the bottom side. Apparently the rope must have been severed.

The blocks are replaced on the table. The performer grasps one projecting end of the rope and pulls it free from the blocks. Peculiarly enough, the other end comes along with it. The rope is restored!

The blocks are unprepared. Not so with the rope. First it will be necessary to procure a quantity of the rope which has a core running through the center. The core is easily removable, and must be removed from a four-foot length of the rope. This piece of rope is then cut in two. The cut ends are dipped in paraffin and allowed to dry. This prevents their fraying.

A bodkin is constructed of a two-foot length of stiff wire. To one end of this bodkin attach a piece of heavy black thread, four feet eight inches long. Run the thread through the two pieces of rope. Remove the bodkin. One end of the thread must be attached to one end of the rope. This may be done by tying or by affixing same in place by winding a small piece of adhesive tape around both the end of the rope and the thread. Figure 405. The other end of the thread hangs loose. See B in Figure 405. Thus the two pieces of rope may be drawn together on the thread and held in place by pressing the loose end of the thread against the end of the rope. The extra thread, which hangs down, will not be noticed.

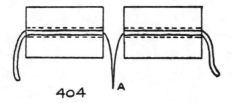

404   A

When the rope, thus prepared, is threaded through the blocks, the joint in the rope is made to come just at the point where the blocks meet. The knife that is pressed down between the blocks is sharp, except for about an inch of the blade. This portion of the knife has been thoroughly dulled. The downward pressure of the knife will merely cause the thread to be pushed down with it. See A in Figure 404.

Finally, by pulling on the thread at the moment when the rope is withdrawn from the blocks, the two pieces of rope will be joined together. Need we remark that the rope cannot be passed for examination?

THE GESSING-GORDON ROPE TRICK

Effect: Two 20-inch ropes are held, one in each hand. Slowly the ends of the ropes slide together and

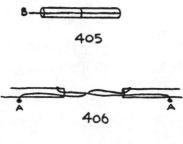

B

405

A   A

406

meet. They are now displayed at the tips of the fingers to have joined themselves together into one rope.

Secret: The ends of the ropes are first bound with white thread, to keep them from fraying.

A strong black thread is fastened securely to the end of one rope, threaded lengthwise through the second and brought out an inch from the end of this second rope.

A second thread is fastened securely to the end of this second rope, threaded lengthwise through the first for one inch and brought to the outside just this inch from the end of the first rope.

The threads are 1 foot long and have heavy knots formed at their free ends to supply a ready grip for the fingers. See A-A in Figure 406.

Presentation: The two ropes are held, one in each hand, with the prepared ends uppermost. The black threads, in front of your dark suit, are unnoticed. The knots, A-A, are gripped between the first fingers and thumbs and the remaining fingers curl around the ropes themselves.

Now, retaining a firm grip on the knots, separate the hands slowly. Allow the ropes to slide over the curled second, third and little fingers. When the ends touch, drop the rope from your left hand, hold the unprepared end of the other rope at the tips of the fingers of the right hand, display for a moment and then place aside.

THE SLOW MOTION RESTORATION BY HARRY BJORKLUND

Effect: A piece of rope, about two feet in length, is cut in half and the magician holds one half in each hand in front of him. At his command the cut ends slowly curl upwards and join, the rope being displayed again in one piece.

Required: Two pieces of rope prepared with a thread, scissors and excelsior clip.

Preparation: Take a piece of soft rope two feet in length, cut it in half and from one half take out the core. Thread a length of black silk about three feet long through this piece, pass it through one end of the other piece and fasten it with a knot on the outside. Pull the thread taut, bring the two pieces together at the cut ends, and attach an excelsior clip hook to the free end of the thread, Figure 407. Coil up the loose thread and insert it with the clip in the hollow end of the threaded piece, Figure 408. Pull out a small loop of the thread, Figure 408, at the point where the pieces join to allow for the insertion of the scissors. Lay the prepared rope on your table and put a small pair of scissors in your lower right hand vest pocket.

Presentation: Pick up the rope by the prepared end with the right hand, show it hanging at full length, transfer it to the left hand, at the same time securing the clip, thrust your right hand into your vest pocket, attach the clip and bring out the scissors. Pull out a loop of the thread about three inches long, Figure 409, then apparently cut the rope at the joint and do it naturally, neither too quickly nor too slowly, being very careful not to cut the thread. Replace the scissors, then pull the two pieces apart, letting them hang down, one piece in each hand, separating the hands about 9 inches, Figure 410.

Now by slowly raising and separating the hands the two lower ends of the pieces will be drawn together and join, Figure 411. Drop the left hand piece and show the rope restored, Figure 412.

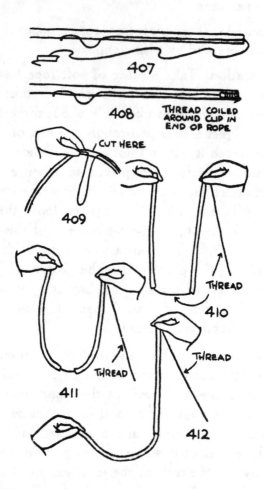

THE MARVEL CUT AND RESTORED ROPE

Effect: The performer holds a length of rope by the ends, Figure 415. A spectator cuts it in two at the center, Figure 416. The two cut ends are tied together, the knot is trimmed away, and the rope is restored.

Preparation: A 3 foot length of soft rope is used. A 6-inch piece of the same kind of rope is tied around it exactly 1 foot from one end, Figure 413. Scissors are in right hand coat pocket.

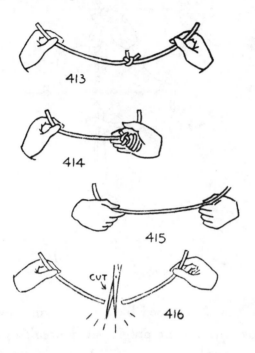

413

414

415

CUT

416

This fake knot, and the foot of rope, are concealed in the right hand, Figure 414. The appearance to the audience is as in Figure 415.

Presentation: Advance with the rope held as explained which makes it appear as only 2 feet long. Spectator unmistakably cuts it, Figure 416, apparently at the very center.

You now appear to tie the two cut ends together. What really happens is that the end of the 1 foot length is concealed and the fake knot is pulled into view, Fig-

ure 417, and an extra knot tied in the ends of the short
piece that forms it.

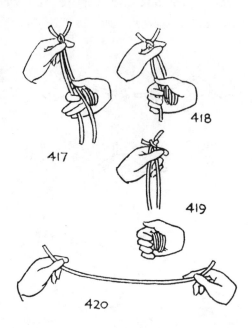

This knot is grasped by the left hand and slowly
drawn upwards. As the previously concealed portion of
the rope appears, the 1-foot length of rope is worked up
into the right hand and palmed in place of the rope just
brought to sight. Figure 418.

Pull the 2-foot length completely free of the right
hand which immediately goes to the right hand coat
pocket and removes the scissors. The palmed piece of
rope is left in the pocket, Figure 419.

Two spectators each hold one end of the rope. You
clip away the fake knot and show the rope restored,
Figure 420.

ENCYCLOPEDIA OF ROPE TRICKS

THE "J. M." ROPE TRICK

Effect: A 6-foot length of rope is held as in Figure 423. A metal ring is threaded over one end of the rope and allowed to fall to the center. The rope is cut and the ring naturally falls to the floor which is additional proof the rope has actually been severed, Figure 424. The two lengths of rope are now knotted together at both ends. One knot is then cut away and the other dissolves so that the rope is once again in one piece and may be presented to some one as a souvenir.

Preparation: It will be necessary for you to procure the following:

Six feet of soft rope or heavy cord.

A 12-inch length of the same rope, knotted at one end.

A 6-inch length of the same rope with a knot at one end.

Two small metal rings or one ring faked with a split.

A spool of white thread and the usual pair of scissors.

Place one metal ring on the long length of rope.

Splice or tie both ends of the six foot length of rope together by placing the ends side by side and binding them tightly with the cotton thread, winding the thread around a number of times so as to make an invisible joint, at least one that will not be discerned at a short distance.

Make a loop in the actual center of the rope opposite to the two bound ends by tying a slip knot, Figure 421.

Insert the 12-inch length of rope through this loop and pull it through so that the knot of the short length is up against the loop in the long rope, Figure 421.

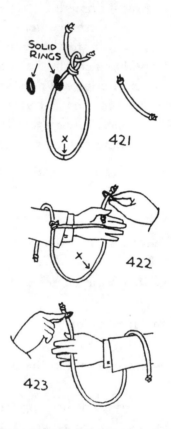

SOLID RINGS

421

422

423

Clip the short 6-inch rope between the first and second fingers of the left hand and then hold the entire rope in this hand by the large loop as in Figure 422. The 12-inch piece hangs over the arm as though one end of the rope. The ring already threaded on the rope is concealed in the palm of the same hand. Notice that quite a portion of the actual rope is hidden from the view of the audience by the left hand and sleeve, Figure 422. So prepared, you are ready.

Presentation: Face the audience with the left hand and arm held over the chest.

With the right hand, grasp the rope with the 12-inch length on it and move the rope over the arm in a casual manner, always keeping the end hanging over the arm. Figure 423 shows what the appearance is to the audience.

Take the metal ring and appear to place the ring on the rope over the end that hangs at the finger tips of the left hand. After the ring is placed on the rope, appear to pull it down slowly. Really leave it in the palm of the left hand while the other ring, actually threaded on the rope, is allowed to slide down to what appears to be the middle, Figure 423.

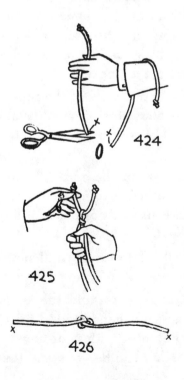

424

425

426

Then you cut the rope, Figure 424.

The ring drops to the floor and the rope appears to the spectators, as it hangs over the arm, to be two separate pieces of rope.

Grasp, in the right hand, the rope (looped end) that hangs in the crook of the arm. Bring this end together with the small end at the finger tips and hold all in the left hand. It appears that all you did was to bring the two pieces of rope together in the left hand.

With both hands, crumple the short 6-inch length of rope into the right hand. Then untie the knot in the long 12-inch rope (all this taking a bit of time) and pull it half way through the loop. It now appears to be the ends of the actual rope, Figure 425.

The right hand then palms the duplicate ring that is still concealed in the left hand and the short piece of rope and this ring are disposed of as the scissors are picked up. It is also possible to get rid of them by disposing of them in the pocket.

Now tie the actual ends of the rope (where the cut was made) and allow the apparently already-tied ends to hang down. The rope now appears to be two lengths tied together.

Clip or cut bits of the ends off the rope, first one end and then another. Completely cut away the knot from the actual ends. This disposes of any tell-tale trace of the thread binding.

Cut away the false ends until nothing is left but the slip knot.

Two spectators now hold the actual ends of the rope. You close your hand around the slip knot in the center and work it loose with your fingers. Remove your hand, reveal the knot to be gone and the rope restored.

BURLING HULL'S "MIRACLE" ROPE
RESTORATION

Effect: The rope is thrown into the audience at the start in one straight solid piece. It is cut and tied together by a spectator who tosses it back to the performer who receives it in his bare hands that contain nothing else whatever. He now proceeds to immediately restore the rope to one straight length by causing the knot to VISIBLY DISSOLVE.

Secret and Presentation: Always use a piece of rope about 6 to 7 feet long. Nothing but the one length is used. Cut the ends down to a sharp point and treat them with a good rope cement for about a ¾ inch. Obtain a pair of shears and you are ready.

"I will take one of you right out of the audience and nominate him as a magician—and let him do the whole feat himself."

Select a lady near the front—or a man if preferred. A lady is more effective. "Here Madam, will you oblige?"

Step back to your box or table and take out the piece of rope. Lay it right in her hands as in Figure 427. The exact center is in the one or other of her hands

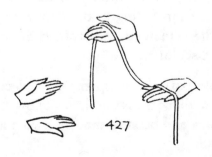

427

and not right between them. This is so that when party cuts rope it will not be cut exactly in the center but to one side of the center. (While not essential to the trick it adds to the nicety of the effect.) Hand party the shears or give them to a second party and ask them to cut the rope. As they go to do so, say: "Wait, I want to step over here several feet away so that there will be no suspicion that I influence you in any way. Now cut."

Another way is to hand party one end of the rope and ask him to hold it high in the left hand, Figure

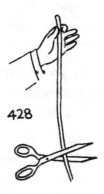

428

428. Place the shears in his right hand, pick up the other or lower end of the rope in your finger tips and tell the party to cut anywhere. This is to prevent the lower portion from falling to the floor after cutting and to prevent the cemented end from gathering dirt from the floor to discolor it.

Have the party hold up the two pieces and show them to the audience, Figure 429. Show there are two separate pieces and be sure that the two cut ends are at the upper end.

Tell party to cross the two cut ends and tie them together in a strong knot. Watch here to see that he understands that he is to cross the pieces and tie them, not lay the two together parallel and tie a knot around them. Have the party tie a clean square knot, not too tightly nor too loosely.

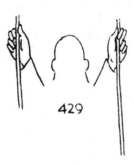

429

The knot will be at one side of the center of the rope.

Take the shears and trim the ends off just as close into the knot as you possibly can, Figure 430. This is important to the working. Force the shears right into the knot and get the ends off close into the knot.

You may let the spectator cut them after you have the trick down fine. Simply see that he cuts the ends close enough to the knot. For the first few performances you had better do the cutting yourself and be safe.

Then show your hands, palms toward audience, absolutely empty and say, "I will now take the rope in my bare hands, for the first time."

Take it in left hand by the end "A" which is nearest the knot, Figure 431.

With right hand take hold of knot "J", Figure 432.

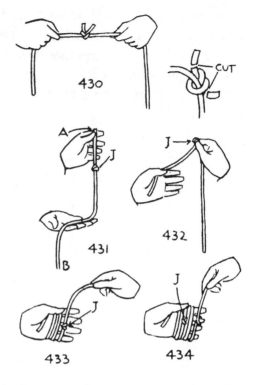

Start winding rope, as in Figure 432, slowly and leisurely around the spread out fingers of the left hand. Spread the fingers wide so as to keep the loops loose.

"I am going to make a number of magic circles in order to create as much magic power as possible."

Turn gradually to the right so that the left side is toward the audience. Conceal the left palm.

By this time you have reached the knot which must come inside of the left hand, Figure 433. If necessary, make the coil a little looser or tighter as needed to make the knot land inside the left hand.

Continue a couple of coils more until you have reached a distance from the approaching end which is about the same distance as the knot is to the other end. Read this over and get it clear. It is for this that we suggested that you have the rope cut between the center and one end, rather than in the exact center.

Having reached this point, bend your second finger inward and, as the rope comes up past it on the inside of left hand (in the winding of the next coil), just give the rope a turn around the left second finger, Figure 434.

Stand with left side toward audience while doing the winding, Figure 435, so that no one can see the

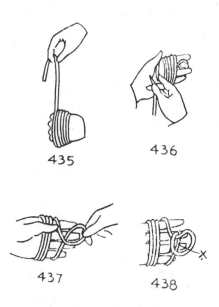

435

436

437

438

bending of this finger. The turn around the finger is taken in one-fourth of a second, as the right hand passes behind left, so there is no fear of it showing. Right hand continues on right up over the top of left hand as formerly in winding all the other coils.

As you come to the end, take it in the finger tips and bring it up inside the left palm and place it against the other end where it will stick instantly and firmly because of the cement, Figure 436.

Take care to lap just the sloping points of the ends so that they will make a neat and invisible join. Do not look at your hands too much while doing this. Just locate the join and look away while you press together and roll into a neat connection.

You may move these ends over toward left fingertips as soon as lightly joined. Then take the right hand away and let the left fingers complete the pressure and rolling "movement" in order to make a neat join.

Now to kill a moment or two. "With your permission I will just tighten your knot a little."

But you really take the loop which is around the left second finger, Figure 437, slip it off, turn it downward on itself, Figure 438, seize the portion of the rope

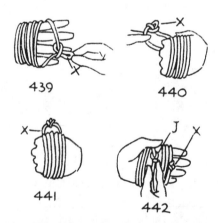

439

440

441

442

marked "X" through the loop, Figure 438, and pull it right through the loop, Figure 439. Pull it tight. Adjust it by drawing upward so it assumes the appearance of a regular knot, not the loop or slip knot that it is.

"That is a pretty tight knot at that, Madam."

Bring the knot up so it shows over the top of the left hand, Figure 440 and Figure 441, and leave it there. Everyone will take it to be the knot tied by the spectator.

In the meantime you have brought your right hand inside the left and rolled the other real knot "J" between your fingers so that it opens. Owing to the fact that the ends were trimmed off so far down into the knot, there is nothing to hold it. Figure 442 and Figure 443.

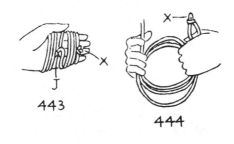

443

444

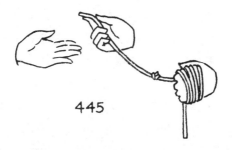

445

Take hold of the coils at the back of the left hand. Draw them off and hold them between the two hands, Figure 444, with fingers holding opposite sides of coils.

This keeps the hands together and enables you to do anything necessary, such as work the knot open (in case you failed to do it cleanly the first time), or straighten out the curved ends which have just come from the knot so they will not be revealed as these ends, or to tighten or adjust the fake knot "X", in case you did not get it tight the first time. When you are new at the trick, you may need this little cover and leeway to clean up any slips made.

To provide time, you continue, "Now Madam, select two nice gentlemen from the audience for your committee to hold the rope."

When party indicates two persons, or you select them for her, have one step up and take one end of the rope. Or you may dispense with that and hand one end to the lady and hold the other end yourself.

As party comes forward, take end of the rope nearest knot "X" and, letting part of rope uncoil from left hand, hand it to him, Figure 445.

Take hold of the rope yourself on the other side of the knot but safely in front of the secret join "A" and "B". Take a turn of rope around your fingers so that the rope will not slip past when you pull hard.

Take party's other hand and guide it over the knot, Figure 446, telling him to recite, "Alla Oom-Mahalla-O-La-La-."

Say, "Watch—watch the knot. It is getting smaller and smaller."

Do not pull it out too soon as everyone should be watching the knot for a few seconds so that they may all see it visibly dissolve and the rope join whole again in full view. Figure 447.

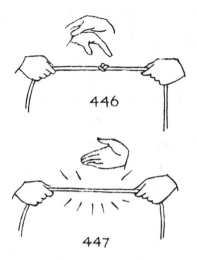

The harder the pull required to get the slip knot to come out, the more effective. This proves the great strength of the "restored" rope. Therefore, make your slip knot "X" as tight as you can and, when pulling at the climax in order to make it come out, pretend to be pulling harder than you are in order to increase the effectiveness.

Here is illustrated a masterly piece of misdirection. An extra fake knot is provided on the rope for the spectators to see and watch. They presume it to be the original knot tied on the rope by the spectator who cut it. Naturally that was the ONLY knot as the real knot has been easily pulled open and is no more. They naturally examine the rope at the point where the knot was, where there is nothing to see. When the rope is being restored by PULLING, the audience sees the full length of the rope with the one knot (the same one, as they suppose) and they naturally concentrate their attention on that point, which they are SURE must be the place where the rope was cut apart and retied. When this is pulled so hard, the great strength of the rope proves to them that there cannot be any fake joints under such conditions. Then the knot dissolves and the rope is whole in one length again—well, a real miracle has apparently been accomplished, right before their eyes.

There is nothing left for them to pin a suspicion on. They are completely lost.

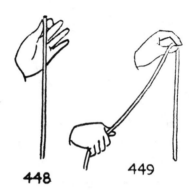

448   449

Immediately hold the rope up, Figure 448, and walk right to the front of stage or platform and show it to the audience — DRAMATICALLY — in one straight piece again.

ALTERNATIVE CONCLUSION. Where it is desired to dispense with anyone holding the rope, in order to speed up the trick, simply hold the rope yourself on either side of the knot, Figure 449. Ask everyone to watch closely, draw the ends apart very slowly until the knot dissolves and leaves the rope in one straight length again. Immediately show the rope all around from end to end. Toss it aside and proceed with the next trick.

PRESENTING THE ROPE TO THE AUDIENCE

"I find that many of you were so attentive that I am

going to present a souvenir of this rare Indian Rope to as many of you as possible. It is a sure preventative for all kinds of separations and divorces, etc."

Here is how Mr. Hull does just that. Picking up the shears, he slips a blade under as many strands as he thinks he can cut through at one clip, Figure 450. He

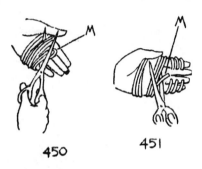

450   451

also nips the place where the ends were joined, indicated by "M", under the blades and snips it off the rope. To get this in position for the cut, he simply (when taking hold of the rope to wind it about his left hand) took hold of it at that point (the secret join) and thus it was doubled over as he wound it around.

Another method he sometimes uses is to cut several strands through, Figure 451, simply seeing that he cuts above the secret join with the first cut. Then he makes another cut to clip through the rest of the strands and simply catches the end containing the join in the shears again. Cutting through the rope (with the others), the secret join is cut right off in a small bit, Figure 451.

He then takes the shears in his left hand and lifts the short pieces away in the right hand, Figure 452, holding them up high to attract attention to the hand and the pieces, and as he passes his table on the way forward, he deposits the shears on the table along with the small bit, under or behind the shears. (Or behind a handkerchief lying on the table.)

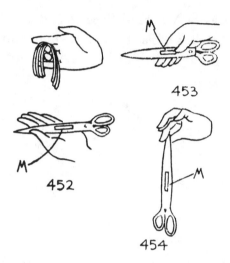

453

452

454

For Magicians' Clubs he uses an even more subtle move.

Here they are looking for the slightest get-away— even between the fingers. Mr. Hull satisfied them by handling everything with the finger tips only. We give you his secret here.

The shears are coated on the left side at the cross-piece with a thin coat of cement. Now when he has clipped off the last bit and cut through the strands, his right hand passes over the little bit of rope, in the act of cutting the strands, and the left thumb places the bit against the coated side of the scissors.

And because the bit of rope is also coated with the same cement, it naturally sticks right onto the shears.

His right thumb, drawn out of the shears, now presses on the piece and adjusts it to a neat parallel position, Figure 453. Then the left hand comes over (palm empty, fingers wide apart), and takes the shears by the extreme point with only the tips of the finger and thumb—and drops the shears down on the table.

Nothing could be cleaner. The bit was carried away stuck on behind the blade of the shears and entirely invisible from the front, Figure 454.

"CUT YOURSELF A PIECE OF ROPE"

This is a sure-fire routine employing a newly perfected method, obviating the use of metal snaps, thus permitting the use of any size woven clothes line, sash cord, wrapping twine, tape or ribbons, and was developed by the late Caryl S. Fleming.

A complete novel routine is explained in which a spectator examines, handles and actually cuts the rope, emulating the magician in a "Do As I Do" interlude, but despite his efforts, attains different results, leading to a climax in which the spectator actually cuts the magician's rope at any chosen place and a final restoration.

Two routines are given herewith. In general effect, they are naturally quite similar, both employ the same simple sleight, the same general basic preparation.

Preparation: The special adhesive—FLEMING'S LIQUID ROPE GIMMIC—supplied with the effect is water-proof, non-poisonous, transparent, stainless, non-inflammable and instantaneous in working.

It will remain flexible and ready for instant use for two or three weeks after applying and the ends once used may be renewed by a single thin application over the old surface.

Its principal active adhesive ingredient is similar in character to an expensive chemical compound used in dentistry and is not intended nor guaranteed for use on metal as some alloys may set up a chemical reaction and consequent discoloration.

If the cement becomes too thick it may be thinned by adding a few drops of either Chloroform (C. P.) or Carbon Tetrachloride (C. P.).

It is not a common commercial rubber cement. Tests of over twenty popular makes gave very unsatisfactory results which did not compare with LIQUID ROPE GIMMIC.

Inasmuch as rope tricks seem to be the current vogue, instructions will be given therefor, but it is understood that the application is relatively the same no matter whether the effect is performed with rope, twine, tape or ribbon.

With a sharp knife, or better still, a single edge safety razor blade—cut the ends of the rope where the Liquid Rope Gimmic is to be applied on a long diagonal so that as much surface presents itself as possible. This naturally gives a greater effective area for the adhesive to work and thus insures against possible failure. In preparing two surfaces that are later to be brought together it is wise to loop the rope around so that the two desired places are parallel and a single synchronous cut made across both sections so that the diagonal angles match exactly.

Apply the Liquid Rope Gimmic with a clean, flat, wooden toothpick sparingly and allow about ten minutes for drying in between coats. Two or three coats should be applied at first to the raw surfaces so as to thoroughly impregnate the porous material, and the prepared ends kept apart until time for actual use. For tape or ribbon, merely coat from one-quarter to one-half inch of the surface to be joined for an overlapping joint.

Be sure the hands are clean and that the treated surfaces do not come into contact with dust or dirt as it will pick up and cause a telltale discolorartion.

Sleight: Only one sleight is employed and this of a simple character. The one described in Prof. Hoffman's "Modern Magic," Chapter XVI, first effect— "The Cut And Restored String"—is excellent (read "The 'Hindoo' Rope Restoration" Chapter 5 and refer to Figures 166 and 167) but for the benefit of those few who may not possess this most valuable work I give here my favorite method of working same.

The two ends of the rope are held between the first and second fingers of the left hand so that they protrude toward the audience from the back of the hand and the loop falls down from the palm toward the performer.

Right hand takes the center of the loop, brings it up to the palm and lays it across the section next to the finger joint—left thumb is brought down upon this cross and the right hand, as if in a continuous movement, grasps the single piece below the cross and carries it up above the left hand into view while the left hand now fully closes to hide the actual center which is still in place and covered by the left thumb. This loop, or false center, is the one that is cut and, of course, is really close to one end, instead of as it appears to be, in the middle.

Note: Instead of the special soft or unsized rope, it has been found that the common cheap starch-filled clothesline procurable in any Five and Ten or hardware store is far better to be used owing to the fact that the filler tends to bind the prepared ends together in a more compact form and affords a more flat even surface or face which gives a smoother joint. No. 7 rope is an excellent size for convenience in handling and visibility.

ROUTINE NO 1: Employs three separate pieces of rope of equal length (would suggest each to be eight or nine feet long); two are unprepared and the third has the diagonal cuts on each end and two or three coats of LIQUID ROPE GIMMIC applied as per directions.

The performer displays three pieces of rope and requests the spectator to select any one of them. If the spectator selects the prepared rope, the performer then places it on his table for later use and hands the remaining two ropes to the spectator asking him to retain the one of his choice and to return the other to the performer.

However, if the spectator selects one of the unprepared ropes, this is laid aside for the moment and the spectator now asked to select a second one.

If this time he selects another unprepared rope, the performer places the remaining piece of prepared rope on his table for later use and gives the spectator his choice of the two ropes thus remaining (the first and last), or if for a second choice the spectator determines upon the prepared rope, the magician places this aside and gives the spectator his choice of the two unprepared ropes.

In other words the magician forces the use of the two unprepared ropes for the first part of the effect and retains the prepared rope for the finale.

Next the magician loans the spectator a pair of scissors and says "Now we are both going to perform the same trick and I am going to instruct you step by step—all you have to do is 'Do As I Do'."

"First you will take the two ends of the rope and hold them between the fingers of your left hand—thus" performer holds his rope ends as described in the paragraph under the heading of "Sleight" and shows same to the spectator.

"Next, with your right hand, pick up the center of the rope which is hanging down and bring it up—so." The spectator will naturally bring the actual center up and close his fist on it, while the performer apparently does likewise, but instead brings up the false center as described.

"Now, take your scissors and cut the loop you have thus formed right in the middle and then loan me the scissors." Spectator cuts his rope and hands the scissors to the performer who cuts his loop and then lays the scissors down on his table.

"Now, please tie any two of the four ends together while I do the same—in a double knot." Performer naturally ties the ends of his false loop around the actual center of the rope and drops the two loose ends.

Spectator follows suit and drops the two loose ends of his rope and stretches it to pull the knot tight, the same as the performer.

"Kindly take your ropes by one end and wrap them around your fist the same as I do."

Both engage in the same action, but the performer secretly, under cover of his right hand, draws the fake knot clear of the rope and palms it in his closed right fist.

"Well, sir, you have followed directions intelligently and we are at present quite equal, but now we are going to have a unique little race. At the count of three we shall both see how fast we can remove the knot from our rope. Are you ready? One, two-three."

The spectator will naturally unroll his rope and struggle to untie his knot while the performer simply holds fast to one end and drops his single piece of rope toward the floor.

Looking at the spectator with his two separate pieces of rope, the performer remarks, "Something seems to have gone wrong for you have two pieces of rope and I have mine restored to a single strand. Too bad, but I'll present you with my knot as a sort of consolation prize."

Performer opens his right hand and extends the knot concealed therein to the spectator. Takes both the spectator's ropes and offers his own restored rope for examination. When the fact is established that the rope is actually in one piece to the satisfaction of the spectator, the performer collects and rolls all the ropes into a ball and disposes of them on his table and picks up the prepared length of rope and again speaks to the spectator.

"I suppose you feel that everything we just did was not exactly to your satisfaction—that is to say, there is

some doubt in your mind as to whether I actually cut
my rope or not, isn't there? And yet we both followed
identical actions throughout, didn't we?"

"Well, maybe you are right and maybe you are
wrong—but—would you feel any better about it if I
held the two ends of this rope wide apart—so—and permitted you to cut it in any place you cared to?"

Spectator decides upon some place on the rope and
upon request of the performer closes the scissors on it
and lets the cut ends fall free.

Performer, holding the two pieces of rope with his
hands well apart so as to prove unmistakably that it is
cut in two separate pieces, speaks: "Inasmuch as we
are now finished with the scissors, will you kindly return them to the table?"

Performer turns to indicate the table, brings his
hands together, places the two prepared faces into position opposite each other and gives them a tight squeeze,
and as he faces the spectator who now looks up,
stretches his restored, single piece of rope between his
hands, gives it a little pull to demonstrate that it is again
in one piece, throws it off stage or on to his table and
ushers the spectator to the runway, thanking him for his
kind assistance and assuring him that there is still much
in the oft repeated saying that "The more you watch a
magician—the less you sometimes see."

ROUTINE NO. 2: In theory and basic dramatic
progression this second routine is substantially the same
as the foregoing but has a few twists that may appeal
to some.

The performer approaches the spectator with a
single piece of rope about sixteen or eighteen feet long
doubled in half.

This rope has been prepared by treating a diagonal slice on one end with the Liquid Rope Gimmic and another diagonal cemented joint about eight or nine inches back from the center of the long double strand toward the prepared end.

The rope is displayed to the spectator and he is then requested to cut same into two equal lengths at the loop in the exact center as presented to him by the performer. This results in an eight or nine-foot length for each.

Now the performer forces a choice of the ropes so that the spectator will have the unprepared piece while the performer retains the prepared one.

The same general progression and speeches are employed as per Routine No. 1 except that the performer must be careful to place the end of his rope that has the cemented joint between his first and second fingers closest to his knuckled joint so that when he brings up his false center loop this joint will be at the middle of same.

Two pairs of scissors can be used here, a sharp pair for the spectator and a duplicate for the performer, which has been prepared by dulling a one-inch section of both blades close to the center so that when the rope is placed therein the scissors will not actually cut but merely grab so that the cement joint can be pulled apart in simulation of a cutting movement.

Or, some comedy may be injected by giving the spectator the sharp scissors as before and the performer picking up a huge hunting knife which has been dulled on the portion of the edge close to the handle.

After the "Do As I Do" cutting episode the action leaves the spectator, as before, with two short pieces knotted together and the performer a piece shorter by the length of the loop he severed at the cemented joint and the two ends both carrying the diagonal treated cuts.

Naturally, the performer discards his knot and the spectator's pieces of rope and proceeds the same as in the first routine with his own remaining piece of rope to the same climax.

So now, "Cut Yourself A Piece Of Rope"—and I hope you like it.

L. W. DOUBLE RESTORATION

We found that the softer, woven, types of rope dyed very well, looked highly effective and seemed most suitable for magical purposes. In the course of experimentation, we evolved the following:

The performer introduces three lengths of rope, each of a different color—red, white and green. These ropes are gathered up in the center and the three loops apparently thus formed are cut. Indeed, to show that the cut was genuine, the performer removes the white rope entirely and shows, to the satisfaction of everyone, that it is truly severed in the center.

The white pieces are tossed aside. An incantation is uttered over the red and green ropes. It is commanded that they retake their original form. Slowly the hand that has apparently been holding the cut centers is opened. The performer's command is found to have been obeyed. The ropes are restored.

If you are sufficiently interested to attempt the performance of the experiment, hie yourself to the nearest store and purchase half a dozen hanks of woven clothes line. Four of these hanks are cut into six-foot lengths. The other two hanks are cut into six-foot, four-inch lengths. We recommend the wholesale purchasing and cutting for soon we will send you on your way to the dyer's and he will charge you but little more for all the rope above mentioned than he would for but one-sixth of the amount.

The six-foot, four-inch lengths, we shall have dyed as follows: Four inches in the center is dyed red. The four inches immediately adjoining, on either, but not both, side, is dyed green. The rest of the rope is left white. Figure 455.

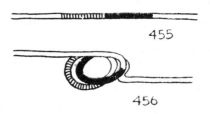

455

456

Half of the six-foot lengths are dyed green; the other half red.

Now, loop up the six-foot, four-inch, rope at the center so as to form three loops, one green, one red, and one white. A thread tied around these loops will serve to keep them in place until it is necessary to make use of the rope. Figure 456.

Lay this rope, thus prepared, over the table. A red and a green rope are laid beside it.

Pick up the ropes with the left hand and lay them on the right hand in the following order: Looped rope first (loop being concealed by the right fingers which are slightly cupped), then the green, finally the red. Show the ropes without exposing the loops.

457

With the left hand, gather up the ends of the ropes. The right hand apparently grasps the center of the ropes. Actually it does grasp the centers, but it is the loops that are allowed to come into view above the right fist. The left hand, having facilitated this move by pulling the ropes taut, comes up to aid in pulling the ropes into view.

It is these loops which are cut. The reader will readily follow that in so doing, one of the ropes is actually cut. The colored ends are completely trimmed away leaving in the performer's hands the red rope, the green rope and the severed white rope. The white rope is pulled free of the hand and tossed to the floor.

It but remains, now, to open the hand and show that a restoration of the other ropes has been effected.

THE L. W. ZENITH ROPE RESTORATION

An impromptu version of the feat was described in Chapter 5.

In this method a length of rope about two yards long is used. The ends are tied. A spectator determines the center of the resulting loop—a procedure which incidentally gives him the opportunity of examining this portion of the rope. A cut is made at this point, and the spectator examines and knots the ends, the rope being thus apparently divided into two equal portions. The performer now takes the rope and cuts the double center of the loop, giving—apparently—four pieces of equal length. He now has eight ends, as he shows. All the ends are trimmed away, when suddenly the performer separates his hands, and is seen to be holding between them the rope in a single length, fully restored! It may be examined!

Use soft woven rope. Cement the ends together. This gives an endless loop. Take an extra piece of rope, six inches long, and place it about the rope, at the point where the ends are cemented, in such a manner that it will appear to be the two ends, the join being hidden by the left hand. Come forward with the rope thus held, and calling attention to it, appear to tie the two ends together. Actually tie the extra piece about the rope, passing the ends twice about each other, instead of once as usual, so that the resultant knot will appear to be a double knot. This knot will slide freely on the rope.

Have a spectator come forward to assist, and ask him to locate the precise center of the rope. Without calling attention to the fact, this demonstrates that there is no fake join in the center of the rope, puzzling those who may have heard of that method. Now apparently the left hand takes the rope by the center—actually it secretly slides the knot down to the center, right hand retaining the cemented ends. Left hand now brings up center of loop and places that portion in right hand, keeping fact that knot is on it concealed, apparently to leave left hand free to pick up scissors to hand to spectator for examination. Right hand now drops center of loop, but as the knot is on that portion, it appears the ends of rope have been dropped and the center retained.

The spectator is invited to hold the "knotted ends." See that he holds the knot tightly with his hand, giving him no opportunity of investigating it. Place supposed center of loop in left hand, but instead of simply holding it spread, double over end of loop and grip with thumb, as in Figure 458. Taking scissors in right hand, apparently cut through loop, but actually cutting in an upward direction to give the illusion of a simple cut, you cut through double rope at point marked in Figure 458.

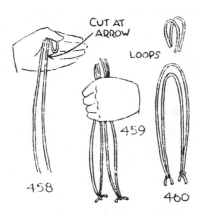

This leaves you, unknown to anyone, with a small double loop of rope thumb-palmed in left hand. It is instantly concealed by passing the scissors to the same hand.

Have the two ends of rope tied by the spectator. As the cemented ends have been cut off, he may of course examine ends. Call attention to the fact that the rope is divided into two equal parts.

Take back rope, holding scissors in right hand again, and place center of double rope in left hand, apparently pulling double loop into view. This position, after the next cut is made, appears to the spectators as shown in Figure 459. The actual state of affairs is shown in Figure 460. It is a small extra loop that is brought into view above hand.

Call attention to the fact that if the double rope is cut at a point equi-distant from the knots, the rope will be divided into four equal pieces. Apparently so cut it, actually cutting the small loop. Point out that you now have eight ends to the rope. Figure 459. Bring up the two knots and hold them also in the left hand, so that all eight ends project above the left hand, and say that you will trim off all the ends. Cut away the fake piece entirely. Cut away the extra piece which, tied about the rope, makes a fake knot. (Make sure that you know which is the fake knot!) Cut off the real knot entirely, as this is more effective than untying it. Put down the scissors. Apparently you are holding four unjoined pieces of rope. Catching an end in each hand, separate the hands; you have a single length of rope stretched between them, and it may be examined!

THE "MAXAM" TRIPLE CUT ROPE TRICK

Here is a rope trick in which the rope is cut and restored three times. The rope is ACTUALLY cut into TWO pieces—the pieces held far apart and yet the rope is restored to one piece and immediately given for examination.

Effect: A straight rope is shown. It has two knots of red twine tied eight inches apart, on each side of the center. The rope is doubled at one section of red twine, and loop containing knot is cut off and thrown out. This loop is positively cut out of the original rope. Pulling on one piece of rope, one short cut end is drawn into the hand. A pull on the other half draws the other short cut end down beside it. Without any further action, the rope is revealed restored and may be pulled upon to prove it! Absolutely nothing has been secretly removed from the rope.

The other section of red twine is cut off, cut ends drawn down into the hand as before, and again the rope is instantly restored.

NOW FOR THE CLIMAX. A loop is formed at the center and cut off. The skeptic's doubts are quelled as the two SEPARATE cut pieces are taken far apart, actually cut entirely in two; not tied at one end, etc. Two ends are now tied together by a square knot, and the left hand grasps the knot and rubs it along the rope BLENDING THE TWO ROPES INTO ONE, as the knot vanishes. There is no exchange of the rope, as the same rope that is cut three times is the one restored and THROWN OUT FOR EXAMINATION.

SPECIAL ROPE: Winston Freer has originated a specially constructed rope that makes this routine possible. It appears to be a little over three feet long but is actually over six feet in length. Refer to Figure 461. Careful examination will reveal that the rope is actually doubled back on itself. Both ends are actually at one end. What appears to the audience to be the second end of the rope is actually its center. See A in Figure 461.

Two slits are made in the outer, sheath-like half of the rope. These tiny slits are about three inches to each side of the apparent center. A piece of red twine is passed through one of the slits, tied around that portion of rope within the sheath, the ends passed around the sheath itself and tied with a bow-knot. The same thing is done at the second slit with another piece of twine. The knots conceal the slits. Figure 461.

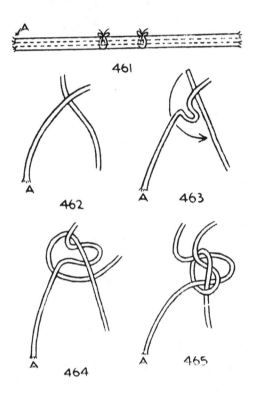

461

462   463

464   465

PRESENTATION: Place a fan in your pocket, or near a well or other place of concealment on your stand. Toss the rope to an elderly person at your LEFT for examination. Take it back, and hold it by the ends of one of the red-bow strings, making certain that these strings rise directly from the bows, and that neither passes under the rope on the way to your fingers. Double the rope sharply at this bow, and as you hold back the sheath, or outer casing of the rope, with the left fingers pull up the strings with the right hand, pulling first on the one that seems to "give" first and then on the other. First the bow will untie, then the strings will release from around the rope, and finally they will draw the core through the slit in the sheath of the rope, exposing a duplicate loop to be cut off. Cut off this core-loop with the string on it, and throw it out to your right. Now for a beautiful move that is possible only in this method.

Holding the ropes with the long ends hanging down, and with the short cut ends showing above the left fingers, pull down on first one long rope and then the other VISIBLY drawing each of the short ends in turn down into the finger-grip, actually into the sheath of the rope itself. Stop when the ends are just flush with the opening of the sheath. Use the fan to cause the restoration and instantly shake out the rope and show it restored. You have absolutely nothing to dispose of.

Now, repeat this, using the other string in the same way. One short end will not draw down this time, however, as it was severed from the rest of the core by the first cut. You merely cut that short end off flush with the opening in the sheath, draw the other end beside it, fan, and again show the rope instantly restored. Pull hard on it now to prove this.

SUPER FINALE: All this merely leads up to the final ACTUAL CUT and complete separation of the rope. Trim away all hollow parts of the rope. Hold the complete half of the rope in the left hand, END A DOWN; the waste piece of rope in the right hand. Tie the two pieces of rope together with this knot. Refer to Figures 462, 463, 464, and 465.

With this knot, you get the waste piece tied around a loop near the upper end of the complete half, so that, by pulling slightly on the complete half you will release the knot and can palm off the knot and the waste rope. These you dispose of as you go for the fan to 'fan in' the last restoration as you did the first two.

TO RESTORE THE ROPE to its original length, grasp the core at the cut end of the complete half with the right fingers, and with the left hand still pretending to hold the knot, you reach up and skin the sheath back under the pretext of "blending the rope together by rubbing the knot along them." Skin the sheath back in one motion extending the whole length of the rope with the rope pointing endwise at the audience. This will stretch the rope to its original length.

After pulling on it you toss it out to those at your EXTREME RIGHT, so that the first examiner may not have the chance to notice the fact that the rope, while substantially the same in appearance as at first, now "feels different" and is softer, though being the same rope!

PATTER STORY: "The Hindu Mystic knows how to weave the cut ends of a rope back together by a mere touch of his fingers, a feat that has been absolutely baffling to western devotees of the Magic Art. Recent developments, however, enable me to perform that feat in a way peculiar to the Hindu. He uses a rope of this sort (toss out), and he cuts it while the identifying markers are in view. Besides his ceremonial knife or scissors, he uses a fan, of which I have recently become the custodian. (Show fan; replace it in your pocket or on the table, and take the rope back.)

Permit me to cut off the markers as I once saw an old Yogi do! You may have it as a souvenir of the strangest mystery your eyes have ever witnessed! Toss out cut piece with string tied on it. And now came an odd ceremony. (Pull ropes down, and fan them.) Suddenly, to our amazement, that rope became restored in one, unbreakable piece! (Pull hard to prove this, and to keep rope moving.)

We pleaded with the old fellow to do it again for us, and in return for a couple of rupees tossed into his collection basket, he did this. . . (Pull up and cut off other string, toss out, pull down on one rope, snip off other even, fan and restore as before.)

So it is, with the fan, and the secret of how the Yogi worked, I can now reproduce this feat to your entire satisfaction. It seems that he had a piece of rope which he doubled over and cut off at the fold, so: (Cut; throw away piece.) If that cut were not enough, he could have cut pieces from all four ends. . . (ACTUALLY SEPARATE THE ROPES with a dramatic pause. Cut away the "hollow parts" of ropes but be very careful not to cut off end A.) He knotted the ends together . . . so . . . (Tie special knot.) And he wound the rope around the knot. (Palm knot and waste piece. Dispose of them when you get fan). Then he would fan the knot in his left hand for a moment (replace fan) and he could blend the knot and ropes together into one solid, perfect rope which we could examine to our satisfaction and find no sign of the three cuts!"

CHAPTER 8
MISCELLANEOUS ROPE TRICKS

Chapter 8. MISCELLANEOUS ROPE TRICKS

STABBING THE LOOP

A length of soft rope is laid on the table as shown in Figure 466. The performer sets the tip of one finger

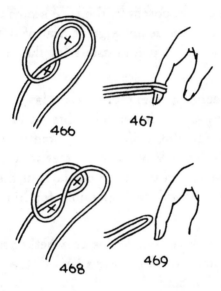

466   467

468   469

in either one of the circles of the "Figure 8" (indicated with a cross). He then tells someone to draw away the ends of the rope together. The result is that the performer's finger is caught in a loop, possibly in the very manner depicted in Figure 467. The string is retained differently according to which loop the finger has been placed within.

After doing this for a few times and showing that the rope invariably loops about the finger, the performer again lays down the rope. He puts his finger in a loop, either one marked with cross in Figure 468, and this time, when the rope is drawn away, it comes clear of the finger. Figure 469.

A study of the drawings will make everything clear. When he lays down the rope for the last time, the performer places it just a little differently from the first few times. It is laid as shown in Figure 468, instead of the way shown in Figure 466.

To the casual observer, the rope seems to be laid as before, but there is really a great deal of difference, because in this case it is impossible for the loops to catch the finger.

An effective presentation is to lay out the rope several times as in Figure 466. Stab a loop each time with an ornamental knife. Each time you succeed in retaining the loop. When a volunteer is convinced how easy it is, hand him the knife but lay out the rope as in Figure 468. It will be impossible for him to be successful.

You can have him bet as to whether he will succeed or fail and you can always lay out the rope so that he will lose his bet.

The proper methods of laying out the rope can be learned in a few minutes, by following the diagrams carefully with a piece of rope. If you wish, the ends of the rope may be tied together at all times. The trick depends for its success on the careless manner in which it is performed.

THE BACHELOR'S NEEDLE

A piece of soft rope, about two feet in length, is knotted at one end. This knotted end is allowed to hang down over the thumb of the left hand, the rope passing through the crotch of the thumb and forefinger close to the base of the thumb as shown in Figure 470. About

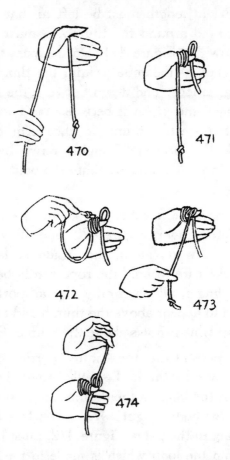

one-third of the rope at the end of which the knot is tied, should hang down below the left hand thumb, Figure 470, while its other end is grasped in the right hand as shown.

The portion of the rope held in the right hand is now wound around the thumb. Wind the rope towards you, bringing it down around the thumb, Figure 470, and up into the crotch between the left thumb and fore-finger until several turns of rope have been wound around the thumb.

A sufficient length must be left to that portion of the rope wound around the thumb to make a loop as follows, shown in Figure 471. Do not pass the last six or eight inches of the rope around the thumb but, in-stead, bring its loose end down between the left thumb and forefinger and pinch it between the two so that it will project above the thumb in the form of a loop, Figure 471, the loop end hanging down between the thumb and forefinger and touching the palm at the base of the fingers.

Now grasp the knotted end with the right hand thumb and forefinger, Figure 472, and allow the slack to scrape, as it were, along the inside surface of the thumb. Take care to hold the rope firmly between the thumb and finger, allowing only a small portion of the knotted end to appear above the thumb and to lie along-side the loop which shows above the thumb, Figure 472.

It is important that the knotted portion of the rope which is above the thumb be pulled toward your body and run past the loop on the thumb side of the loop that is nearer your body, Figure 472. The free end of the rope showing in the palm, Figure 472, must be between the palm and the loop which is made in the palm, Fig-ure 472, as the knotted end is pulled up between the forefinger and thumb, Figure 472.

You should now let go of the knot for a moment. Then suddenly grasping it between the thumb and fore-finger of the right hand, as shown in Figure 503, give it a quick pull. The rope is thereby mysteriously threaded in the loop as shown in Figure 473 and 474.

To repeat without arousing suspicion, pull the knotted end from out the loop and bring it up inside the thumb just as before, remarking, as you do so, that you will make it a still more difficult matter to thread the loop. Accordingly drop the knotted end and, taking hold of the loose end in the palm, Figure 472, pull it downward so that the loop above your thumb will become still smaller. You now take up the knotted end and give it a quick pull. The rope is again threaded in the loop.

SAME RING—SAME FINGER

Select a light, skeleton type chair, preferably one with a smooth seat, but particularly one of the kind which has an open space between the seat and the back. In other words, the back does not extend all the way down to the seat but only to within about four inches,

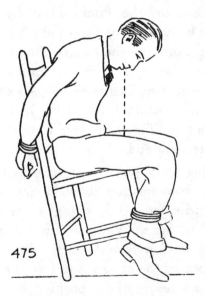

475

leaving that much open space between the two. Figure 475.

Seat yourself in this chair. Extend your arms around the back of the chair and request a spectator to tie your wrists together in that position. Next, request that one ankle be tied to each front leg of the chair.

A borrowed ring is placed between your teeth. After a screen is placed in front of you, ask the spectators to tell you which finger of either your right or left hand that they wish the ring to appear upon.

While they are deciding, tip the chair backward as far as you can, by extending the feet and toes downward, leaning forward at the same time to keep your balance. Now extend your neck and head downward as far as possible and let the ring drop into your lap, between your legs and thence down on to the seat of the chair. This can be easily and noiselessly done by opening the knees after the ring has been dropped into the lap. Next assume your original position with all four legs of the chair on the floor. Now by putting the weight of the body on your feet, and lifting yourself up and off the seat of your chair and a little forward at the same time, you can by a series of repeated motions of the body force the ring backward on the seat of the chair so that it is soon within reach of the hand. Once it is obtained, it is not difficult to place it on the desired finger of the selected hand.

While this body pushing process is taking place, continue your conversation about having no assistants, except the spirits, etc., but doing so with the teeth tightly closed so that the voice sounds the same as it did when the ring was between the teeth. Drop the ring into your lap as soon as the screen is in front of you.

As soon as the ring is in position, ask to have the screen removed. Allow anyone to remove the ring from the finger on which it was requested to appear.

SEYMOUR DAVIS' "SINBAD'S ROPE"

THE LOOKS: The performer exhibits a length of rope, said to have belonged to Sinbad, the Sailor, and invites a spectator to assist him in illustrating a sea story. The rope is measured with the aid of a tape measure, and a piece about 40 inches long is cut off. The story is now begun and, as it progresses, the rope is effectively used to illustrate Sinbad's tale. The spectator is asked to cut off 2 inches of the rope, thus shortening it to 38 inches. However, when the story is finished, the rope is again measured, but it is found to measure 42 inches instead of 38.

THE HOW: Any tape measure may be used. Soft, cotton rope, such as is obtainable at almost any hardware store, is used. Have a 4-foot piece and a pair of scissors ready.

When spectator comes on platform, trim off one frayed end of the rope, and hand him the scissors. Place trimmed end of rope even with end of tape measure, holding tape measure between first and middle fingers of right hand, the left fingers keeping end of rope and measure even. Now slide right hand along to measure the rope, holding tape measure taut but letting rope slide loosely between right thumb and first finger. Of course the rope should not be held so loosely that it dangles, but it should be kept just taut enough so that it will lay along tape measure. Spectator is allowed to cut off rope at exactly 40 inches. Performer begins Sinbad's actual story at this point of the trick. He allows spectator to measure and cut off exactly 2 inches of the rope. The 2-inch piece is then cut into bits and burned, or the pieces scattered along the rope as one would scatter salt.

Performer calls attention to the fact that the rope is now 38 inches long. Continuing his story, performer again measures rope in the following manner: Spectator is asked to hold one end of rope even with end of tape measure. The performer then measures the rope in the same manner as at first, except that he keeps the rope taut and the measuring tape loose this time, thus stretching the rope to the 42-inch mark.

Sounds simple, doesn't it? Just try it move by move. It works!

THE SAY: Build a story around the following plot, using your own words and manner best fitted to your particular personality: Sinbad, the Sailor, was at sea. There came a terrific storm. The small sailing craft must be anchored to shore. Great Scott! The rope won't reach! (Rope measured, 40 inches long.) The boat is floating away. Ha! Sinbad to the rescue. He cuts off one end (2 inches cut off rope), ties it to the other end (2-inch piece burned or vanished in any way desired), swims ashore and anchors boat by tying rope to a telephone pole (pole found to be 42 inches long). Sinbad given engraved collar button for valor. (If rope ever fails to stretch to the 42-inch mark, a good excuse is that Sinbad used up some of the rope in tying the knot.)

H. BERSON'S MIRACLE ROPE GROWTH

EFFECT: The performer, after the presentation of one of the many cut and restored rope trick routines, adds an additional climax by taking the rope he has just finished using and has it marked with a tag, piece of gummed paper, or in any other way that suggests itself. In full view of the audience, he draws the rope through his hand and shows it has increased to twice its original length. The markings are still attached to prove conclusively that there has been no substitution. Rope tricks have proven very popular and this additional effect will be welcomed by all.

HOW IT IS DONE: An extra piece of rope is used. It must be an exact duplicate in color, texture and appearance. This duplicate may be any reasonable length but we suggest that it be the same length as the one first displayed. Treat both ends of both ropes, so it will not matter which ends are used, with a good rope cement. Let this dry thoroughly.

Take off your coat and place one piece so that when the coat is put back on the rope will be concealed up the sleeve with one end near the cuff. The balance of the rope is so arranged and pleated that it may be drawn from the sleeve easily and without tangling.

If you wish, you many attach a loop of flesh-colored catgut to the lower end of the rope up the sleeve. Let this loop come down and over the middle finger. Even a loop of pink silk thread may be used for this purpose. The thread or catgut will facilitate getting the extra piece of rope down into the hands without any fumbling or hesitancy.

The effect, as it now proceeds, is the showing of the visible length of rope, having it marked in some manner to preclude substitution, and then taken back by the performer. The end of the extra piece in coat sleeve is pressed to the end of the visible rope and, as they have both been treated with rope cement, a rolling pressure between the fingers causes them to join firmly together.

If done in a proper manner, the joining is invisible and a good rope cement will hold sufficiently that a good pull may be made later to prove that the rope is all in one piece.

With the two rope ends securely attached, the performer closes his hand but allows the end to protrude through the opening of fist made by the curled thumb and forefinger. Gradually pulling on the rope, the two pieces are brought into view as one, much to the astonishment of the audience. The part that is marked should be produced at the beginning by having the marker near the end you proceed to pull from the fist first. Having produced the rope, you display its doubled length. Because the fact that its increased size is so very evident, no measuring should be necessary to prove that it has been caused to grow to twice its size.

Suitable patter should be arranged. You might remark that this rope wasn't long enough for the Hindu boy to quite reach heaven when originally tossed in the air. By some unseen power he was able to increase its length. Thus he passed on to the Great Happy Hunting Ground of the Mighty Allah that had gone on before, etc.

WINSTON FREER'S ALAGEN ROPE

EFFECT: The magician displays a three-foot length of rope and simply by pulling it through his hands it stretches to more than six feet in length. After the stretched rope has been examined, the magician may use same in a rope cutting routine.

In this method there is no exchange and no body or sleeve work. You simply pull the rope through the hands and it stretches.

SECRET: The rope is constructed exactly the same as the "Maxam" rope described in Chapter Seven. Refer to Figure 461. Of course, the "Alagen" rope lacks the slits and red strings included in that illustration.

The working will be obvious. You simply grasp the "core" and pull it out as you skin the "sheath" back. The rope not only doubles in length but may be immediately examined.

An odd variation, suggested by Mr. Freer, is to color the "sheath" a bright red. Now, the rope not only increases to twice its original length but changes from red to white.

WINSTON FREER'S MASTER MUSCLE

EFFECT: The magician places a short piece of rope, it need only be five or six inches long, on the table in front of anyone. They are requested not to touch it but they may look it over from end to end as closely as they wish. Now, the magician picks it up on each side of the center with the forefinger and thumb of each hand only. Slowly and deliberately, HE PULLS IT APART. It looks like a return engagement of Samson.

SECRET: The rope used is a piece of that left after working either the "Maxam" or "Alagen" tricks. A slit is made half way through the rope with a sharp razor blade. This slit is on the underside when the rope is placed on the table for visual inspection. The rope frays out when it is pulled apart. This fraying conceals the fact that the rope had previously been tampered with.

WINSTON FREER'S "TUG-OF-WAR" ROPE

Imagine a tug-of-war contest between three or four members of the audience and the magician. The odds look very much against the magician but he has no trouble holding his own. For some unknown reason the rope seems to slide through the hands of his opponents and, without being able to prevent it, they all fall to the floor in a heap.

The magician is the victor with all the rope in his hands and stranger yet, the rope is more than twice its original length and can immediately be used in a rope cutting routine.

SECRET: The original length of the rope is six feet. It is constructed the same as the "Alagen" rope. In other words, you have a rope within itself with both ends at one end and the center at the other. If the core is grasped by one man, and another man tries to pull against him by pulling on the outer rope, or sheath, the second man will be unable to prevent the rope from pulling out through his hands. Several opponents may be vanquished in this way, as each falls off the faked end of the rope, not realizing that his team mate has just fallen off behind him.

PRESENTATION: Have a silk or cotton handkerchief at hand. Invite three volunteers, young men preferred, to have some fun with you. Start out with a tug of war contest in which you and one chap pull against the other two.

Now, have them all pull against you. As in any tug of war contest, you tie the handkerchief around the rope near your end, between you and your nearest opponent.   As you tie this, whisper to your nearest opponent to keep a good hold on the rope near this handkerchief—not to grip too hard, nor let go.

You skin back the outer sheath a bit as the handkerchief it tied right over the place where the sheath ends on the core. You grasp the core in one hand, gripping the sheath lightly too with the thumb and forefinger.   Have it understood that only a straight grip is allowed as it would be unfair to you for them to wind the rope around their hands, etc.

Now, start pulling easily.   There are three against you, the magician.   See that they are all near the wing and you are about the center of stage. Suddenly you release your hold on the sheath and continue pulling on the core. Run away from them quite rapidly until they are all seated on the floor looking surprised and foolish. You hold all the rope, hank and all. Apparently the rope has "stretched" out to more than twcie its original length.

It is well to have a cushion or carpet for them to fall on.   See that they do not stand near any tables or hard objects they might strike their heads on as they fall.

THE HYPNOTIZED ROPE

EFFECT: A novel interlude that was described to me by John Lippy, Jr.

Suppose the magician is going to present the "Vase Of the Orient" mystery.   He first picks up the short length of rope from his table and holds it vertically in front of him by the very ends at his extreme fingertips. The right hand is at the top.   Slowly he removes this hand and the rope remains erect held only by the left hand at the lower end.

Once more the upper end is grasped in the right hand and again it is released. This time the rope falls limp and may be used in any trick that requires an ordinary, short length of rope.

SECRET: A quantity of sugar is dissolved in a basin of water. The rope is soaked in this solution and then hung up to dry. When dry, the rope will stand stiff and erect by itself.

PRESENTATION: Have the rope laid out perfectly straight on your table. Pick it up by one hand at each extreme end. Hold it out straight and horizontally for a moment and then shift it to a vertical position with the right hand at the top. The right hand is removed, as explained, and the rope rises straight and firm from the left hand. When the right hand again grasps the rope, it is between the forefinger and thumb which slide along it to the top, starting at just above the left fingers. This action permits the thumb nail to press against the side of the rope away from the audience and break the crystalized shell that supports the rope. This time, when the right hand lets go, the rope falls limp.

GRANT AND MAILLOW'S ROPES OF BENGAL

A piece of cardboard, 6 x 9 inches, is formed into a cylinder in full view of the audience and a rubber band snapped around it to hold it in place. Two unprepared ropes are next handed out for examination and threaded through the cylinder. The performer cuts one of the ropes short, then merely pulls on it and it stretches back to full length. This is repeated twice more.

A spectator is handed a slip bearing a written prediction. Another length of rope is cut from one of the ends making a short and a long rope. The spectator is allowed free selection of either rope and is permitted to remove it from the tube himself. Whichever rope he has selected agrees with the prediction.

SECRET AND PRESENTATION: The moves are as follows: Two four-foot ropes are displayed as in

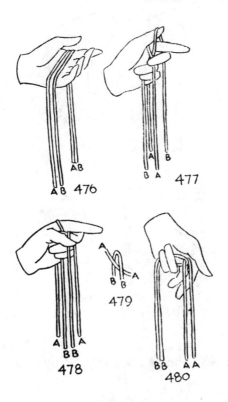

Figure 476. The ropes are crossed and the thumb slipped under rope "B". Figure 477.

The thumb is brought down, Figure 478, which brings both "B" ends together.

Figure 479 illustrates the position of the ropes at this stage.

The hand is dropped to the side. This brings both "A" ends together. Figure 480.

The fingers are closed around the ropes to conceal their "linked" nature. Figure 481.

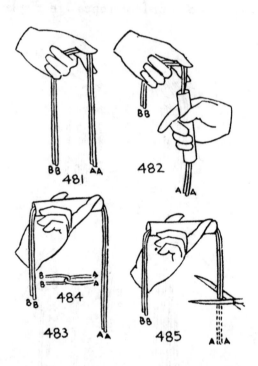

Figure 482 shows the ropes being threaded through the tube.

Figure 483 pictures the ropes ready for cutting. The ends "A-A" extend much farther from the tube.

Figure 484 reveals the actual position of the ropes in the tube.

Equal lengths are cut from the ends "A-A" and passed for examination. Figure 485.

Cut a foot length from one "A" end. This makes a short and a long rope. Figure 486.

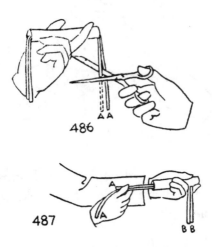

486

487

The tube is reversed. The "A-A" ends are concealed behind the arm while "stretching" the rope. Figure 487.

Cut a foot length from a "B" end making a short and a long rope.

The "B-B" ends are concealed behind the arm while stretching the rope. Same as Figure 487 with the exception that the position of the rope ends are reversed.

Again cut a foot length from one "B" end.

A prediction has been written which states that the spectator will select the short rope. If the tube is offered as in Figure 488, it matters little which end he chooses as both ends, "B-B", belong to the short rope.

If the tube is reversed, and the prediction made accordingly, the spectator will select the long piece. In either case, the performer holds one end of the rope at the opposite end of the tube and pulls at the same time that the spectator does.

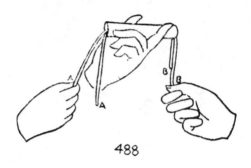

488

NOTE: The moves depicted in Figures 477, 478, 479, 480, and 481 are made while picking up the tube from the table.

HERMAN HANSON'S CLIMAX ROPE TRICK

This feat of apparent restoration has been reserved until now because of its similarity to the preceding trick.

EFFECT: A length of rope is openly cut into two equal parts. These are placed in a cylinder made from an unprepared magazine, or sheet of paper, with an elastic band around it to keep it in shape. The two ends of the rope above the cylinder are taken by a spectator on one side and the performer on the other, they slowly pull the rope out and it is found to be again in one piece. All trace of the cut has disappeared.

PRESENTATION: Show the magazine, roll it into a cylinder about two inches in diameter, and put the elastic band around it. Stand this on your table. Pick up the rope and test it by jerking it sharply between the hands. Take the scissors and cut it in half. Hold the two pieces in the right hand between the thumb and forefinger, Figure 489. Take the center of the first rope be-

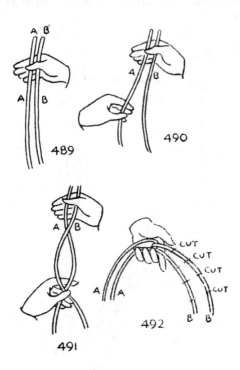

489

490

491

492

tween the first finger and thumb of the left hand, pull it a little to the left and count "One," Figure 490. Now take hold of the second rope at its center in the same way, taking care to cross this second piece over the first one and insert the second and third fingers between the ropes at the point at which they cross over each other, Figure 491. Count "Two."

Let both ends of the rope fall from your right hand and at the same time turn your left hand over slightly, bringing its palm toward the floor. The two ropes will

now be looped together as in Figure 492, the two ends
of one piece being on one side of the hand and those of
the second piece being on the other. As far as the audience is concerned, you have simply taken both pieces
by their middles. In order to divert any suspicion at

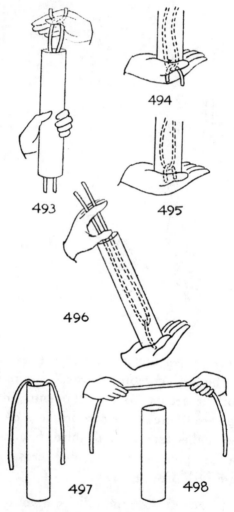

493   494   495   496   497   498

this point, however, it is advisable to ask for the assistance of a spectator as you make this move.

A volunteer having come forward, hand the scissors to him and, with the ropes held in your left hand, concealing the loops, invite him to cut off several pieces of both ropes and offer the ends of rope BB, Figure 492. When he has done this, take the scissors and cut off several more pieces from the same ends, thus ensuring that the loop in Figure 491 will be very short. Hand the scissors back to the spectator and take the ropes in the right hand, holding them as shown in Figure 493.

Pick up the cylinder with the left hand, lower the ends of the ropes into it, Figure 493, and, as the right hand touches the top of the cylinder, turn it upside down, using both hands, Figure 494 and 495. Pull the ends now in the left hand upwards a little and at the same time release one end of the loop, gripping the other end in the right thumb crotch. Correctly done the audience sees, apparently, the two ends of the ropes being pulled up into the cylinder, Figure 496.

The situation now is this: You are holding the cylinder in the left hand and two ends of the rope are hanging down outside as in Figure 497. You have the small piece of the original second rope hidden in your right hand. Ask the spectator for the scissors, take them from him with your right hand and put them in your pocket, letting the small piece of rope drop with them.

Ask the spectator to take hold of one end of the rope, seize the other end yourself and pull the rope slowly out of the cylinder. The climax is reached when the middle of the rope comes into view and it is seen to be in one piece again, Figure 498. Unroll the cylinder, show it empty, and hand the restored rope to the spectator as a souvenir.

PERCY ABBOTT'S "EASY-DO" ROPE TRICK

The effect is to make two cuts in a six foot length of rope, and bring about a restoration without resorting to the business of trimming the knots and palming the fake pieces and so on.

Here are Mr. Abbott's instructions:

Refer to Chapter Six for the moves I use in the cutting—I have used this method of rope cutting for many years and simply added the Brema fake when the Convincing Rope Trick was given to the magic fraternity.

The supposedly cut rope is draped around the neck and a 5-pound paper sack is shown. One small corner is cut from the bottom of the sack and one end of rope is threaded through from the inside of the sack. The first knot in the rope prevents the rope from going all the way through. More rope is stuffed into the sack until the second knot is out of sight of all spectators.

The mouth of the sack is now twisted around the rope, and ends of rope can now be held by two members of the audience. Here you stress the point that it is impossible for you to tamper with the rope at the cut sections as same is sealed within the confines of the paper sack, therefore, the paper sack is their protection against trickery on your part.

You now grasp the mouth of the sack, requesting the spectator holding the end of rope that passes through the hole in the bottom of the sack to release his hold. The other spectator holding his end of the rope, you skin the sack completely off the rope, crush it, and nonchalantly throw it to one side. The rope is completely restored.

U. F. GRANT'S AMAZING ROPE TRICK

Now for the first time this amazing rope trick is revealed to the magicians of the world. It is one used by its originator, U. F. Grant, on special occasions only when magicians were not present, with the thought of keeping it exclusive. Only a few magicians were let in on the secret, one being Max Holden, who saw Grant perform it on a special show in 1928.

Always it has been the magician's dream to take a single length of rope and, without any loops or false ties, to cut it in half and hold the two pieces separately; then, without exchanging the rope, to completely restore it, and at the finish to be able to throw the rope to the audience as a souvenir.

That is exactly what happens in this effect, which Grant has dubbed the Amazing Rope Secret. It is a rope trick that has stood the test and actually fooled every audience before whom it has been worked, including the few magicians who have witnessed it.

So, after reading the secret, do not discard it and say, "I am afraid I could not get away with it."

SECRET AND WORKING: At the outset let us stress the point that certain conditions are necessary and as this is a feature trick, it is not to be used as a pocket stunt, but to be used only on special shows where you have a fairly large audience and you are at a short distance from them, and if possible on a platform or stage.

First of all, decide upon the rope you intend to use. Any soft, pliable rope, such as used in most cut and restored rope tricks, will do.

Take a piece of BLACK felt and sew it into a tube just large enough to slip over the rope and about two and a half inches long. Slip this to the center of the rope. Then take the two ends of rope and cement them together.

NOW if you are wearing a dark brown or blue suit, or a Tuxedo, hold the rope at the cemented ends and allow the rope to hang down in front of your body so it hangs in front of trousers, the black tube, invisible against the dark suit, causing the appearance of two ends of the rope. In other words, it appears as if you are holding the center of the rope and the two ends are hanging down in front of you. Hold the rope fairly close to the body.

Cut at the top at cemented section and trim off a little at each end to get rid of all the cemented surface. Hold the ropes at top, one in each hand, about two and a half inches apart, and, the audience apparently sees the two separate ends at the bottom. They see two separate distinct ropes.

Bring the two ends at top together in one hand. Other hand reaches down and apparently catches the two ends, but actually covers the tube part in palm of hand with each end of rope coming out of the fist thus formed.

NOW pull the rope through the hand. As you do, the tube remains in the hand and the rope comes out in one piece. Cloth tube is crushed in the hand and the completely restored rope is thrown out to the audience for thorough examination—and may be taken away.

You have performed a Miracle rope trick the audience will long remember.

PATTER SUGGESTION. Step forward with the rope and patter to the effect that magicians for years have dreamed of a rope trick where they could take one single length of unprepared rope such as you are holding and actually cut it in half without any false moves or ties, and hold each piece separate and away from the other; then without exchanging this rope, restore it in full view and allow that same rope to be taken home as a souvenir by any spectator. That is exactly what you are about to perform, a trick you have developed after many years of experimenting.

Then go on to say they are to watch you closely and see that everything is open and above board—you will even work it in slow motion. By working it slow-motion and deliberately, it will help, as then it will not be noticed that you are careful not to move the rope too much after it is cut. To the audience it will appear as if you are holding it still and handling it slowly so they can follow more closely.

Now go ahead and work trick as explained with normal serious patter. As you pull the rope through the hand to be restored, cry out, "A MIRACLE," and at the same time throw the rope into the audience with a wide sweep, and take a bow.

CHAPTER 9
THE HINDOO ROPE TRICK

Chapter 9. THE HINDOO ROPE TRICK

RUPERT SLATER'S MOTH AND ROPE

The instructions that follow are in Mr. Slater's own words.

EFFECT AND PATTER: The first and last verses should be spoken in the performer's natural voice and the intermediate verses in the local dialect of the place where performing.

> From Greenland's icy mountains,
> To Buckingham Street in the Strand,
> They say that the Indian Rope Trick
> Is the myth of a Mystic Land.
>
> Will I have a drink sir?
> Not arf I won't with you,
> Make it a couple of pints, sir,
> And I'll tell you what I'll do,
> I'll show you the Indian Rope Trick,
> Then you'll know that the thing is true.
>
> I was only a private soldier sir,
> In eighteen eighty three,
> A' trying to do my duty,
> At Bombay by the sea,
> And when I thinks of the Rope Trick
> I laughs to myself with glee.
>
> I shall never forget the day sir,
> Out on the Barrack Square,

The officers, men and the ladies
Were all of 'em gathered there,
When in the midst of the crowd sir,
A rope went into the skies,
And a boy climbed up the rope sir,
Then vanished afore our eyes.

Now this was done in the open,
Under the blazing sun,
And yet the kiddie vanished,
And I didn't know how it was done.
But I said to myself I'd find out sir,
If it cost me a month of pay,
(Tho' we didn't get much at that time,
Only a penny a day).

So after the show was over,
I spoke to that Magic Wallah,
And he showed me how it was done sir,
When I gives him a half a dollar,
What: You don't believe me!
Then stand me a drop more beer,
And I'll show you the trick at once, sir,
In front of your eyes right here.

Look: an ordinary piece of rope sir,
    (Performer picks up rope)
And a moth of a brilliant hue,
    (He picks up moth)
Now if you watch me closely
I'll prove what I said was true,
I place the moth on the rope sir,
    (Performer does so)
Near the bottom end, just so,

Please notice sir what happens,
The moment I say "Go."

See: it's climbing up the rope sir,
Just like that Indian did,
It's going up the line sir,
Like the war-time soldiers did.
Higher and higher and higher,
It's nearly reached my hand,
BLIMEY SIR IT'S VANISHED!
NOW DO YOU UNDERSTAND?
      (Performer places rope on table.)

And from Greenland's icy mountains,
To Buckingham Street in the Strand,
They say that the Indian Rope Trick
Is the myth of a Mystic Land.

PREPARATION: I obtained a length of thick rope
from a marine store; it contained an inner cord which
I found could with careful manipulation be removed
leaving a kind of hollow rope which would just hold a
tube ¾ of an inch in diameter. I colored an 18-inch
length of this rope medium grey and when dry I mot-
tled it with black.

I made a cardboard tube 10 inches long and ¾ of
an inch in diameter. One end of the tube I plugged with
a piece of cork. In the side of the tube, near the opposite end, I made an oblong hole. I slightly smeared
the tube with Ste-fix, around the hole, and then inserted
it into the rope. I left it for a day and then with a razor
blade I cut a hole in the rope to correspond with the hole
in the tube.

I passed the end of a long piece of thin thread through the rope (from the opposite side to the hole and opposite to the top of the hole—Figure 499) then out

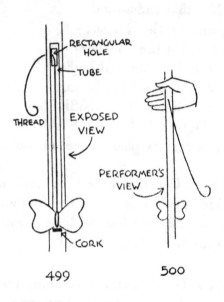

499   500

through the hole. To this end of the thread I attached the moth and I fastened the other end of the thread to the table.

The body of the moth I made from a cylindrical piece of lead, ½ an inch long and ¹⁄₁₆ of an inch in diameter, which I covered with a piece of colored tissue paper, and to which I attached wings made from a feather flower. If you take great care in putting it together a very large moth can be made which will function perfectly.

TO PERFORM: Pick the rope up with the forefinger and thumb of the left hand, the hole towards you, and exhibit. Transfer the rope to your right hand

and hold it as shown in Figure 500. As you place it into the right hand move the thumb towards the right so that the rope will make half a revolution, thus bringing the hole to the front. The audience will not see the opening because the right hand conceals it from their view.

Take the moth with the left hand; move forward till the thread adjusts itself so that you can suspend the moth near the bottom end of the cord or tube. Now slowly move the right hand forward, and the moth will appear to climb up the rope till it is hidden behind the right hand. Continue the pull and the body of the moth will pass through the hole; then bring the rope towards you and the weight of the lead will cause the moth and feathers to descend into the rope. Take the rope in the left hand, giving the half twist to bring the hole towards you again; exhibit and place on the table.

THE POCKET HINDU ROPE TRICK

Several years ago, Sid Lorraine showed me this interesting novelty.

EFFECT: A short piece of rope, about two inches long, is displayed. The performer seriously asserts that it is a sample of the actual type of rope used in the famous Hindoo Rope Mystery. The story of what really occurs, he explains, has been grossly exaggerated. The native wonder worker does toss the end of a coil of rope in the air. A small boy does climb the rope which mysteriously remains suspended vertically in the air BUT THE FEAT SUDDENLY TERMINATES WITH THE MAGICIAN CLAPPING HIS HANDS AND THE BOY AND ROPE SUDDENLY VANISHED FROM VIEW.

This remarkable trick, so it is said, can only be performed in the morning or in the evening. The reason for this is that the apparent disappearance of the boy and the rope is an illusion created by the slanting rays of the sun.

To illustrate his meaning, the perrormer holds the short piece of rope at the tips of his left fingers. A match is lighted and the right hand moves it slowly downward past the rope to simulate the slanting rays of the descending sun. This make-shift expedient is more successful than anticipated FOR THE ROPE ENTIRELY DISAPPEARS.

SECRET: Most of you are familiar with flash paper. In this trick a piece of flash rope is used. The patter concerning the slanting rays of the sun is to supply an excuse for the use of the lighted match to touch off the flash rope.

NOTE: The flash rope is also very effective when used as the sliding knot in numerous cut and restored rope routines. A candle flame, for instance. visibly welds the rope together again—or so it appears when the knot so completely vanishes.

THE VANISHING BOY

Collins Pentz describes a trick where a rope is thrown in the air and a small boy climbs up the rope and disappears, somewhat on the order of the much talked of Indian Rope Mystery. It may be presented on almost any stage, is easily accomplished and does not require much time or material to build.

By making a careful study of Figure 501, you will be able to see every detail of its working without much description.

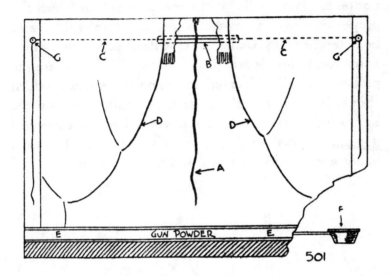

When the rope is thrown into the flies it drops to the floor and another trial is made. This time a person concealed in the flies catches and ties the upper end of the rope. The boy climbs to the top and while all of him but his hands and wrists are in view the powder is set off by a push button which produces a flash and smoke. Just as soon as the smoke rises and conceals the boy from the view of the audience, the cable "C" is quickly pulled and the boy is drawn behind the wings. From there he descends and runs around to the front of the house and comes running down the aisle.

Just as the boy starts on the journey for the wing, the rope is dropped to the stage.

For your further information, please consult Figure 501 again. "A" represents the rope which should be quite large. "B" is a piece of gas pipe attached to the cable. "C" which runs over pulleys at each end. "D" to "D" is the opening between the wings, which should not be too large. "E" is the metal trough in which the proper quantity of powder is placed. This will have to be determined by trial. "F" is a flash pan, from which wires run to an electric push button. "G" is where the pulleys should be located to support the cable, which should be tied securely at each end until the time the boy is to be drawn behind the wing. The short piece of gas pipe is used so the cable will not hurt the boy's hands and to give an easier and more solid grip.

502

504   503

DUNNINGER'S EAST INDIAN ROPE TRICK

The effect of this illusion is in line with the various ideas that have been planned to duplicate the Indian Rope Trick—namely, the vanish of a boy from a suspended rope in the center of the stage. The following is one of the most practical methods yet devised.

505

A coiled rope is on the stage. One end rises. Figure 502. When it is out of sight in the flies, a boy climbs the rope. The magician mounts an ordinary ladder and

385

covers the boy with a cloth. Figures 503 and 504. He descends the ladder; fires a pistol; and the cloth and rope fall. Figure 505. The boy is gone.

SECRET: The rope is drawn up by a strong piano wire. The end is fastened or retained when the rope reaches the flies. There is a batten above the top of the curtain which forms an opening behind which the rope is raised. From this batten a strong piano wire runs to the rope. Figure 506.

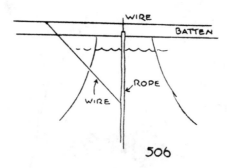

The boy climbs the rope. Attached to him is a skeleton wire frame or form. Figure 507. When he reaches the required spot, he attaches the form to the rope; and also attaches the piano wire to a special belt which is around his body. Figure 508.

The ladder is set by the curtain. When the performer extends the cloth, he momentarily covers the space between the rope and the curtain. The boy simply lets go of the rope. The weight of his own body instantly swings him off behind the curtain, as the wire comes down at a sharp angle. Figure 509. The magician does not hesitate. He wraps the cloth about the wire frame and leaves it hanging on the rope. When the pistol is fired, the rope is released from above and everything drops to the stage. Figure 505.

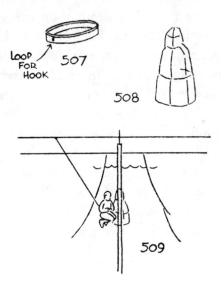

Note the great feature of this illusion—namely that the getaway of the boy is instantaneous. He swings off like a flash. Cumbersome back drops, hoisting winches or trick ladders are eliminated. The whole thing takes place in the fraction of a second—as rapidly as if the boy leaped out of sight. The covering between the curtain and the rope is no more than momentary.

A thin strong wire will do the work. The lighting should all be from in front, thus rendering the wire invisible. A back drop of a mixed design is preferable. Despite the remarkable effect of this illusion, the props required are inexpensive. With a rope, two wires and a skeleton form, the illusion can be adapted to almost any stage.

SVENGALI'S ROPE CLIMBING TRICK OF INDIA

Mr. W. T. Lawhead offers the following version:
EFFECT: The performer comes on the stage with a twenty-foot coil of rope on his left arm. He is accompanied by a small boy. On reaching the center of the stage he stops and, taking one end of the rope in his right hand, tosses it into the air. To the amazement of all, the rope does not drop back to the stage but remains stationary in a perpendicular position with no visible means of support. One end of the rope is on the stage. The other end dangles in the air some twenty feet above the performer's head. The boy then climbs to the top of the rope, where he remains a few seconds, and slides back down. The performer then grasps the rope and commands it to fall. It immediately drops back to the stage.

It is significant to note that the entire rope, the performer, and the boy, are in full view of the audience at all times. No confederates or back-stage assistance is required. There are no mirrors or sheet glass used. The trick can be performed in the open air, as it was originally.

SECRET: Twenty feet above the center of the stage, a piano wire is stretched across in a horizontal position. This fine wire will not be visible beyond the footlights and yet it will be sufficiently strong enough to hold up the weight of a boy or even a man. The rope used by the performer should be frayed at one end. Imbedded and concealed in the frayed part, securely fastened to the rope, fix a steel hook with four prongs. Two of the prongs are at right angles to the other two.

The prongs should be about the size and shape of ordinary fish hooks. That end of the rope which contains the hooks is the one the performer throws into the air. Standing directly under the piano wire, the performer throws the rope into the air in such a manner that the frayed end will come in contact with the wire and, as there is a hook reaching out in each direction imbedded in this frayed part, one of the hooks will catch on the wire. The boy, who has been trained to climb the rope, then climbs to the top. To all appearances, from the point of view of the audience, the rope and boy are suspended in the air with no means of support whatever.

After the boy slides back down the rope, the performer gives the rope a twirling motion which dislodges the hook from the wire and the rope drops to the floor. If the trick is performed in the open air, the wire should be stretched between two trees and the audience kept at a distance.

THE DISCOVERY: Many years have elapsed since the Rope Trick was performed in India. The secret of this trick, no doubt, is unknown to the present day fakirs and magicians of India. It probably belonged to the preceding generation. It is quite possible that the aged Hindoo fakir who did perform the trick some four decades ago thought that the secret of the modus operandi died at the time he did. He guarded his secret most carefully. Indian magicians of recent years have told travelers fanciful and weird tales of the rope trick but they have failed to demonstrate it when put to the actual test by real investigators.

After twenty years of research, interviewing travelers and East Indians, and listening to all kinds of impossible explanations ranging from hypnotism to the absolute denials that it was ever performed, the writer (Mr. W. T. Lawhead) has finally learned the secret from the lips of a high caste Brahman. He is of a wealthy East Indian family, was educated in America and England, and is one of the most influential personages in all India. I doubt if any magician, aside from the writer, has ever had the privilege of interviewing this leader of thought in the Far East.

When this Indian leader was a small boy in his native town, his father gave him a very elaborate birthday party one year. An aged fakir was hired for the occasion to perform his mystifying feats. The tricks were performed in the open parkway in front of the boy's home. When it came time for him to perform the rope trick, the boy's older sister excused herself from the guests and retired to the house. From a concealed position, she looked through an extra strong pair of binoculars and discovered that the rope was hooked on to a fine wire that extended from the dense foliage of one tree, across the open parkway, and into the dense foliage of a second tree. The fakir, evidently, had secretly strung the wire sometime the night before and so was "all set" for the party the next afternoon. The audience was kept at a considerable distance so it could not detect the wire.

As the trees were many feet apart, being on opposite sides of the open area, and as there were no branches or foliage directly above the upright boy and rope, it seemed as if nothing intervened between the top of the rope and the open sky, which made the illusion perfect.

J. K. WRIGHT'S INDIAN ROPE TRICK

The Indian Rope Trick, mentioned in every itinerary of the Orient, has been made world-famous by the fakirs of India, and as with all other unexplainable feats of legerdemain, the performance has usually been ascribed to hypnotism or even crowd-mesmerism. The rope, in accordance with this version, is merely cast aloft, and in the interval of the throw and before its descent, the spectators are hypnotized, their eyes seeing not, their minds retaining only what is told them by the fakir.

India is the land of a thousand iron-bound castes, no caste will enlighten the other, each looking upon the caste lower as a defilement if even thought of; but all the various strata are combined to defeat the foreigner. The natives of India keep their secrets. To this day it is unexplainable how the natives were kept advised as to the movement of the troops, the fall of cities, and other information which the British with the aid of heliographs and messengers were days in forwarding.

An Indian fakir is generally a descendant in a profession, be it entertainment, plain alms-seeking or disguised under some fanatical religious devotion. From childhood he assimilates knowledge concerning his particular bent, and practices with the patience only had by the Orientals, considering himself extremely well provided for if he obtains a single, simple meal every day. Hence his public appearance may be certain to be as perfect as humanly possible.

The performer of this rope trick must first of all have his rope, which if ever closely examined will be discovered to be a jointed affair, flexible in one direction only. This rope in the old days of the trick had to be assembled from carved pieces of selected teak. Even after the most careful assembly it might have broken in a dozen different places. When it was tested to the builder's satisfaction, it was given a woven sheath so that in appearance it was identical with other coils of rope in his possession. Then for months on end, the fakir would practice the handling and casting of the pseudo and ordinary ropes. When it was possible for him to cast the jointed rope to such perfection that it simulated that of the ordinary, he would then obtain an agile boy of small size and weight, and initiate him into the mysteries. Under-nourished and ill cared for, so that all growth had ceased, the boy selected for the work could be counted upon to maintain utter silence and to perform his part to perfection. To him it meant the realization of a Cinderella dream—he would have food each day and a place to sleep at night.

The performance would take place in a narrow alley, flanked with low buildings, or else in the end of a blind alley. Natives with tom toms and shrill pipes would serve to attract a crowd. When enough spectators were gathered one of the attendants would carefully increase the smudge from the incense until a suitable smoke screen was built up. The performer the meanwhile would be untangling, coiling and arranging his ropes with care and great display, and then unostensiously the prepared rope would be selected and thrown into the air. It would uncoil and remain in the air with a slight arc, the incense ascending in carefully regulated clouds, so that the end extending into the air was visible at times and completely obscured in other intervals.

At a command from the fakir the boy would run forward and begin to clamber up the rope, the fakir revolving in a circle meanwhile. When the boy ascended the roofs of the shops he would pause until the rope swung over the edge of a roof and, making certain that a billow of smoke hid his action, would drop to the roof and scuttle away. The fakir would continue to revolve, the smoke would grow less and the fakir would command the boy to descend. Upon receiving no reply he would seemingly grow angry and so jerk the rope that it would descend in a natural rope manner. The spectators would of course gasp and then display astonishment because the boy had not come hurtling down with the rope.

At a call from the fakir, a muffled voice would reply, which when traced would emanate from a wicker basket placed against the building wall, outside of the circle of spectators, and when opened with great show of unwrapping of rope and unlocking of fastenings, the boy who had ascended the rope, would be found by an assistant, locked and sealed in the basket.

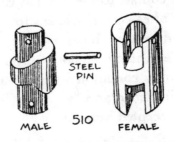

MALE   510   FEMALE

When performed by one of the Indian fakirs, an artist in his craft whose every motion commands attention, the rope trick is unsurpassed for effect. The construction of the rope is indicated in Figure 510. The sections are best machined from duraluminum or from nickel steel rods, with hardened pins of the same material. Even with the best of high tensile-tested material, breakage may occur several times before a rope is ready for use; for the object is to keep the diameter of the finished rope down to normal size. The sheath may be of braided cotton, stained to the proper shade, and should be woven thick and firm enough so that upon flexure of the rope no bumps or protrusions of sections are visible.

DAVID DEVANT'S HINDOO ROPE TRICK

The following account is that given by Mr. Devant himself.

It is a sad reflection upon the limitation of human practitioners of the magical art that the one trick in which the public never seems to lose interest, and about which there has been more argument and controversy than any other magical manifestation, should be an illusion which the public has never seen.

I refer, of course, to the "Indian Rope Trick," that legendary feat of eastern magicians for whose reproduction in England I once offered a salary of 5,000 pounds a year. There are many versions current regarding this trick and the only condition I made was that it should be presented in accordance with the broad outline of the generally accepted version.

The magician was to stand in the open air surrounded by spectators and was to throw one end of a rope into the air, the other end remaining on the ground. The rope was to remain suspended in mid-air while a boy climbed up, suddenly to vanish into space.

If the magician cared to embellish his performance in accordance with some of the more highly-colored versions of this illusion, such as by himself climbing up the rope after the boy, cutting his assistant to pieces amid blood-curdling screams and sending the pieces of his body hurtling to earth, then, so much the better value we would be receiving for our 5,000 pounds.

But, alas! For the annals of magic, it was not to be. Though my challenge was given the widest possible publicity, even to the extent of circulating specially-printed copies in India, no one came forward to claim the reward by achieving the impossible. For that is my considered opinion of the Indian Rope Trick—that, to present it in the form of my challenge, which basically agrees with most of the reported versions of the trick, is altogether beyond the limitations of scientific illusion and therefore, humanly impossible.

That no one has ever seen an Indian Rope Trick performed I do not for one moment assert. The evidence of its existence in some form or another is altogether too strong to dismiss the whole thing as a myth, but I believe that the trick is largely a tale that has grown in the telling and that those who have seen rope tricks in India are confusing many partial memories into one general and erroneous impression.

I have had personal experience of this tendency to unconscious exaggeration, particularly as regards magical illusions, in hearing some of my own tricks described after a long interval. The narrators have almost invariably colored the facts with their own imagination, and credited me with achieving the most enviable of miracles. In fact, I have even been hailed as the only living magician ever to have produced the Indian Rope Trick on a London stage!

As it happens, this tale has rather more basis of truth than more stories concerning the Indian Rope Trick because I did actually invent and present an illusion which reproduced the effects of this legendary trick as closely as any known principle of scientific illusion would permit.

In my version of the Indian Rope Trick, I first drew attention to a basket, about the size of a large suitcase, which was resting upon a stand, clear of the ground. Airily flourishing the basket to demonstrate its lightness, I then proceeded to unpack from it the dismembered portions of a man's body, a head, a trunk and the normal complement of legs and arms.

After the various portions had been publicly displayed and privately deemed "fakes" by my distrustful audience, they were carefully re-packed into the case and covered with a piece of cloth. Whereupon the covering gradually rose up to disclose, at length, a full-grown, living Indian standing in the basket.

The dismemberment and reunion of the Indian having been presented in accordance with the best traditions of the rope trick, if not altogether in the correct sequence, it remained only for me to vanish the Indian from a rope that was hanging from the flies in the center of the stage and which had previously been shown to be both genuine and flexible.

At this juncture, however, a diversion occurred and attention was called to a dining-room table which had been standing on the stage. After the table had been shown to have no connection with the ground other than its four legs, it was momentarily surrounded by two screens which, when removed by the Indian, disclosed no prosaic dining-table but a coral cave in which reclined a pleasing princess of India.

That lady having been duly admired, and her artistic setting emphasized by a momentary turning-off of the stage lighting and the illumination of the cave by blue limelight, the presentation of the rope trick was resumed.

Apologizing for my inability to defy the law of gravity to the extent of poising a rope vertically in mid-air, I once again drew attention to the rope hanging from the flies and sent the Indian climbing up it hand over hand. When he was some ten feet from the ground and in full view of the audience on the lighted stage, I fired a revolver—and instantly the Indian vanished into a puff of smoke. Down from the flies fell the dismembered portions of his body whereupon the princess, with a proper sense of delicacy, also vanished from the chair on which she had been sitting, leaving the magician alone upon an empty stage.

And now to make retribution to some of the many thousands of people whom, for many years, I deceived with my "vanishing" Indians.

First, the Indian's emergence from the basket called for no great feat of magic, for he was actually in the basket, in company with his dismembered body, from the outset. It is surprising into how small a space the human body can be packed and though the basket was by no means of unusual size it could accommodate, admittedly with a squeeze, the Indian and the dummy limbs. Its weight, of course, was more than I could lift, and my airy brandishing of the basket when I lifted it from its stand was facilitated by an iron rod which projected from the stool and had attached to it, beneath the stage, a heavy weight so counterbalanced that I was able to lift the basket up carelessly with one hand.

The Indian princess had a rather more comfortable resting place than the Indian. She was concealed in the top of the dining-room table which, though it appeared (and actually was) of normal thickness in front was, at the back, in the form of a wedge. The widest part afforded sufficient space for her to lie down in comparative comfort.

The conversion of the table top into a coral cave involved several seconds of rather hectic work on the part of the princess who, in the brief interval between the screens being placed around the table and their removal, had to reverse the table's flaps (on the uderside of which the cave scenery was painted) set up a number of ground rows and yet be discovered reclining gracefully in her cave, evidencing no shortage of breath as the result of her not inconsiderable exertions.

Incidentally, the introduction of this princess interlude was no purposeless elaboration of the illusion, but was essential to the presentation of the Indian Rope Trick. It provided me with my only possible opportunity for substituting a specially-prepared rope for the rope which had been changing from the flies from the outset and whose flexibility and general innocence I had already demonstrated to the audience.

The substitution took place during the momentary blackout when the stage lights were lowered for the subdued blue illumination of the princess's cave and the rope that hung from the flies when the lights came on again was actually a rope-covered metal casing. Concealed within this casing was a pair of "lazy-tongs" or expanding scissors, between the points of which hung a sheet of red velvet whose purpose will shortly be seen. The lazy-tongs could be actuated by a sliding rod inside the casing which also carried a strong hook.

The Indian wore a special harness with a large ring attached to it, and when, in climbing the "rope," he reached the hook, he dropped his ring over it, and let the hook take the whole of his weight. Immediately, the sliding rod, impelled by his suddenly-applied weight, actuated the lazy-tongs which shot out to their fullest extent, spreading the sheet of red velvet. This red velvet, completely covering the Indian and blending perfectly with the red velvet back-cloth of the stage, effectively concealed him from view, the illusion being helped by the wreathing smoke from the flash-powder that was electrically set off as I fired my revolver.

The princess, at this stage, had long since disappeared—quite unobtrusively, through a lift beneath the stool on which she had been sitting. Her exit—even had it been watched during the diversion caused by the Indian climbing the rope—would scarcely have been noticed as her flowing outer garments were mounted on a wire framework out of which she slipped, via the lift and in "deshabille" into the nether regions, leaving a lifelike framework dummy still seated on her stool.

When the moment came for this dummy to disappear, under the same cover of smoke that had aided the Indian's disappearance, the framework closed up with a spring-like suddenness and, with the entire inner part of the stool, was dropped through a trapdoor whose momentary opening was covered by a spring blind.

Trapdoors, it will be seen, are to the modern magician what charms and potions were to the wizards of an earlier age. The only difference is, perhaps, that when a modern magician employs a trapdoor he does at least know where he is sending his victim, whereas the old-time wizard could only speculate as to the probable destination of the victims of his less successful potions.

A CATALOGUE OF SELECTED DOVER BOOKS
IN ALL FIELDS OF INTEREST

A CATALOGUE OF SELECTED DOVER BOOKS
IN ALL FIELDS OF INTEREST

AMERICA'S OLD MASTERS, James T. Flexner. Four men emerged unexpectedly from provincial 18th century America to leadership in European art: Benjamin West, J. S. Copley, C. R. Peale, Gilbert Stuart. Brilliant coverage of lives and contributions. Revised, 1967 edition. 69 plates. 365pp. of text.
21806-6 Paperbound $3.00

FIRST FLOWERS OF OUR WILDERNESS: AMERICAN PAINTING, THE COLONIAL PERIOD, James T. Flexner. Painters, and regional painting traditions from earliest Colonial times up to the emergence of Copley, West and Peale Sr., Foster, Gustavus Hesselius, Feke, John Smibert and many anonymous painters in the primitive manner. Engaging presentation, with 162 illustrations. xxii + 368pp.
22180-6 Paperbound $3.50

THE LIGHT OF DISTANT SKIES: AMERICAN PAINTING, 1760-1835, James T. Flexner. The great generation of early American painters goes to Europe to learn and to teach: West, Copley, Gilbert Stuart and others. Allston, Trumbull, Morse; also contemporary American painters—primitives, derivatives, academics—who remained in America. 102 illustrations. xiii + 306pp.
22179-2 Paperbound $3.50

A HISTORY OF THE RISE AND PROGRESS OF THE ARTS OF DESIGN IN THE UNITED STATES, William Dunlap. Much the richest mine of information on early American painters, sculptors, architects, engravers, miniaturists, etc. The only source of information for scores of artists, the major primary source for many others. Unabridged reprint of rare original 1834 edition, with new introduction by James T. Flexner, and 394 new illustrations. Edited by Rita Weiss. 6⅝ x 9⅝.
21695-0, 21696-9, 21697-7 Three volumes, Paperbound $15.00

EPOCHS OF CHINESE AND JAPANESE ART, Ernest F. Fenollosa. From primitive Chinese art to the 20th century, thorough history, explanation of every important art period and form, including Japanese woodcuts; main stress on China and Japan, but Tibet, Korea also included. Still unexcelled for its detailed, rich coverage of cultural background, aesthetic elements, diffusion studies, particularly of the historical period. 2nd, 1913 edition. 242 illustrations. lii + 439pp. of text.
20364-6, 20365-4 Two volumes, Paperbound $6.00

THE GENTLE ART OF MAKING ENEMIES, James A. M. Whistler. Greatest wit of his day deflates Oscar Wilde, Ruskin, Swinburne; strikes back at inane critics, exhibitions, art journalism; aesthetics of impressionist revolution in most striking form. Highly readable classic by great painter. Reproduction of edition designed by Whistler. Introduction by Alfred Werner. xxxvi + 334pp.
21875-9 Paperbound $3.00

JOHANN SEBASTIAN BACH, Philipp Spitta. One of the great classics of musicology, this definitive analysis of Bach's music (and life) has never been surpassed. Lucid, nontechnical analyses of hundreds of pieces (30 pages devoted to St. Matthew Passion, 26 to B Minor Mass). Also includes major analysis of 18th-century music. 450 musical examples. 40-page musical supplement. Total of xx + 1799pp.

(EUK) 22278-0, 22279-9 Two volumes, Clothbound $25.00

MOZART AND HIS PIANO CONCERTOS, Cuthbert Girdlestone. The only full-length study of an important area of Mozart's creativity. Provides detailed analyses of all 23 concertos, traces inspirational sources. 417 musical examples. Second edition. 509pp.
21271-8 Paperbound $4.50

THE PERFECT WAGNERITE: A COMMENTARY ON THE NIBLUNG'S RING, George Bernard Shaw. Brilliant and still relevant criticism in remarkable essays on Wagner's Ring cycle, Shaw's ideas on political and social ideology behind the plots, role of Leitmotifs, vocal requisites, etc. Prefaces. xxi + 136pp.

(USO) 21707-8 Paperbound $1.75

DON GIOVANNI, W. A. Mozart. Complete libretto, modern English translation; biographies of composer and librettist; accounts of early performances and critical reaction. Lavishly illustrated. All the material you need to understand and appreciate this great work. Dover Opera Guide and Libretto Series; translated and introduced by Ellen Bleiler. 92 illustrations. 209pp.
21134-7 Paperbound $2.00

BASIC ELECTRICITY, U. S. Bureau of Naval Personel. Originally a training course, best non-technical coverage of basic theory of electricity and its applications. Fundamental concepts, batteries, circuits, conductors and wiring techniques, AC and DC, inductance and capacitance, generators, motors, transformers, magnetic amplifiers, synchros, servomechanisms, etc. Also covers blue-prints, electrical diagrams, etc. Many questions, with answers. 349 illustrations. x + 448pp. 6½ x 9¼.
20973-3 Paperbound $3.50

REPRODUCTION OF SOUND, Edgar Villchur. Thorough coverage for laymen of high fidelity systems, reproducing systems in general, needles, amplifiers, preamps, loudspeakers, feedback, explaining physical background. "A rare talent for making technicalities vividly comprehensible," R. Darrell, High Fidelity. 69 figures iv + 92pp.
21515-6 Paperbound $1.35

HEAR ME TALKIN' TO YA: THE STORY OF JAZZ AS TOLD BY THE MEN WHO MADE IT, Nat Shapiro and Nat Hentoff. Louis Armstrong, Fats Waller, Jo Jones, Clarence Williams, Billy Holiday, Duke Ellington, Jelly Roll Morton and dozens of other jazz greats tell how it was in Chicago's South Side, New Orleans, depression Harlem and the modern West Coast as jazz was born and grew. xvi + 429pp.
21726-4 Paperbound $3.95

FABLES OF AESOP, translated by Sir Roger L'Estrange. A reproduction of the very rare 1931 Paris edition; a selection of the most interesting fables, together with 50 imaginative drawings by Alexander Calder. v + 128pp. 6½x9¼.
21780-9 Paperbound $1.50

LAST AND FIRST MEN AND STAR MAKER, TWO SCIENCE FICTION NOVELS, Olaf Stapledon. Greatest future histories in science fiction. In the first, human intelligence is the "hero," through strange paths of evolution, interplanetary invasions, incredible technologies, near extinctions and reemergences. Star Maker describes the quest of a band of star rovers for intelligence itself, through time and space: weird inhuman civilizations, crustacean minds, symbiotic worlds, etc. Complete, unabridged. v + 438pp.   (USO) 21962-3 Paperbound $3.00

THREE PROPHETIC NOVELS, H. G. WELLS. Stages of a consistently planned future for mankind. *When the Sleeper Wakes,* and *A Story of the Days to Come,* anticipate *Brave New World* and *1984,* in the 21st Century; *The Time Machine,* only complete version in print, shows farther future and the end of mankind. All show Wells's greatest gifts as storyteller and novelist. Edited by E. F. Bleiler. x + 335pp.   (USO) 20605-X Paperbound $3.00

THE DEVIL'S DICTIONARY, Ambrose Bierce. America's own Oscar Wilde—Ambrose Bierce—offers his barbed iconoclastic wisdom in over 1,000 definitions hailed by H. L. Mencken as "some of the most gorgeous witticisms in the English language." 145pp.   20487-1 Paperbound $1.50

MAX AND MORITZ, Wilhelm Busch. Great children's classic, father of comic strip, of two bad boys, Max and Moritz. Also Ker and Plunk (Plisch und Plumm), Cat and Mouse, Deceitful Henry, Ice-Peter, The Boy and the Pipe, and five other pieces. Original German, with English translation. Edited by H. Arthur Klein; translations by various hands and H. Arthur Klein. vi + 216pp.   20181-3 Paperbound $2.00

PIGS IS PIGS AND OTHER FAVORITES, Ellis Parker Butler. The title story is one of the best humor short stories, as Mike Flannery obfuscates biology and English. Also included, That Pup of Murchison's, The Great American Pie Company, and Perkins of Portland. 14 illustrations. v + 109pp.   21532-6 Paperbound $1.50

THE PETERKIN PAPERS, Lucretia P. Hale. It takes genius to be as stupidly mad as the Peterkins, as they decide to become wise, celebrate the "Fourth," keep a cow, and otherwise strain the resources of the Lady from Philadelphia. Basic book of American humor. 153 illustrations. 219pp.   20794-3 Paperbound $2.00

PERRAULT'S FAIRY TALES, translated by A. E. Johnson and S. R. Littlewood, with 34 full-page illustrations by Gustave Doré. All the original Perrault stories—Cinderella, Sleeping Beauty, Bluebeard, Little Red Riding Hood, Puss in Boots, Tom Thumb, etc.—with their witty verse morals and the magnificent illustrations of Doré. One of the five or six great books of European fairy tales. viii + 117pp. 8⅛ x 11.   22311-6 Paperbound $2.00

OLD HUNGARIAN FAIRY TALES, Baroness Orczy. Favorites translated and adapted by author of the *Scarlet Pimpernel.* Eight fairy tales include "The Suitors of Princess Fire-Fly," "The Twin Hunchbacks," "Mr. Cuttlefish's Love Story," and "The Enchanted Cat." This little volume of magic and adventure will captivate children as it has for generations. 90 drawings by Montagu Barstow. 96pp.
                              (USO) 22293-4 Paperbound $1.95

THE RED FAIRY BOOK, Andrew Lang. Lang's color fairy books have long been children's favorites. This volume includes Rapunzel, Jack and the Bean-stalk and 35 other stories, familiar and unfamiliar. 4 plates, 93 illustrations x + 367pp.
21673-X Paperbound $2.50

THE BLUE FAIRY BOOK, Andrew Lang. Lang's tales come from all countries and all times. Here are 37 tales from Grimm, the Arabian Nights, Greek Mythology, and other fascinating sources. 8 plates, 130 illustrations. xi + 390pp.
21437-0 Paperbound $2.75

HOUSEHOLD STORIES BY THE BROTHERS GRIMM. Classic English-language edition of the well-known tales — Rumpelstiltskin, Snow White, Hansel and Gretel, The Twelve Brothers, Faithful John, Rapunzel, Tom Thumb (52 stories in all). Translated into simple, straightforward English by Lucy Crane. Ornamented with head-pieces, vignettes, elaborate decorative initials and a dozen full-page illustrations by Walter Crane. x + 269pp.
21080-4 Paperbound **$2.00**

THE MERRY ADVENTURES OF ROBIN HOOD, Howard Pyle. The finest modern versions of the traditional ballads and tales about the great English outlaw. Howard Pyle's complete prose version, with every word, every illustration of the first edition. Do not confuse this facsimile of the original (1883) with modern editions that change text or illustrations. 23 plates plus many page decorations. xxii + 296pp.
22043-5 Paperbound $2.75

THE STORY OF KING ARTHUR AND HIS KNIGHTS, Howard Pyle. The finest children's version of the life of King Arthur; brilliantly retold by Pyle, with 48 of his most imaginative illustrations. xviii + 313pp. 6⅛ x 9¼.
21445-1 Paperbound $2.50

THE WONDERFUL WIZARD OF OZ, L. Frank Baum. America's finest children's book in facsimile of first edition with all Denslow illustrations in full color. The edition a child should have. Introduction by Martin Gardner. 23 color plates, scores of drawings. iv + 267pp.
20691-2 Paperbound $3.50

THE MARVELOUS LAND OF OZ, L. Frank Baum. The second Oz book, every bit as imaginative as the Wizard. The hero is a boy named Tip, but the Scarecrow and the Tin Woodman are back, as is the Oz magic. 16 color plates, 120 drawings by John R. Neill. 287pp.
20692-0 Paperbound $2.50

THE MAGICAL MONARCH OF MO, L. Frank Baum. Remarkable adventures in a land even stranger than Oz. The best of Baum's books not in the Oz series. 15 color plates and dozens of drawings by Frank Verbeck. xviii + 237pp.
21892-9 Paperbound $2.25

THE BAD CHILD'S BOOK OF BEASTS, MORE BEASTS FOR WORSE CHILDREN, A MORAL ALPHABET, Hilaire Belloc. Three complete humor classics in one volume. Be kind to the frog, and do not call him names . . . and 28 other whimsical animals. Familiar favorites and some not so well known. Illustrated by Basil Blackwell. 156pp.
(USO) 20749-8 Paperbound $1.50

EAST O' THE SUN AND WEST O' THE MOON, George W. Dasent. Considered the best of all translations of these Norwegian folk tales, this collection has been enjoyed by generations of children (and folklorists too). Includes True and Untrue, Why the Sea is Salt, East O' the Sun and West O' the Moon, Why the Bear is Stumpy-Tailed, Boots and the Troll, The Cock and the Hen, Rich Peter the Pedlar, and 52 more. The only edition with all 59 tales. 77 illustrations by Erik Werenskiold and Theodor Kittelsen. xv + 418pp. 22521-6 Paperbound $3.50

GOOPS AND HOW TO BE THEM, Gelett Burgess. Classic of tongue-in-cheek humor, masquerading as etiquette book. 87 verses, twice as many cartoons, show mischievous Goops as they demonstrate to children virtues of table manners, neatness, courtesy, etc. Favorite for generations. viii + 88pp. 6½ x 9¼. 22233-0 Paperbound $1.50

ALICE'S ADVENTURES UNDER GROUND, Lewis Carroll. The first version, quite different from the final *Alice in Wonderland,* printed out by Carroll himself with his own illustrations. Complete facsimile of the "million dollar" manuscript Carroll gave to Alice Liddell in 1864. Introduction by Martin Gardner. viii + 96pp. Title and dedication pages in color. 21482-6 Paperbound $1.25

THE BROWNIES, THEIR BOOK, Palmer Cox. Small as mice, cunning as foxes, exuberant and full of mischief, the Brownies go to the zoo, toy shop, seashore, circus, etc., in 24 verse adventures and 266 illustrations. Long a favorite, since their first appearance in St. Nicholas Magazine. xi + 144pp. 6⅝ x 9¼. 21265-3 Paperbound $1.75

SONGS OF CHILDHOOD, Walter De La Mare. Published (under the pseudonym Walter Ramal) when De La Mare was only 29, this charming collection has long been a favorite children's book. A facsimile of the first edition in paper, the 47 poems capture the simplicity of the nursery rhyme and the ballad, including such lyrics as I Met Eve, Tartary, The Silver Penny. vii + 106pp. (USO) 21972-0 Paperbound $1.25

THE COMPLETE NONSENSE OF EDWARD LEAR, Edward Lear. The finest 19th-century humorist-cartoonist in full: all nonsense limericks, zany alphabets, Owl and Pussycat, songs, nonsense botany, and more than 500 illustrations by Lear himself. Edited by Holbrook Jackson. xxix + 287pp. (USO) 20167-8 Paperbound $2.00

BILLY WHISKERS: THE AUTOBIOGRAPHY OF A GOAT, Frances Trego Montgomery. A favorite of children since the early 20th century, here are the escapades of that rambunctious, irresistible and mischievous goat—Billy Whiskers. Much in the spirit of *Peck's Bad Boy,* this is a book that children never tire of reading or hearing. All the original familiar illustrations by W. H. Fry are included: 6 color plates, 18 black and white drawings. 159pp. 22345-0 Paperbound $2.00

MOTHER GOOSE MELODIES. Faithful republication of the fabulously rare Munroe and Francis "copyright 1833" Boston edition—the most important Mother Goose collection, usually referred to as the "original." Familiar rhymes plus many rare ones, with wonderful old woodcut illustrations. Edited by E. F. Bleiler. 128pp. 4½ x 6⅜. 22577-1 Paperbound $1.00

CATALOGUE OF DOVER BOOKS

PLANETS, STARS AND GALAXIES: DESCRIPTIVE ASTRONOMY FOR BEGINNERS, A. E. Fanning. Comprehensive introductory survey of astronomy: the sun, solar system, stars, galaxies, universe, cosmology; up-to-date, including quasars, radio stars, etc. Preface by Prof. Donald Menzel. 24pp. of photographs. 189pp. 5¼ x 8¼.
21680-2 Paperbound $2.50

TEACH YOURSELF CALCULUS, P. Abbott. With a good background in algebra and trig, you can teach yourself calculus with this book. Simple, straightforward introduction to functions of all kinds, integration, differentiation, series, etc. "Students who are beginning to study calculus method will derive great help from this book." Faraday House Journal. 308pp.
20683-1 Clothbound $2.50

TEACH YOURSELF TRIGONOMETRY, P. Abbott. Geometrical foundations, indices and logarithms, ratios, angles, circular measure, etc. are presented in this sound, easy-to-use text. Excellent for the beginner or as a brush up, this text carries the student through the solution of triangles. 204pp.
20682-3 Clothbound $2.00

BASIC MACHINES AND HOW THEY WORK, U. S. Bureau of Naval Personnel. Originally used in U.S. Naval training schools, this book clearly explains the operation of a progression of machines, from the simplest—lever, wheel and axle, inclined plane, wedge, screw—to the most complex—typewriter, internal combustion engine, computer mechanism. Utilizing an approach that requires only an elementary understanding of mathematics, these explanations build logically upon each other and are assisted by over 200 drawings and diagrams. Perfect as a technical school manual or as a self-teaching aid to the layman. 204 figures. Preface. Index. vii + 161pp. 6½ x 9¼.
21709-4 Paperbound $2.50

THE FRIENDLY STARS, Martha Evans Martin. Classic has taught naked-eye observation of stars, planets to hundreds of thousands, still not surpassed for charm, lucidity, adequacy. Completely updated by Professor Donald H. Menzel, Harvard Observatory. 25 illustrations. 16 x 30 chart. x + 147pp.
21099-5 Paperbound $2.00

MUSIC OF THE SPHERES: THE MATERIAL UNIVERSE FROM ATOM TO QUASAR, SIMPLY EXPLAINED, Guy Murchie. Extremely broad, brilliantly written popular account begins with the solar system and reaches to dividing line between matter and nonmatter; latest understandings presented with exceptional clarity. Volume One: Planets, stars, galaxies, cosmology, geology, celestial mechanics, latest astronomical discoveries; Volume Two: Matter, atoms, waves, radiation, relativity, chemical action, heat, nuclear energy, quantum theory, music, light, color, probability, antimatter, antigravity, and similar topics. 319 figures. 1967 (second) edition. Total of xx + 644pp.
21809-0, 21810-4 Two volumes, Paperbound $5.75

OLD-TIME SCHOOLS AND SCHOOL BOOKS, Clifton Johnson. Illustrations and rhymes from early primers, abundant quotations from early textbooks, many anecdotes of school life enliven this study of elementary schools from Puritans to middle 19th century. Introduction by Carl Withers. 234 illustrations. xxxiii + 381pp.
21031-6 Paperbound $4.00

TWO LITTLE SAVAGES; BEING THE ADVENTURES OF TWO BOYS WHO LIVED AS INDIANS AND WHAT THEY LEARNED, Ernest Thompson Seton. Great classic of nature and boyhood provides a vast range of woodlore in most palatable form, a genuinely entertaining story. Two farm boys build a teepee in woods and live in it for a month, working out Indian solutions to living problems, star lore, birds and animals, plants, etc. 293 illustrations. vii + 286pp.

20985-7 Paperbound $2.50

PETER PIPER'S PRACTICAL PRINCIPLES OF PLAIN & PERFECT PRONUNCIATION. Alliterative jingles and tongue-twisters of surprising charm, that made their first appearance in America about 1830. Republished in full with the spirited woodcut illustrations from this earliest American edition. 32pp. 4½ x 6⅜.

22560-7 Paperbound $1.00

SCIENCE EXPERIMENTS AND AMUSEMENTS FOR CHILDREN, Charles Vivian. 73 easy experiments, requiring only materials found at home or easily available, such as candles, coins, steel wool, etc.; illustrate basic phenomena like vacuum, simple chemical reaction, etc. All safe. Modern, well-planned. Formerly *Science Games for Children*. 102 photos, numerous drawings. 96pp. 6⅛ x 9¼.

21856-2 Paperbound $1.25

AN INTRODUCTION TO CHESS MOVES AND TACTICS SIMPLY EXPLAINED, Leonard Barden. Informal intermediate introduction, quite strong in explaining reasons for moves. Covers basic material, tactics, important openings, traps, positional play in middle game, end game. Attempts to isolate patterns and recurrent configurations. Formerly *Chess*. 58 figures. 102pp. (USO) 21210-6 Paperbound $1.25

LASKER'S MANUAL OF CHESS, Dr. Emanuel Lasker. Lasker was not only one of the five great World Champions, he was also one of the ablest expositors, theorists, and analysts. In many ways, his Manual, permeated with his philosophy of battle, filled with keen insights, is one of the greatest works ever written on chess. Filled with analyzed games by the great players. A single-volume library that will profit almost any chess player, beginner or master. 308 diagrams. xli x 349pp.

20640-8 Paperbound $2.75

THE MASTER BOOK OF MATHEMATICAL RECREATIONS, Fred Schuh. In opinion of many the finest work ever prepared on mathematical puzzles, stunts, recreations; exhaustively thorough explanations of mathematics involved, analysis of effects, citation of puzzles and games. Mathematics involved is elementary. Translated by F. Göbel. 194 figures. xxiv + 430pp. 22134-2 Paperbound $4.00

MATHEMATICS, MAGIC AND MYSTERY, Martin Gardner. Puzzle editor for Scientific American explains mathematics behind various mystifying tricks: card tricks, stage "mind reading," coin and match tricks, counting out games, geometric dissections, etc. Probability sets, theory of numbers clearly explained. Also provides more than 400 tricks, guaranteed to work, that you can do. 135 illustrations. xii + 176pp.

20335-2 Paperbound $2.00

MATHEMATICAL PUZZLES FOR BEGINNERS AND ENTHUSIASTS, Geoffrey Mott-Smith. 189 puzzles from easy to difficult—involving arithmetic, logic, algebra, properties of digits, probability, etc.—for enjoyment and mental stimulus. Explanation of mathematical principles behind the puzzles. 135 illustrations. viii + 248pp.
20198-8 Paperbound $2.00

PAPER FOLDING FOR BEGINNERS, William D. Murray and Francis J. Rigney. Easiest book on the market, clearest instructions on making interesting, beautiful origami. Sail boats, cups, roosters, frogs that move legs, bonbon boxes, standing birds, etc. 40 projects; more than 275 diagrams and photographs. 94pp.
20713-7 Paperbound $1.00

TRICKS AND GAMES ON THE POOL TABLE, Fred Herrmann. 79 tricks and games—some solitaires, some for two or more players, some competitive games—to entertain you between formal games. Mystifying shots and throws, unusual caroms, tricks involving such props as cork, coins, a hat, etc. Formerly *Fun on the Pool Table*. 77 figures. 95pp.
21814-7 Paperbound $1.25

HAND SHADOWS TO BE THROWN UPON THE WALL: A SERIES OF NOVEL AND AMUSING FIGURES FORMED BY THE HAND, Henry Bursill. Delightful picturebook from great-grandfather's day shows how to make 18 different hand shadows: a bird that flies, duck that quacks, dog that wags his tail, camel, goose, deer, boy, turtle, etc. Only book of its sort. vi + 33pp. 6½ x 9¼.   21779-5 Paperbound $1.00

WHITTLING AND WOODCARVING, E. J. Tangerman. 18th printing of best book on market. "If you can cut a potato you can carve" toys and puzzles, chains, chessmen, caricatures, masks, frames, woodcut blocks, surface patterns, much more. Information on tools, woods, techniques. Also goes into serious wood sculpture from Middle Ages to present, East and West. 464 photos, figures. x + 293pp.
20965-2 Paperbound $2.50

HISTORY OF PHILOSOPHY, Julián Marias. Possibly the clearest, most easily followed, best planned, most useful one-volume history of philosophy on the market; neither skimpy nor overfull. Full details on system of every major philosopher and dozens of less important thinkers from pre-Socratics up to Existentialism and later. Strong on many European figures usually omitted. Has gone through dozens of editions in Europe. 1966 edition, translated by Stanley Appelbaum and Clarence Strowbridge. xviii + 505pp.   21739-6 Paperbound $3.50

YOGA: A SCIENTIFIC EVALUATION, Kovoor T. Behanan. Scientific but non-technical study of physiological results of yoga exercises; done under auspices of Yale U. Relations to Indian thought, to psychoanalysis, etc. 16 photos. xxiii + 270pp.
20505-3 Paperbound $2.50

Prices subject to change without notice.
Available at your book dealer or write for free catalogue to Dept. GI, Dover Publications, Inc., 180 Varick St., N. Y., N. Y. 10014. Dover publishes more than 150 books each year on science, elementary and advanced mathematics, biology, music, art, literary history, social sciences and other areas.